Date Due

THE EGYPTIAN
WAY OF DEATH

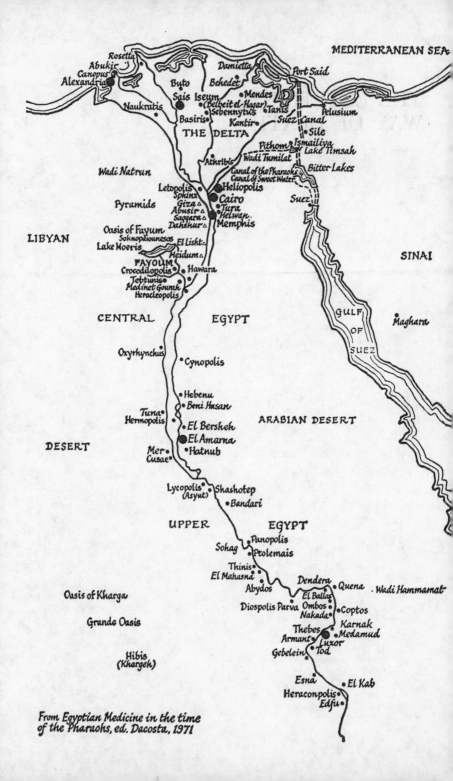

From Egyptian Medicine in the time of the Pharaohs, ed. Dacosta, 1971

THE EGYPTIAN WAY OF DEATH

MUMMIES AND THE CULT OF THE IMMORTAL

By Ange-Pierre Leca

Translated by Louise Asmal

DOUBLEDAY & COMPANY, INC., Garden City, New York
1981

Library of Congress Cataloging in Publication Data

Leca, Ange-Pierre.
   The Egyptian way of death.
   Translation of Les momies.
   Bibliography: p. 277.
   Includes index.
   1. Mummies—Egypt.   I. Title.
DT62.M7L413   1981   393'.3'0932

ISBN: 0-385-14609-4
Library of Congress Catalog Card Number: 78–68362
Copyright © Librairie Hachette 1976
English Translation copyright © 1979 by Louise Asmal
First British Edition published 1980 by Souvenir Press, Ltd.
43 Great Russell Street, London WC1B 3PA and simultaneously
   in Canda (under the title THE CULT OF THE
   IMMORTAL)

CONTENTS

LIST OF ILLUSTRATIONS

(Drawings by the author)

Fig.

LIST OF PLATES

INTRODUCTION

The Egyptians were obsessed with death, and their civilisation was coloured by a belief in life after death which led to their elaborate funeral rites, their splendid monuments, and the mummies themselves that are the subject of this book. For centuries the Egyptian mummies have exercised a strange fascination over us. Nor has this interest in Egyptology declined in recent years. Quite the reverse. It seems that people living in an age, in which scepticism about spiritual matters is on the increase, often need to reach out to the religious practices of other races as if to compensate for some deficiency in their own cultures.

But mysticism apart, there are other reasons why the study of Egyptian mummies is of continuing interest to us. Egyptology is less than two hundred years old, but because the privilege of mummification, at first the prerogative of the royal pharaohs alone, was gradually extended to the nobility and then to all classes of citizen, and finally to the sacred animals too, the study of mummies sheds light on every facet of Egyptian life as well as on the course of Egyptian history. By examining some of these remains, we have been able to discover what food the Egyptians ate, the state of their teeth, the diseases they died from and many other facts, some of which we have been able to apply to present day problems. For instance we now know that illnesses which were previously believed to have been caused by factors peculiar to the twentieth century existed in Ancient Egypt. Experts have found evidence of heart disease, high blood pressure and other so-called "modern" diseases in mummified bodies, making it necessary for doctors to seek other causes for these phenomena. Similarly the experiments conducted on mummies by Sir Max Ruffer at the beginning of the century gave us information about the effects of marrying blood relations which is still of value today.

The period with which this book deals spans about three thousand years. The history of this fascinating era was revealed to us by the Egyptian historian Manetho of the Third Century B.C. who compiled a list of pharaohs, dividing the kings into groups called "dynasties." There were thirty dynasties in all and they did not correspond to the rise and fall of the ruling houses but to political acts or events. Later on further divisions were made into Old, Middle, New and Late Kingdoms, with two divisions during which the leadership collapsed, known as the First and Second Intermediate Periods.

The earliest mummies to have been found in Ancient Egypt date from the Fourth Dynasty of the *Old Kingdom*. At this time too the pharaoh was at his most powerful, and the great pyramid, the biggest of all the pyramids which still stands on the edge of the desert at Giza, was built by King Cheops as his tomb. From the Seventh to the Eleventh Dynasties disorder reigned in Egypt, followed by the reunification of the country by the Theban rulers in a period known as the *Middle Kingdom*. Both art and science flourished at this time and the zenith was reached in the Twelfth Dynasty under the kings Amenemhet and Seostris.

After a further period of misrule the Theban King Ahmosis took over the whole country once again, as the first king of the *New Kingdom* which lasted from the Eighteenth to the Twentieth Dynasties. It was at this time that Egypt extended her terriories into both Asia and Nubia and the capital Thebes became very rich and powerful. Kings Amenophis and Tuthmosis were the first rulers to call themselves pharaohs. At the close of the Eighteenth Dynasty came the reign of Akhenaten, the king who tried to establish the religion of one god. He was succeeded by Tutankhamun, the boy-king, whose magnificent tomb was discovered so dramatically by the English archaeologist Howard Carter in 1922.

The Nineteenth and Twentieth Dynasties saw a long procession of pharaohs, all called Ramesses. It is to Ramesses II, the great builder, that we are indebted for the remains of many temples. Egypt was subject to invasions by Ethiopians and Assyrians during the *Late Kingdom* which covered the Twenty-fourth to the Thirtieth Dynasties, and from the Twenty-seventh Dynasty onwards the art of mummification began to decline. In 342 B.C. the last Egyptian king Nectanebos was ousted by the Persians who ruled Egypt for ten years until Alexander "liberated" it. The Ptolemaic Period followed with the Macedonian Kings ruling the country. After 30 B.C. came the Roman Period with Egypt finally becoming absorbed into the Roman Empire. By this time the practice of embalming, which had been an art form of some considerable dimensions, had become very crude indeed.

But although death was very important to the Egyptians, life was considered to be more desirable. One sage of the period advised: "Enjoy your days. Delight your nose with balm and sweet perfume, offer lotus garlands to your wife to adorn her arms and neck. Let her whom you cherish be seated at your side, and let singing and music delight your ears. Cast care from you; think only of your pleasure until the day comes to enter into a world where silence reigns. . . . For you must understand that no-one can take his worldly goods with him, and no-one has ever returned after his departure." The worst fear though was that the corpse might be destroyed, which would also destroy its chance of eternal life. "Die not a second time" was written hopefully at the bottom of some coffins.

So how precisely did the ancient Egyptians set about preserving the corpses of their loved ones from decay? If we open an old dictionary of the Académie française, we can read the following definition of the word mummy: "Corpse embalmed by the ancient Egyptians. Can be used by extension for the bodies of those who were buried under the quicksands formed by the wind in the Arabian and Egyptian deserts, and which were later found dried by the heat of the sun . . . Mummy can also be used of the brown colour extracted from the pitch used to smear mummies."

This definition is wrongly based on an interpretation for which it is difficult to find the source. The term does not appear in any Egyptian text, nor in modern Coptic vocabulary. Egyptians used two expressions to denote a dead body: "khet" for the corpse and "wi" for the embalmed and wrapped mummy. The word "mummy" which is to be found in Byzantine Greek and in Latin derives in fact from the Persian "mummia" which means bitumen, and has also come to signify a mummy embalmed in bitumen. In fact it was long held that the ancient Egyptians preserved their dead through the use of this material, as for example in the description given by Ibn el Baïtar (1197–1248), a famous doctor and pharmacologist from Cairo: "The name mummy is given to the drug of which we have just spoken and also to what is called Judean bitumen, and to the mummy in tombs which is found in great quantity in Egypt and which is none other than the mixture that the Byzantine Greeks used to embalm their dead so that the bodies would remain in the state in which they were buried and not undergo any decay or change." Abd al-Latil (1162–1231), a Baghdad doctor, paid half an Egyptian dirham in Cairo for the contents of three skulls, and declared that the substance inside them was closely related to bitumen. From then onwards, simply because the mummies looked black, generation after generation repeated that the Egyptians treated their dead in this way, although they never did so during the classical period and only rarely in the Greco-Roman period.

THE EGYPTIAN
WAY OF DEATH

CHAPTER 1

WHY MUMMIES?

DISMEMBERED CORPSES

Mankind lived for thousands of years in Egypt before mummification was introduced during the Fourth Dynasty, yet as far back as the neolithic period around 4500 B.C. the people who lived there had developed a very advanced culture, passed from a nomadic life to an agricultural one, settled on their chosen sites, and started to make pottery. After five hundred years, a cult of the dead began to develop in the so-called Nagada civilisation, as is evident today from the exquisite objects such as jewellery, schist vases, make-up palettes and carved ivory which have been found in their graveyards. Their tombs were not elaborate but were simple trenches of an oval or rectangular shape dug out of the sand, in which the corpse lay on his left side with his knees drawn up to his chin, his head facing south and his face turned towards the west. The body was usually covered with animal skins or matting, occasionally wrapped in a piece of cloth; very rarely there are signs of a coffin having been used. Of course the human remains consist only of bones, but in the intact tombs which have not been disturbed at all there can sometimes be found skeletons which are either completely broken up or which have parts missing.

The cult was widespread but a few examples can be taken

El Amrah tombs of the early Nagada period to show
the bodies were arranged. At El Amrah, for instance, the
s were placed in a heap around which lay the funerary ma-
als, while at Abydos one skeleton was discovered in two
halves buried at a little distance from each other, and the bones
of another were piled up with the skull on top. Some bones were
found dyed with red ochre. All these facts point to the likelihood
that the corpse was dismembered before being buried, but the
origin of this curious practice remains uncertain. However, various theories have been put forward. Petrie, an English pioneer in
Egyptology, saw it as a sign of cannibalism and conjectured that
the deceased's family ate his flesh at a macabre banquet with the
idea that they would thus acquire his qualities. Maspéro, former
French head of the Antiquities Service in Egypt, postulated that
it was fear of the dead person returning which lay behind the
barbarous custom of dismembering his body, which would prevent him from coming back to haunt the living by stopping the
union of body and soul which was essential to life; he found
nothing implausible in the contradiction between this practice
and the Egyptian custom of ensuring an after-life to the deceased by burying him with food and funerary equipment. Yet
another theory was put forward by Wainwright who thought
that some bones might have been removed for use as amulets,
but this hypothesis has no basis in fact or in any archaeological
finding. Lastly Hermann, who could find no firm foundation for
any of these explanations, presumed merely that some religious
observance must be involved, a curious rite intended to purify
the deceased and ensure his salvation and continued existence in
heaven.

OSIRIS, GOD OF THE DEAD

In any case, it is from the establishment of this custom that was
born the legend of Osiris, god of the dead, in which one can
recognise both features from the custom of dismembering the
corpse and signs of the beginnings of the practice of wrapping it
(Fig. 1).

Fig. 1. Osiris, god of the dead. Wrapped in his cover like a
mummy, his hands crossed on his breast and holding a
sceptre and a whip, his forehead bearing a white mitre
flanked with two plumes. Bronze statuette of the late
New Kingdom.

The story of this god began as popular tradition, and then developed with various additions and changes until it was finally
stabilised as part of the official religion. There are various ver-
sions in existence, of which the most common seems to have
been that given by Plutarch. He says that Osiris was the son of
Nut, who personifies the heavenly dome of the sky, and Geb the
earth-god, and that he was the brother of Isis, Nephthys and
Seth. He married his sister Isis and at first reigned over earth

with benevolence, continually extending Egypt's frontiers and maintaining justice and happiness within its borders. However his brother Seth became jealous of his renown and decided to supplant him. One day Seth invited him to a banquet to which he had summoned seventy-two conspirators and showed him a chest which he had had secretly made to Osiris' measurements. He declared that he would present it to whoever could fill it completely by lying down in it. None of the guests who tried could satisfy the conditions; Osiris then tested it himself, and as soon as he was well and truly in the chest the conspirators hastily slammed the lid and nailed it down. Then they tied up the chest with rope and threw it into the Nile.

In great distress, Isis wandered the world in search of her husband and finally found him washed up on the bank of the river Byblos. She brought his body back to the marshes of the Delta region, where Seth discovered it again, cut it up and scattered the pieces throughout Egypt. Once more Isis set out in search of the fragments, which she succeeded in reassembling with the exception of the male organ which had been swallowed by an oxyrynchus fish. At this point Plutarch's account comes to an end, but fortunately it is supplemented by Egyptian texts, which state that the sun god Re sent Anubis, the jackal-headed god, down from the sky in order to watch over all embalming in future. Anubis carefully put the body together again and wrapped it in its own skin. Osiris thus appeared as we know him now, clothed in a shroud which covered his legs, his arms folded on his chest, and his head dressed in a white bonnet with two large feathers at the sides. Isis and Nephthys then waved their broad-winged arms up and down in order to fan the body back to life, and so Osiris was born a second time, though his reign on earth had now come to an end and he was henceforward god of the dead. Every dead person became in a sense Osiris. In many inscriptions written on the sarcophaguses one can read invocations such as "Greetings O thou who art chief of the great . . . I am Osiris," or "Nut, stretch out over me and open me . . . I am Osiris." The dead person had changed into an Osiris.

The practice of dismembering corpses did not continue for long, and in the pre-dynastic period the idea grew up that the body should be preserved whole as it was in life as far as possible. In any case the dry Egyptian sand acted as a remarkable preservative, and the sun was so hot that the corpses, instead of rotting slowly, became dehydrated and thus conserved a life-like appearance. When the sand shifted or some animal interfered, the corpses appeared miraculously dried and so perhaps either induced or reinforced a belief in an afterlife in the next world. Certainly the burial grounds far from the Nile on the edge of the mountains, in Upper Egypt or among the sand-dunes of the Delta, were deliberately constructed there out of reach of floods, with the object of preserving the bodies.

THE IMMORTAL SOUL AND BODY

Very quickly the idea developed that man consisted of an immortal soul or ka contained in a covering of flesh, though the word soul is inexact because the Egyptians saw being as having three parts, the body, the ka and the ba, all of which were essential to man's survival in the afterlife. The concepts involved are confused for us, as maybe they were in some degree for the Egyptians themselves, and can only be explained here in a very simplified form. The ka is a small fragment of divine essence issued from the universal spirit which gives life to all matter; the body, the material part, and the ka, the spiritual part which gives the body its personality, are born out of the chaos of the world. It may be noted that the ram-headed creator of life, the god Khnum, who models men from clay, always has two similar figurines on his potter's wheel, of which one is the physical body and the other the ka. Indeed the ka is often referred to as man's double, and though it is a prerequisite for his life and being it is still in some way separate from his physical body. It could be called his life-force.

The ba, which appears at the moment of union between the ka and the body, is truly the soul, man's moral sense; it is this which bears the responsibility for man's behaviour when he comes to face the gods, and which is his individual conscience. After death, the ka and ba leave the corpse which is then no more than the bodily remains. The ba, which belongs to man, can only sur-

vive if it is closely united with the ka which is by definition immortal because it forms part of the divine essence. On the other
hand the body must be ready for the ka to come and be reincarnated in it after death, though the ka can also do this through a
funerary statue in the likeness of the dead person, the ka statue.

Because great importance was attached to the survival of the
body, the form of burial gradually changed. Nourishment had to
be left in the tomb so that the body did not lack food and drink
when it was needed by the ka. This meant that the trench had to
be enlarged, which in turn led to the danger of sand caving in
and destroying the body. At the end of the neolithic age therefore, during the Gerzean civilisation, the walls of the grave were
coated with mud or lined with wood in order to prevent such a
catastrophe, and the opening was covered by a kind of lid made
of wood, branches and clay, so that the corpse did not get
crushed. Here we see the beginnings of the first funerary chamber.

Later the walls were strengthened with unbaked bricks, and in
some kinds of tombs the ground was earthed up into banks on
which the offering vases were placed. These tombs had not yet
evolved into the monumental vaults of Egypt's heyday, but they
took another step on the way when a screen was erected between the part reserved for the corpse and the part devoted to
offerings, which became a primitive funerary chapel. The arrangements grew still more elaborate with extra rooms being dug
out in order to house the furnishings, which all had to be shored
up with more wood, and with flat stone slabs replacing the unbaked bricks. At each fresh development the funerary complex
went deeper underground, and soon the dead had to be brought
down through a shaft which was afterwards filled in with sand
and stones. The whole structure was covered with a mastaba,
which was a huge oblong embankment faced with limestone inside which one or two rooms were built and decorated with
scenes of daily life. Here the ka could come and enjoy the here-
after as if he were still among the living. A small room, the serdab, sheltered the deceased's statue and communicated with the
outside through a slit for the incense smoke (Fig. 2). This statue
had to be as lifelike as possible, in case it were called on to
assist in the reincarnation of the ka. Another very important

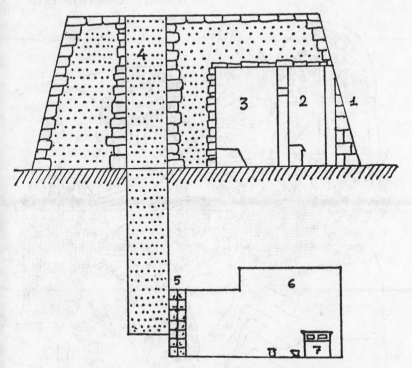

Fig. 2. Section of a mastaba: 1. Door; 2. Chapel; 3. Serdab;
4. Filled-in shaft; 5. Portcullis; 6. Burial vault; 7. Sarcophagus.

function was performed by the stela with a false door, which
allowed the corpse to leave its tomb from time to time; a table
for the offerings stood in front of this and was engraved with
pictures of exotic dishes which could provide the necessary
nourishment if the family forgot to bring real food (Fig. 3).
When the pyramids were built, the burial chamber was
constructed right at the centre, reached by a secret corridor
which was carefully disguised, protected with traps and finally
blocked with huge masses of granite.

Thus belief in the body's survival after death meant that great
care was taken to minister to its needs inside the tomb. The

Fig. 3. Offering table (Nakht's tomb). On it there can be seen grapes, a goose, various vegetables, antelope haunches, a calf's head, bread and flowers.

rooms increased in both size and number, and they were hidden from the depredations of looters by building them deeper, secreting them in the heart of the pyramids, and blocking up the access shafts. Unfortunately this meant that the natural conditions for preserving the body were lost; the heat of the dry sand which prevented the body decomposing could no longer penetrate to the corpse. This was the more so because the simple rush matting, coarsely woven linen or goatskin which previously had roughly covered the corpse were now replaced by a coffin in which the body was wrapped in several thicknesses of cloth. Later the coffin itself was enclosed in one or more sarcophaguses and the layers of linen and wrappings multiplied. These produced ideal conditions for hastening the decomposition of the body, with the result that in the end the most sumptuous funerary complex held nothing better than a skeleton.

Since the Egyptians believed that the deceased survived after death in virtually corporeal form, they were naturally eager to find some artificial means of preserving the body. However, it took them a long time and many fumbling attempts before they attained the skill in mummification which we see in the New Kingdom.

CHAPTER 2

MUMMIES AND SCIENCE

Archaeologists who laboured at their task a hundred years ago would have been amazed by the sophisticated technology at the disposal of those who study mummies today. Nevertheless its possibilities were glimpsed at the turn of the century by a pioneer who was fascinated by the rich potential offered by science and who had begun work with the limited means available at the time: Sir Max Armand Ruffer. He was born in Lyons in 1859, but chance brought him to England to study medicine, and he later completed his studies in Paris which was the centre for his special interest, bacteriology, which was then a new branch of medicine. In the course of his research he had the misfortune to contract diphtheria, complicated by paralysis from which he only barely managed to recover, and so he went to convalesce in Egypt where the climate was reputed to be healthy. Here his work won him the chair of bacteriology in Cairo. It was not long before he realised the value of his medical knowledge in studying mummies, and henceforward devoted most of his life to this field. His publications, which range from the discovery of parasite eggs on two thousand year old bodies to the problems arising out of the pharaohs' custom of consanguineous marriages, are still relevant today. He died tragically in 1917 when, in his capacity as director of the Red Cross, he was carrying out a mission in a ship which was torpedoed off the coast of Salonica. His work was incomplete when he died, but his studies were continued by Elliot Smith and Wood-Jones, and the former edited the volume of the *General Catalogue of the Antiquities of Cairo Museum* which deals with mummies.

AUTOPSY

Ruffer set Egyptology on a path which was to bring it an enormous distance from its beginnings. A century ago, the only way of examining a mummy was by autopsy which involved no equipment at all, and consisted in unwrapping the mummy by hand and making a careful visual examination of the body. At one time this operation was rather a ceremonial event and the honoured guests who came to view the spectacle were not by any means all scientists. The official report of one out of many such occasions, drawn up by Georges Daressy, assistant keeper at Cairo Museum, reads as follows: "On 26 March 1903, at two o'clock in the afternoon, in one of the rooms of the Museum of Egyptian Antiquities at Cairo, through the good offices of M. Maspéro, Director-General of Egyptian Museums and of the Department of Excavations, M. E. Brugsch bey, Keeper of the Museum, and M. Daressy, Assistant Keeper, the mummy of King Thutmosis IV was unwrapped. Present at the operation were: Count and Countess Cromer, Messrs. Ahmed bey Kamal, Bénédite, Spiegelberg, Newberry, Theodore Davis, Quibell, Carter, Lacau, Drs. Lortet, Keatinge, Elliot Smith, Fouquet, Wildt, Campbell, and Mesdames Andrews, Keatinge, Elliot Smith, Campbell, and Dewey, and Mademoiselle Jouhandeau." This list includes some of the most celebrated names of the day in Egyptology, as well as others who had no connection at all with the subject. Well-known personalities or political figures were often invited to be present on such occasions, but later on interest seems to have declined and there were only four observers present at the unwrapping of Sit Amun in 1939. Perhaps the numbers were restricted in the interests of scientific research, perhaps the lower social rank of the mummy excited less curiosity, or perhaps the public realised in advance that the operation would not be very interesting, for "one could feel the skull and a few sparse bones through the linen, and it was obvious that this was a mummy which had been re-wrapped after the original mummy had been damaged."

At this stage, Egyptologists had to rely on the naked eye for their information, though from early on it was the custom to note down in meticulous detail what they saw. We still have Maspéro's interesting account of how the mummy of Ramesses II was first revealed on 1 June 1886:

> The first layer of cloth was removed and revealed successively a strip of material, about eight inches wide, wound round the body, then a second shroud sewn together and kept in place by narrow strips attached at intervals, then two thicknesses of bandaging and a piece of fine linen stretched from the head to the toe. A picture of the goddess Naut, about three foot high, was drawn on the latter in red and black as prescribed in the ritual. A fresh bandage was placed under this amulet, then a layer of pieces of linen folded in squares, and stained with the bituminous matter the embalmers had used. When this last wrapping was removed, Ramesses II was revealed. He was tall (nearly six foot after embalming), well made, and perfectly symmetrical. His head was elongated and small in proportion to his body, and the top of his skull was completely bald. His hair, which was thin over his temples, became thicker towards his neck and fell in smooth straight locks about two inches long; it had been white when he died but was stained light yellow by the perfumes. His eyebrows jutted out from a low narrow forehead. He had thick white lashes, small close-set eyes, a long thin nose, hooked like a Roman and slightly flattened at the end by the weight of his wrappings, hollow temples, prominent cheekbones, rounded protruding ears with a delicate fold to the edge and holes pierced in the lobes for earrings, a strong and powerful jaw, and a very high chin. His mouth was wide open and had thick fleshy lips; it was filled

with blackish paste, and when some of this was removed with a chisel we could see a few well-worn teeth which were quite fragile in spite of their white well-kept appearance. His moustache and beard, which were sparse and carefully shaved during his life, had grown either during his last illness or after his death. The hairs were white like those on his head and eyebrows, but coarse and spiky and barely a tenth of an inch long. His skin was a sickly yellow, caked with black stuff. His mask gave us a good idea of his facial expression when he was alive: he had unintelligent features which bordered on the animal, but they were coupled with a proud and determined air of sovereign majesty. The rest of the body was equally well preserved, but had not kept its original appearance so well because the flesh had shrunk, and his neck for instance was no thicker than his spine. His chest was ample, his shoulders held high, his arms crossed on his chest, and he had long delicate hands reddened with henna, with very beautiful nails cut level with the flesh and cared for like a kept woman's. There was a gaping wound on his left flank where the embalmers had taken out the viscera. His genital organs had been removed with the aid of a sharp instrument, and according to custom must have been buried separately in the hollow interior of a wooden figure of Osiris. His thighs and legs were emaciated, with long thin feet, rather flat, rubbed with henna, like his hands. His bones were weak and fragile and the muscles had atrophied through senile decay; indeed we know that Ramesses II reigned for a number of years with his father Seti I and then for seventy-two years alone, so he was nearly a hundred when he died.

There is no doubt that this description was quite satisfactory by the standards of the last century, for it faithfully recounts every detail of Ramesses II's appearance, but it bears no comparison with the results that can be achieved by modern procedures, even when these are limited to the macroscopic. In this area Cockburn's autopsy of a nameless mummy, baptised Pum II because he had been loaned by the Pennsylvania University Museum, was a model one. It was carried out in Detroit on 1st February 1973 by a multidisciplinary team which had access to all the most modern scientific and technological resources, and their amazing results will be cited in more detail in the course of the following chapters. No mummy had ever been the object of such meticulous attention. Even to remove the wrappings was extremely difficult, because over the years the resin which permeated them had hardened and together they had set into a solid mass. Great care had to be exercised to ensure that the body was not damaged, and it took nine men working with chisel, hammer and electric saw seven hours to free the mummy. The whole operation was recorded on videotape and more than a thousand pictures preserve the details of each step.

Many modern medical techniques have been used to good effect on mummies. Recently Dr. Bucaille, with the aid of specialists from Cairo, made use of the endoscope, an instrument which television viewers may have seen on medical programmes being introduced into the body through natural channels such as the trachea, bronchia, oesophagus and rectum. Basically it is a kind of torch which lights up the interior of the body, and offers the great advantage that it allows internal examination without any incision in the flesh. Thus Dr. Bucaille could make an exhaustive examination of the royal mummies without causing them any damage, simply by introducing the endoscope into openings in the thorax, skull and flank which had already been made.

X-RAYING MUMMIES

Another invaluable modern technique is of course the X-ray, which was first used on a mummy by Sir Flinders Petrie in 1898, only three years after Röntgen had made his discovery. This early machine was not powerful enough to do more than take pictures of the mummy's feet and legs, but the experiment was soon followed by others.

In 1903 the first X-ray machine in Egypt was installed in a clinic in Cairo. It was too bulky to take to the museum, so the mummies had to be brought to it. The first to make the journey

was Thutmosis IV, who arrived in a taxi accompanied by Elliot
Smith and Wood-Jones. Later the technique was put to different
use when in 1913 Bertolli tried to discover whether any jewels or
amulets had been inserted between the bandages, and by chance
found an abnormality in the lumbar column of an Eleventh Dynasty body.

Since then the full value of radiography has been amply
exploited by experts such as Moodie, who published a book in
1931 illustrated with numerous X-ray photographs, and Jonck-
heere, whose study of a body thought to belong to Butehamon, a
royal scribe, appeared in 1942. In recent years Gray has written
numerous works on mummies housed in European museums
such as the British Museum and the museums at Newcastle,
Liverpool, Leiden and so on. By 1967 he had carried out one
hundred and thirty-three examinations and had succeeded in
refining his technique to the point where it was possible to vary
the kind of film, the filter and the type of exposure in order to
take into account the thickness of the bandaging or the sarcophagus. For instance, when he analysed the bodies in the Rijksmuseum Van Oudheden in Leiden, he managed to focus on particular parts in great detail through the use of a device called an
image intensifier which, while it reduces the number of X-rays
transmitted, enhances the brightness of the image.

Royal mummies were also X-rayed by Harris and Weeks in
1971, in collaboration with a team from the Universities of Michigan and Alexandria and Cairo Museum. So far they have published only papers concerning the skull and bone structure of the
face, but their main purpose was to examine the jawbones, the
arrangement of the teeth and their condition, to see whether
they could use these to establish the degrees of kinship between
different pharaohs. They used stereo-radiography for the whole
skeleton which, as its name indicates, produces a three-dimen-
sional image of the area examined.

There is another technique called tomography which, by scan-
ning the area to be X-rayed and reversing the plate which re-
ceives the impression, produces images of the desired section on
a selected plane and at a selected depth. An even more sophisticated version of the same process, resulting in more detailed
pictures, was used by Cockburn and his collaborators to show

the opening drilled in the base of Pum II's skull to remove his brain. It had already been discovered during the autopsy, but was only revealed to its full extent through polytomy. Finally the Detroit team used xerography, the latest technique in radiology, which can produce an image of the soft parts of the body on special sensitive paper, whereas classical radiography can only take pictures of bones.

UNDER THE MICROSCOPE

Of course mummies have been examined in minute detail under a microscope. However this is not as simple as it may sound, for even the examination of organic tissues from a living body comes up against enormous difficulties stemming largely from the fact that the structure of the tissues has to be fixed and the cells preserved in a state as close to their natural one as possible. After this fixation, the tissue has to be infiltrated with paraffin, which allows it to be cut by a precision tool called a microtome into slices of around twenty thousandths of a millimetre thick. Finally the section has to be coloured with dyes which have an affinity with the colouring of the cell itself or the tissue which is to be examined. Unfortunately this method cannot be successfully applied to mummies without considerable prior preparation of the tissues.

The first step is to rehydrate the fragments to be analysed, so that the cells are restored to their original size. Czermak tried to do this in 1852 by plunging samples into a solution of caustic soda, but the results were not very happy. Wilder did no better in 1904 with caustic potassium, though Ruffer was a little more successful six years later with sodium carbonate. Other methods were tried out with varying degrees of success, but it was only in 1955 that Sandison laid down the procedure which basically is still used today. It is extremely complex, and starts with the immersion of the sample for some time in a solution consisting of thirty parts of ninety per cent proof alcohol, fifty parts of one per cent proof formalin, twenty parts of five per cent sodium carbonate, and glycerine. When this has succeeded in making the flesh look as normal as possible, then the process of fixing the tissues by controlled dehydration is carried out, in exactly the same way as tissues from a living body are fixed. The sample passes through successive baths of eighty per cent alcohol, then ninety-six per cent, and then one hundred per cent; after further immersion it is ready to be put into a mixture of paraffin, stearin and beeswax.

An amazing sight then appears under the microscope. The whole structure of the skin is restored almost to normal, except for the outer layer which has usually vanished. The cartilage is intact with all its little rounded cells grouped into small columns. The muscles have kept their characteristic striations. In the case of the lungs, the texture of the tissues is so miraculously renewed that it has even proved possible to diagnose any lung diseases that were present before death. The arteries still have their three tunics and sometimes still contain drops of red blood, mostly in the surface blood vessels and particularly in the scalp; this is because after death blood tends to flow to the surface where the dehydration process operates more quickly than it does deeper inside the body, and so preserves the shape of these fragile cells.

When particles of fecal matter are magnified they reveal the deceased's eating habits, or at least the food he ate at his last meal: vegetable fibres were found in the intestine of Mentuheteps' wife Henenet, and muscle fibres in Pum II. Bones are less easy to examine because they are often brittle, and have to be softened in acid solutions before they can be cut into thin sections.

For a long time the eyes were neglected because their sockets looked empty, and it was some time before it was realised that the globe had in fact shrunk right to the back. When Sandison attempted to rehydrate an eyeball, he was surprised to see the socket gradually refilling almost to its normal state, and a greyish circular cornea appearing between the half-open lids. It even looked a bit translucent, though not as much as it would have done in life. He carefully removed it and gave it the usual treatment before examining it, when he found that the front of the eye remained, but the more fragile structures of the choroid and retina had disappeared.

Pum II from Philadelphia was the first mummy to have a

piece of his remains examined under an electron microscope. A magnifying power of three to twenty-four thousand revealed not only the secrets of his tissues but also of his cells, which were examined in minute detail. The technical prowess needed to delve into the smallest elements of these cells, down to the vacuoles which store the enzymes and the crinkled walls of the cells where the energy-transfer system is found, is quite incredible when one remembers that the body being analysed is more than two thousand years old.

BLOOD GROUPS

We all know that we ought to have a card in our wallets noting our blood group, so that in an emergency a blood transfusion of the correct blood can be given without delay. Of course the method of classifying blood was only discovered comparatively recently, in 1900 in fact, so it is hardly surprising that the labels attached to mummies' necks which we have mentioned make no reference to their blood group. Nonetheless it is possible to deduce it from a muscle or bone which has been dissolved into dust through a special process. This requires relatively large fragments, weighing about a gram, and so a different technique was invented by Connoly, who used an enlarging method to analyse tiny amounts of dust from human tissue, and so type the blood.

At first sight it is difficult to see what interest such a study could have, but two examples will soon show us that it has a practical application. When Boyd studied several series of mummies, he found that the blood groups A, B and O recurred with very much the same frequency in ancient Egypt as they do there today. Above all he was able to confirm the presence of group B blood in predynastic mummies, going back more than three thousand years before Christ, whereas it had been thought that group B was only a mutation of group O which first appeared during the Christian era.

The other example concerns the identity of individual mummies. We can now be sure that the human remains once thought to be those of Akhenaten are in fact those of Smenkhkare, Akhenaten's co-regent who succeeded him for a very short reign. The relationship of Smenkhkare to Tutankhamun had always been the subject of debate, and they were thought by Mme. Desroches-Noblecourt to be brothers. An anatomical comparison of Tutankhamun's body with Smenkhkare's showed that anthropometrically their measurements were very similar, and an analysis of their blood has shown that they could indeed be brothers, although it cannot prove this. Both of them belonged to group A2 and also to group MN.

POLLUTION IN ANCIENT EGYPT

Chemical expertise has contributed to our knowledge of mummies and mummification procedures, and it was inorganic chemistry which proved that dehydration was carried out through the use of natron, not salt. The sodium chloride, or ordinary salt crystals, which is found on the bodies or bandages came either from the natron itself or from the water used to wash the body before it was wrapped. This water was supposed to be water drawn from the Nile at Elephantine, but in fact it often came from a holy lake, a local river or even a well, and the latter could easily have contained quite an amount of salt. Iskander's analysis of the waste matter and the material used for stuffing showed that natron had a powerful degreasing effect, and provided the reason for its use in preference to ordinary salt.

Chemical analysis has also thrown a fascinating sidelight on the growth of pollution in our modern environment. The heavy metal salts which we imbibe with our food and drink and above all with the air that we breathe adhere to our bones, and so it is possible to use a spectroscope, a device for observing radiation, to compare the level of pollution in a mummy with that in a present-day corpse. The Chemistry Department of the University of Michigan carried out research along these lines which showed that although the quantity of mercury found is more or less the same in both cases, the bones of a contemporary corpse contain thirty times more lead than those of an ancient Egyptian. This is an amazing and worrying finding.

Interesting information is also being obtained in Prague by a team of biochemists under Strouhal who are examining the resins which had been poured into Pum II's skull and abdomen, and which had also been used to cover his bandages and seal the coffin lids. Their first objective is to determine its precise chemical composition, and they are then taking samples from conifers all over the Middle East to compare the two. They hope thus to be able to pin-point the exact source of the resins, and though this may seem a rather pointless exercise it will in fact throw light on or confirm the old trading routes of ancient Egypt, as well as Egyptian foreign relations. Already they have discovered a tiny scrap of cotton inside the linen, the first time that cotton has been found in the Middle East of that period. This raises an important question, as to whether Egypt itself grew cotton or whether it came from India, and if the latter what the relations between the two countries could have been.

Biochemistry is a new field in archaeology. It covers all the constituents of living matter, that is to say the glucides or sugars, lipids or fat matter, and proteins or nitrogenous substances sometimes grouped into glycoproteins or lipoproteins. All these are very long molecules which can only be examined by means of advanced technology. Some of them, like the gangliosides and the phospholipides which make up the nervous tissues, are very fragile and have broken down, but others like the neutral fats and cholesterol still remain to be found in mummies. The exploration of this area has only just begun.

CARBON DATING

As we have seen, it is possible to assign an approximate date to a mummy by examining the position of its arms, the method of embalming and the way it is wrapped, but this may sometimes be misleading when old techniques were employed at a time when they had generally gone out of use. Similarly the appear-

ance of the coffin is not an accurate guide because coffins were
so often reused. It is necessary therefore to have recourse to
more direct methods.

Carbon dating is one of these methods, and one which is by
now fully developed. We know that all organic tissue, whether
vegetable or animal, contains both ordinary carbon and also a
minute quantity of slightly radioactive carbon known as carbon
14, which comes from cosmic rays bombarding the ordinary carbon. Any radioactive matter will gradually disintegrate through
the loss of its radioactivity until it reaches a stable element, and
the loss of half of the radioactivity reduces it to a state called the
period or half-life of the element: for carbon 14 this is 5,568
years. Since dead tissue no longer accumulates carbon 14, it is
possible to measure the radioactivity in a tissue and then to date
it accurately to within a few dozen years. In order to do this, a
fragment of the tissue is burnt; this gives off carbonic gas from
which the pure carbon can be extracted and its radioactivity
measured by a Geiger counter. The disadvantage of this process
is that it requires several dozen grams of tissue, which may not
be available or which it would not be desirable to burn.

A new dating method is therefore being explored by Barraco,
which uses only a small quantity of matter. This involves the
racemisation reaction of amnio acids, a rather esoteric process
but one which is nevertheless worth explaining because it offers
new and hopefully fruitful avenues of research. Living tissue is
made up for the most part of large molecules, the proteins,
which themselves consist of a varied assortment of small particles called amino acids whose most striking physical feature is
their capacity to deflect polarised light. Dextrorotatory amino
acids, which are not found in nature, deflect it to the right.
Levorotatory amino acids, which are found in living organisms,
deflect it to the left. However, levorotatory amino acids in dead
bodies transform themselves over a long period of time into dextrorotatory form, and this transformation is known as racemisation. The proportion of one form to another therefore shows how
long the body has been dead. The method however has one
drawback, and that is that the rate of transformation varies with
the temperature of the body, and it is therefore vital to know the

approximate thermal conditions of the place where the mummy was buried.

Slowly, as mummies are unwrapped by archaeologists, examined under radiography, explored by means of microscopes, analysed for their reaction to different chemical elements and subjected to fire so that they can give information to the Geiger counter, they are yielding up their secrets to us.

CHAPTER 3

MUMMIES, THEIR LIVES AND TIMES

Each new method of analysis that has been described brings its own contribution to our knowledge of Egyptian civilisation. It has already provided us with a mine of direct information on funerary rites. It has helped us to determine an individual's life expectancy in pharaonic times, and it has shown us the food habits of the ancient Egyptians and the dental troubles to which these led. It has enabled us too to detect their illnesses from the marks left on their bodies and skeletons. Finally, study of the bodies of both the kings and their ordinary subjects has sometimes confirmed our theories about the course of history, and will no doubt in future illumine periods which today are still obscure.

I CIVILISATION AND PATHOLOGY

Pounds of gold

Convention in ancient Egypt dictated that the deceased required a whole variety of trappings and equipment if he were to proceed decently to the afterlife, and these of course have provided archaeologists with a fertile source of research material. Numerous amulets were needed around his neck, waist and limbs, and were slipped between the layers of bandages, for it was considered extremely foolhardy to venture into the unknown regions beyond without protection against all the dangers which were likely to arise. Seven charms together was the general rule, for seven was the magic number, but during the later period one hundred and four were thought necessary to provide the best protection for the body. The best quality embalming also meant more amulets, and Tutankhamun for example was equipped with no less than one hundred and forty-three. Some mummies though, even the best ones, have no talisman at all, due no doubt not to the niggardliness of the family but to fraud or lack of conscientiousness on the part of the embalmer, for there was no-one to check up on him by examining the bandages. Even the funerary papyri which were essential to pass into the kingdom of the dead are not always in due form, and some have been found which begin with the name of one deceased and end with another.

Amulets were made of different materials according to the family's station in life. The best were made of gold, others of bronze, stone, glass, wax, or clay which was first baked and then enamelled. Some families were afraid that they might not have provided enough talismans, and so they placed stone moulds in the tomb which would enable extra ones to be made if required. Every aspect of Egyptian religion is represented in the statuettes of the gods and sacred animals, royal hair arrangements, and hieroglyphic signs. The most common are the Udjat-eye, the djed pillar, the girdle of Isis and the scarab.

The Udjat-eye (Fig. 4), the eye of the falcon god Horus appeared engraved on the seal over the incision made in the flank to remove the viscera: it symbolises clairvoyance and physical prosperity. The djed pillar, emblem of Isis, may have represented a tree stripped of its branches or a post with notches cut into it: it was the principal amuletic sign used to protect the dead. The girdle of Isis (Fig. 5) was often found together with it, and was shaped like an ankh cross with its lateral arms drooping.

Fig. 4.   Faience amulet in the shape of an Udjat-eye or falcon's
eye.

The scarab is found on pectoral seals or worn on rings: pushing its ball of cow dung backwards with its hind legs, it
represented the daily course of the sun round the earth. One particular scarab, the "heart scarab" was essential to the mummy; it
was placed on the chest and was quite large, made from green-
coloured stone reminiscent of vegetation and so symbolising
rebirth; it was often set in a gold band or encrusted with gold.
The flat part was engraved with an extract from the thirtieth
paragraph of the Book of the Dead which guards the deceased
against any false evidence brought before the tribunal when his
heart is weighed and which by force of magic certifies in advance that the heart belongs to a righteous man.

Not all the amulets have such a clear meaning. The little
earthenware objects in the shape of a bonnet or the royal crown,
or the vulture-goddess which watched over the Southern Kingdom and the erect cobra which watched over the Northern Kingdom, gave even the humblest deceased a little of the pharaoh's
powers and may have been intended to impress the members of
the tribunal of the dead when they were giving judgement. The
ankh sign, in the form of a looped cross, gave life; the bundle of
reeds gave strength; and the little heart may have had the same
meaning as the scarab, restoring consciousness to the dead man.

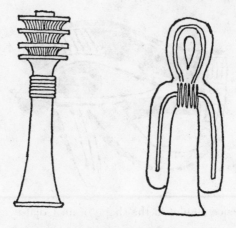

Fig. 5.   Djed pillar and girdle of Isis.

The mummy's head rested on a single piece of wood carved into a curved shape and supported on a straight pillar set into a socket (Fig. 6). In later periods this went out of use and was replaced by a miniature carving which was slipped under the neck. The symbolism of other practical implements such as the set-square and the level is even more obscure, though one can guess that they were intended to ensure eternal equilibrium.

The third finger of the left hand of the body bore a gold ring which was sometimes surmounted by a scarab and symbolised purity and, more significantly, survival as a god. Rich people wore several rings, while the poor had to be content with only one made of wax or gilded plaster.

Once the mummy was complete and properly bandaged, two strips of red leather rather like a scapulary were placed round its neck and over its shoulders. Egyptologists refer to them as mummy's braces. They are wider at the ends and finished in two goffered pieces of white leather bearing the image of a god.

The richer the deceased, the more numerous were the amulets and jewels. The pharaohs themselves were equipped with a treasure-house of objects which have dazzled their discoverers down the ages. Mme. Desroches-Noblecourt, who witnessed the unwrapping of Tutankhamun, has described the astonishing

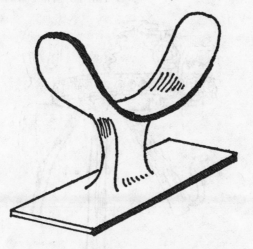

Fig. 6. Mummy's head-rest.

collection of diadems, necklaces, bracelets, rings, pendants and pectorals which were revealed as each bandage was removed. The Pharaoh's skull was covered with two linen headdresses embroidered with beads and decorated with gold leaf cut in the shape of the vulture and the cobra; on top of these, a gold circlet held in position four more gold bands at the back, two undulating cobras at the sides, and the erect cobra and vulture's head at the front (Fig. 7). His neck was protected by several bead necklaces and twenty gold amulets, as well as a large throat-piece representing the sacred falcon with outstretched wings.

Tutankhamun's chest was adorned with five pectorals made of gold leaf or gold cloisonné, inlaid with glass, lapis lazuli and cornelian, and decorated with the eye of Horus, the serpent of Buto, the vulture of Upper Egypt, the winged scarab and the solar falcon. In addition he wore collarettes made of rows of gold and blue glass beads and gold pendants. The rings, finger-stalls and sandals which completed the mummy's attire were also fashioned from the same precious metal. Seven heavy bracelets covered the right forearm, and six the left. His waist was girded first with a belt of gold beads and then with one patterned with chased gold leaf. It would take too long to count and describe

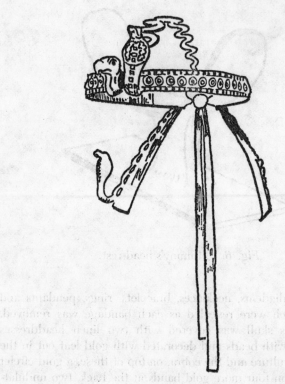

Fig. 7.   Diadem found on Tutankhamun's mummy. On the gold
            circlet is the vulture of the goddess Nekhbet of Upper
            Egypt and the cobra of Lower Egypt.

the jewels which adorned and protected him. The most unusual
ornaments worn by Tutankhamun were made of iron, which was
extremely rare in ancient Egypt. It was used to make a little
amulet in the form of a head-rest and a sacred eye on a bracelet.
Iron was also used for the blade of a magnificent dagger, with a
hilt surmounted by a pommel of rock-crystal, and a gold sheath;
when it was removed from the bandages the metal bore not a
trace of rust and was so clean that it shone like steel.

When to die

There is no doubt that some people did survive into old age in Egypt, for in hieroglyphic writing the sign for old age is a picture of a bent man leaning on a stick (Fig. 8). One of them was the wise man Ptah-Hotep, who lived to a great age but drew no satisfaction from it, for as he said: "Lord, my Master, I am now advanced in years and old age has reached me; decline has set in and the feebleness (of childhood) has returned and made me into a child again so that I sleep all the time. My arms are weak, my legs refuse to follow the bidding of my heart which is tired out. My mouth is dumb and can no longer speak; my eyes are weak, my ears are deaf; my nose is blocked and can no longer breathe. All sense of taste has gone. My mind is forgetful and cannot recall the events of yesterday. My bones ache in old age; to stand up and sit down are both hard. What used to be good has turned bad. Old age brings nothing but sorrow to man."

Fig. 8.   Hieroglyph for "to be old," followed by the determinative sign of an old man leaning on a stick.

Nevertheless the prospect of these misfortunes did not prevent the Egyptians from aspiring to long life, and it was considered courteous to wish that your fellow human-beings might attain the age of one hundred and ten years. Thus the sage Amenemope received the following letter one day from one of his respectful pupils: "May Amenti be granted to you without you feeling the effects of old age, and without you falling sick. May you fulfil one hundred and ten years on earth with your limbs still strong, as is due to a holy man like yourself whom the gods reward."

The best-known example is that of Ramesses II who lived to

be ninety-six years old after having reigned sixty-five years, and having married two hundred women of his harem who presented him with ninety-six sons and sixty daughters. His lasting vigour enabled him to have sexual knowledge of his daughters when they became nubile, and he had many more children by them. However, for each pharaoh who enjoyed exceptional health there were many many ordinary people who died young. It is very difficult to make a precise estimate of the mortality rate in ancient Egypt, because infants were buried separately from adults and there are very few of them in the cemeteries. X-rays of mummies often show up cartilages fused to the bone, which are a sign of an adolescent whose tissues have not completely hardened. In Turin Museum, seven hundred and nine adult skulls from the dynastic sites of Gebelein and Asyut were examined, and Chiarelli found that their average age was thirty-six. The true average would be lower still if the high infant mortality rate was taken into account, as well as the fact that complications in childbirth made the age of death for women lower. Nevertheless the figures do provide a basis of comparison with the life-expectancy of a present-day Swedish child, which is seventy-six for a boy and seventy-eight for a girl. A baby born in India today can expect to reach thirty-four years, while in 1969 in Egypt the average age was 51.6 years for a man and 53.8 for a woman. In three thousand years man has advanced a long way with the help of medicine and hygiene.

Nevertheless the mortality rate cannot have remained static, and must have been higher in periods of famine and lower when food was plentiful. Higher social classes enjoyed a longer life; thus the average age of the Ptolemies when they died, leaving out those who were assassinated, was sixty-four years, which is very near our modern average in Europe.

Eating brick

Egyptians had the most appalling teeth. Palaeopathological examination of mummies' jaws and skeletal remains has shown that dental decay derived from two factors, abrasion and caries.

This wear on the grinding surfaces of the teeth is almost universal, affecting both the pharaoh and the humblest of his subjects. It is not possible that every Egyptian ground his teeth, so one must look for the cause in the bakery. Crumbs of bread from every period have been found in the tombs, and at first it was thought that the fibrous husks of whole grains of corn which they contained were the sole cause of the decay, but then when pieces of bread were broken in half and examined more carefully little specks which reflected light were seen. Mineralogical analysis showed that some of these were smooth grains of sand and others small rough pieces of felspar, mica and sandstone. Evidently this was the cause of the wear, but the reason for the presence of such particles in the bread was not so obvious.

The explanation was discovered by Prag, an English researcher who had read in Pliny that the citizens of Carthage used first to crush their grain with a pestle and then add a small amount of pounded brick, chalk and sand, before they milled it. Prag experimented with crushing corn in an old grinding mill, and found that after a quarter of an hour of effort the grains were still nearly all whole. However, when he added sand in the proportion of 1 to 100, he quickly obtained quite fine flour. Leek, who is a specialist in the dental study of mummies, made a detailed analysis of the mineral fragments in the bread and found that they came from:

the earth in which the corn had grown;

the implement used for the harvest, which was a wooden sickle with silex teeth;

sand raised by the wind during winnowing;

sand which the wind blew into the granaries, which were badly designed and vulnerable to sandstorms;

tiny fragments which constant use wore off the pestles, mortars and mills; and finally

the minute quantity of minerals which were deliberately added to make the flour finer.

Dental caries is not so common and has a different cause. Elliot Smith found very little of it in the predynastic periods, but later on during the Fourth Dynasty it attacked the aristocratic classes though not the common people. Gradually it became more widespread, and during the later period of decline it was present among all sections of the population. Obviously it was linked to food habits: richer and more abundant and varied food which included more cooked items made everyone more prone to it. Abrasion and caries have the same consequences, which are expulsion of the pulpal chamber and then its infection with cysts and abscesses forming round the root of the tooth. Mummies often have large cavities in their jawbones caused by infection spreading from the teeth, sometimes bringing on osteitis or osteomyelitis. In extreme cases infection became general and septicaemia resulted; perhaps this was what killed Amenophis II, whose teeth were in a dreadful state.

"There is a book-keeping scribe who lives with me. All the muscles in his face twitch, he has ophthalmia in one eye, and worms are gnawing at his teeth." Thus the Anastasi IV papyrus described the symptoms of a man afflicted with dental neuralgia; and the case was not unique, witness the body of specialists which grew up to cope with these problems. Herodotus gave an account of them as follows: "The whole country is full of doctors, some for the eyes, some for the teeth, some for the stomach, and some for hidden diseases." The names of a few have come down to posterity, such as Ni-ankh-Sekhmet who was "head of the dentists in the royal palace," as well as being a doctor, and Hesi-Re of the Third Dynasty whose tomb has been discovered.

Their impressive phrases conceal their lack of knowledge and their inability to relieve the sufferings of their contemporaries. The Ebers papyrus, which is a vast medical encyclopaedia and a collection of therapeutic recipes of dubious efficacy, offers several methods for curing tooth-ache: "Another specific for getting rid of an ulcer in your teeth and for strengthening the gums: cow's milk, I; fresh dates, I; dried carobs, I. Leave this outside during the night for the dew to fall on it, and then chew it for nine days." The unfortunate sufferer could not have experienced much relief from such remedies.

There is one last find which has given rise to great excitement among the kind of Egyptologist who is so enamoured of his subject that he is convinced nothing new has been discovered since the time of the pharaohs. The exhibit in this instance consists of two teeth found in a necropolis of the Old Kingdom at Giza, two molars joined by a twisted gold thread which encircled them above the roots (Fig. 9). Here, it is claimed, is the evidence of dental care. The belief is reinforced by the presence of tartar not only on the teeth but also on the gold thread, which would seem to prove that the band had been put in position while the person was alive. However, the tartar has never been examined under a microscope and it is quite possible that mineral accretions from the earth in which the corpse was buried could have brought about the same result; also, the two teeth show a very different

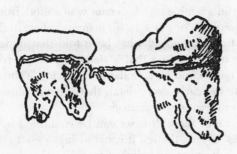

Fig. 9.   Two teeth held together by twisted gold wire.

degree of wear; and finally they appear too far from each other to have been fixed while still in the mouth.

In rare cases, mummies have an artificial tooth carved from ivory and mounted on a wooden pin. The arrangement does not seem very secure and it looks as if in reality it was the embalmers who inserted it in order to make the corpse look as presentable as possible. This theory is borne out by the fact that no royal mummy has ever been found with the mark of any dental operation, though it was the pharaohs who suffered the worst tooth decay and it would be unthinkable for a pharaoh to be left in pain if the dentists had really possessed any effective techniques.

From atheroma to infarction

It is said that one of the plagues of our civilisation is disease of the arteries, which causes infarction, brain haemorrhage and arteritis, and its prevalence is supposed to be due to the richness of our food, the climate of insecurity in which we live, and the stresses which we endure daily. But the Egyptians ate rather frugal meals, although their food was rich in fats, they hardly ever abused alcohol, had no tobacco and lived under less strain than we do, and yet they too suffered from atheroma and arteriosclerosis. They too experienced angina pectoris, with its pain spreading to the arm, as well as infarction, and they were well aware of the dangers of the symptoms for their doctors were taught: "If you examine a sick person who suffers from stomach-ache and complains of pains in his arm and chest and down one side of his stomach, and who has been told that he has the uadj disease, you must tell him that a sickness has entered into him through his mouth and he is in danger of dying." The description is so accurate in nearly every detail that it could almost be taken from a modern treatise on disease.

The presence of these diseases can be confirmed by examining the mummies' bodies, though it is not always easy to make a precise diagnosis because embalming modified the tissues. For example, Ramesses II's heart seemed clear of any serious lesions, but as the embalming process had reduced it to the size of a biscuit about three by one and a half inches square, and as it was so hard that it had to be cut with a saw, it was hardly possible to make a proper examination. Sometimes evidence does come to light, as in the case of Teye, whose mummy was discovered at Deir el-Bahri and which when dissected revealed a thickening of the coronary arteries and fibrous zones in the walls of the heart which are the scars of an infarct.

X-rays of mummies often show up hardening of the arteries in the limbs. Merneptah, who is generally thought to be the same pharaoh as the one mentioned in Exodus who drowned in the Dead Sea, did not seem on first examination to have died in this way. He was one of the first mummies to undergo a full anatomical examination, which revealed that his aorta was dotted with calcareous deposits. The aorta was then sent to London for its tissues to be analysed, and under the microscope it could be seen that the lesions were simply the effect of old age and were not caused by pathological deposits of cholesterol. Nevertheless these deposits have been found on many subjects, not only on large arteries but also on small ones, the arterioles, whose lumen they restrict. One case has also been found where the arteries of the intestine had been attacked; they belonged to the singer Har-Mose of the Eighteenth Dynasty, and were discovered inside a canopic packet.

Finally it is clear that Teye suffered from high blood pressure as well as from coronary troubles. There is no testimony to this from any contemporary doctor, but the evidence in his kidneys is unmistakeable.

Bronchitis and tuberculosis

The Egyptian climate may be hot and dry but it can be deceptive, for the nights are cool and often cause chills which may bring on bronchitis. People seem to have suffered a great deal from coughs, and the Ebers papyrus contains no less than twenty-one potions and one inhalation intended to alleviate the symptoms. Honey was known to provide relief and is a vital ingredient in all the remedies. Many skeletons also bear the evidence of osteoarticular tuberculoses, which leads one to think that pulmonary tuberculosis must also have existed, although so far no direct proof has been found. Periods of famine would certainly tend to produce cases. It is not difficult for today's doctors to examine the mummies' lungs, for the embalmers used to preserve them after treatment in canopic jars from which they can be extracted and analysed for signs of the pulmonary diseases that attacked the pharaoh's subjects. Medical experts were able to deduce that Har-Mose the singer, whose deteriorating arteries threatened to give him an infarct in the intestine, in fact died earlier from bronchopneumonia, because when they put his right lung into a bucket of water it sank instead of floating.

The most frequently encountered lesions derive however from anthracosis and silicosis. Today these illnesses unfortunately still affect miners and quarry workers, who as a result experience difficulty in breathing and become susceptible to tuberculosis. The initial damage comes from breathing in particles of mineral matter that are floating in the air in the mines. In ancient Egypt the same effect was probably produced by inhaling tiny sand crystals during storms, which would give rise to fibrosis of the pulmonary tissue which in turn would cause breathing difficulties. The level of silica in Pum II's lungs reached 0.22%, while the normal level is less than 0.05% and the outside limit is 0.20%.

Carbon deposits are also often found in the lungs. This would not have produced serious ill effects, but it does confirm that many Egyptians lived in small, badly ventilated rooms where candles and fires produced a great deal of smoke.

Pain then as now

The Egyptians may have misunderstood the diseases they suffered from, and they certainly gave them other names from the ones we know today, but nonetheless they experienced many of the same illnesses as we do, for which their mummies provide ample testimony.

In the stomach of one young woman of the Ptolemaic period, we find a thick band of sticky whitish substance from the tip of her appendix across the whole pelvis, which indicates that she suffered from severe appendicitis. Another young girl had had a rectal prolapse, in which the rectum protrudes through the anus, but this must not be confused with the numerous apparent prolapses which are found on bodies in the great graveyard of Hesa island: these are not pathological but are due purely to the effect of intestinal gases accumulating as poorly mummified bodies decomposed, and finally pushing out the intestine.

It seems that liver attacks were not common among Egyptian women, for the symptoms are not mentioned in the Ebers papyrus and Smith and Dawson found only one body out of some thirty thousand examined in which stones were present in the biliary duct; it belonged to a priestess of Amun.

Kidney stones seem to have been a little more common, but no good reason has yet been offered to explain why in one case embalmers had inserted one of these stones into its owner's nostril. Stones can be discovered now without going to the trouble of conducting an autopsy, simply by making an ordinary X-ray which shows them up in the kidney, ureter or bladder. One poor woman of the Twenty-first Dynasty must have suffered all her life from cystitis and lumbar pains for both her kidneys were riddled with holes from abscesses and swarming with colon bacilli.

Both mild and serious skin diseases have left their mark on the skin of some mummies. Ramesses II's forehead was covered in comedones, and Ramesses V's face, stomach and thighs were pitted with smallpox scars. One priestess of Amun who died at an advanced age after having been bedridden for a considerable time still carried on her buttocks and back large ulcer scars which the embalmers had tried to hide with pieces of gazelle skin.

Leprosy and the plague which sowed such terror in the Middle Ages were already spreading in antiquity: evidence of the first has been found on the multilated hands and feet of a Coptic woman, and of the second on an Egyptian from the Greek period who had lesions on his lungs and liver.

A common disease in Egypt both in ancient times and today is bilharzia, which the Ebers papyrus calls the âaâ sickness and which is a parasitic disease caused by a kind of worm which still flourishes today. It lodges in the urinary tract and causes blood stains in the urine, or less commonly attacks the intestine where it makes the spleen swell up. Ruffer discovered calcified eggs from this parasite in the urinary tract of a mummy from the Twentieth Dynasty. Threadworm too has plagued man from the earliest times, for its eggs have been found in a prehistoric saltmine in Austria, and in Egypt for the first time in Pum II's intestine.

The pharaohs were not spared any of these diseases. Ramesses V, who had already caught smallpox, was also the victim of a large inguinal hernia which descended into his scrotum and doubled its size. The royal bearing of Siptah, who succeeded Seti II, must have been seriously affected by the limp which troubled him from his childhood onwards, for his whole right leg was atrophied and ended in a club foot, clearly the consequence of polio (Fig. 10). Another man who must have suffered equally badly was an ordinary citizen discovered by Petrie at Deshasheh, whose femur was three inches short; he could hardly have walked without a prosthesis and must have found life very difficult.

Sometimes the presence of quite a small lesion is sufficient to

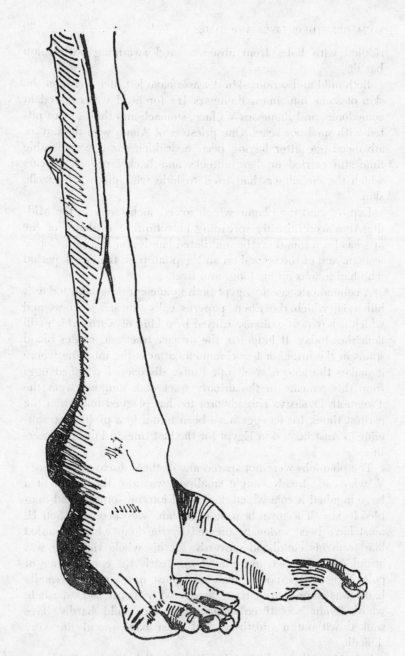

Fig. 10. Considerable shortening of Ramesses Siptah's lower right leg, with club foot, resulting from an attack of poliomyelitis in childhood.

allow a doctor to reconstruct an individual's medical history. Thus a localised thickening of the dome of a skull found in a First Dynasty skeleton indicates the existence of a meningioma, a strange benign tumour in the meninges. It can be deduced from its position on the right hand side of the skull, just above the ear, that the person must have suffered repeated attacks of epilepsy and paralysis of the left hand side which would have affected the leg more than the arm.

Some beings were even more unfortunate. Among the monkey mummies found at Hermopolis there was a tiny human creature who must have been stillborn and who was a victim of anencephalia, that is to say he had no brain and no top to his skull. Dwarfs like those one sees today in circuses, were not unusual in Egypt and have been found dating from the predynastic period. They were highly regarded and the luxurious sarcophaguses and tombs of dwarfs such as Seneb and Puoinhetef bear witness to their elevated social station. It is possible that they played the role of jester at court, for in one list of palace officials there is the title "Director of the dwarfs" and "Master of the dwarfs in charge of clothing."

In 1825, Granville brought back the first description of a gynaeological ailment in ancient Egypt: a malignant tumour in the right ovary which had attacked the peritoneum. Strangely this observation has been the only one of its kind and no other researcher has ever mentioned finding a fibrous tumour or a cyst in the ovary. Supposed vaginal prolapses, commonly known as dropped vaginas, are nothing of the sort but are due to the same cause as the rectal prolapses already mentioned, that is to say the distension of the abdomen with gases produced by decomposition. Engelbach and Derry were struck by the considerable enlargement of the vagina in the mummies of the women of Mentuhotep II's court; but they rejected any improper explanation and decided that the peculiarity must stem from some special method of embalming. Contemporary gynaecology is one branch of medicine that has little to learn from the study of mummies, though it would not be true to say that Egyptian women were safe from genital disorders because the Ebers papyrus gives remedies for treating vulvitis and metritis which it calls "remedies for refreshing the uterus and ridding it of heat."

Doctors had no hand in childbirth, which was the concern of matrons, who might qualify to be called midwives if it were not for the damage they often caused during births. One of the two royal wives of Mentuhotep, Henhenet, may well have died in labour; her bladder was so distended that for a long time anatomists took it for a dilated vagina, but in fact the vagina opened into it through a wide tear. Her pelvis was hardly bigger than a chimpanzee's and so was not wide enough to allow the baby to come out normally, with the result that it had to be extracted by force and made huge tears in the vulva and bladder.

It seems that the Egyptian pelvis was usually rather small, which gave rise to difficult births. Smith and Derry found, in the cemetery at Hesa, the skeletons of three women who had died during their pregnancy, one of them in her last month; the tiny skeleton of the foetus lay in the middle of her pelvis. Elsewhere there is evidence of a dramatic delivery which ended in the death of both mother and child: the remains of a Coptic negress were found buried in the position she was in when she succumbed after terrible sufferings, lying on her back with her thighs outspread and the head of the foetus caught and crushed in her narrow pelvis. Pregnancy was not always welcome, and those young girls who unhappily became pregnant outside marriage were liable to severe punishment. One young Nubian woman who was a few months pregnant was beaten to death for this reason, and she was found with the bones of her hands and feet broken and her skull fractured.

Egyptian medicine had few drugs to deal with illnesses, so in order to ward off death from their children mothers used to intone the following moving incantation:

Disappear, o demon who comes in the darkness and enters
  stealthily, with your nose behind you and your face turned
  backwards, for that which you came for will escape you!
Disappear, o larva who comes in the darkness and enters
  stealthily, with your nose behind you and your face turned
  backwards, for that which you came for will escape you!
Did you come to embrace this child?
I will not permit you to embrace him.

Did you come to calm him?
I will not permit you to calm him.
Did you come to harm him?
I will not permit you to harm him.
Did you come to take him away?
I will not permit you to take him away from me. . . .

If this chant had no effect, then a mouse was cooked and given
to the child or his mother to eat. Its bones were also placed in a
little linen sachet knotted around the neck, unless the case was
so desperate that there was no time to remove them. This explains why some children found in the predynastic cemetery of
Nag-ed-Der still have in their digestive tracts bones from the
mice they consumed just before they died.

Signs of disease in skeletons

Examining skeletons and x-raying mummies has brought to light
the surprising fact that vertebral arthrosis was just as common
then as it is now. Gray found "parrots' beaks" in more than a
quarter of the eighty-eight mummies he examined. This is a very
high percentage, especially given the low life expectancy of the
time. Ancient Egyptians also suffered from slipped discs, for
which nowadays we blame the sedentary habits of people who
go on long journeys by car and take only irregular exercise.

Curvature of the spine in childhood and rheumatism of the
spine in the young adult also left visible marks. One old man
with long hair and a white beard, who had been a member of
the local community of foreign Christians which had established
itself near the temple of Philae, is the oldest example and one of
the best illustrations of a case of chronic gout: enormous whitish
concretions of urate of lime had gathered on his feet, especially
round his big toes and also at the ankle, while chalky masses
could still be seen deforming his knee-caps and ankles. Such
cases used to be common in the recent past, but have now become much more rare since it is possible to eliminate or inhibit
uric acid with the use of drugs.

Arthrosis of the limbs had little time to establish itself when

life was so short; however, cases have been discovered where the
hip and knees were affected, especially when they were predis-
posed to the disease by malformations which already existed.
Arthrosis of the shoulder is surprisingly frequent compared to
today.

Vertebral tuberculosis destroyed the spine of more than one
mummy and fused others, causing major malformations, but its
mark is particularly clear on a young priest of Amun of the
Twenty-first Dynasty. Not only had his four last dorsal vertebrae
and first lumbar one collapsed to form a single irregularly shaped
block, but as a result an enormous abscess had developed of
which the edge was still lodged in the pelvis. Such abscesses are
hardly seen today with the use of antibiotics, but used to be a
frequent consequence of tuberculosis of the bone. They would
attack any joint such as the elbow, knee or hips, and their prog-
nosis was very bad.

The collection of diseases which attacked the skeleton would
not be complete without mentioning benign and malignant
tumours and the much rarer dysplasia, as well as the so-called
disease of glass bones which is a congenital fragility of the bones
resulting in multiple fractures at the slightest shock. A little child
of the Twenty-second Dynasty suffered from this unusual disease
and his skeleton looked so curious and so slender that at first
those who discovered it thought it belonged to a monkey.

Wounds and other injuries

Many mummies show signs of fractures, but some of these especially in the later period resulted from the embalmer's carelessness, or even from deliberate efforts to make the body fit into
a coffin which was too short or too narrow. The consequences are
easily distinguishable from fractures caused by accidents when
the victim was alive. Smith and Dawson were amazed by the
considerable number of cases of bony callosities which they
found in graveyards from every dynasty.

It is strange how the Egyptians' ability to deal with different
fractures varies from our experience today. Some fractures of the
neck of the femur have been found perfectly healed, while others
had apparently not been tended at all, which would certainly

have caused death. Some which are considered difficult to set today, like the neck of the humerus, have been found perfectly knitted together, while others like the collarbone which is supposed to be simple to mend were badly done with the pieces overlapping considerably. This is odd considering that the Smith papyrus, which contains a thorough treatise on the treatment of wounds, provides the correct method of caring for this type of fracture by pulling the shoulders back: "You must put him on his back with something folded between his two shoulder blades; you pull on both his shoulders in such a way as to bring the collar bone outside until his fracture is reduced. You make two bands of linen and put one on each side of the arms, then you dress it with 'imeru' and treat it every day with honey until it is cured." Except for the dressing of imeru and honey, the treatment could not be bettered today.

Fractured bones were held in place by means of splints. We have the proof of this from the mummy of a person who is presumed to be the royal scribe Butehamon, who died of an open fracture of the bones of his forearm, and whose mummy still has this part of the limb kept in place by three cradles of acacia bark. In other cases pieces of wood wrapped in linen were used, and it may well be that the cloth was made heavier with plaster or resin in order to make it more rigid.

Not all these fractures were accidental. The saying "spare the rod and spoil the child" may not have been an Egyptian one, but it was one whose sentiments would have been eagerly concurred with. Education was tough and inculcated by force if necessary, as this exhortation shows: "Scribe, do not be lazy, or we shall soon make you bend . . . We teach monkeys to dance and break in horses." The rod was considered the most suitable instrument of this policy, and was widely used by teachers. Enna the scribe wrote to his master: "I have been with you since childhood, you have chastised my back, and your instructions entered my ears." It was commonly said, too: "A young man has a back, and listens to the person who strikes it." Theft and slander and indeed any minor offence were punished with a beating whose length varied in proportion to the gravity of the crime. In very serious cases, the punishment could be "one hundred blows, of which five shall make gaping wounds." A guilty soldier could be "beaten like papyrus." If a peasant did not pay his dues of corn to the exchequer, he would be beaten unmercifully. Undoubtedly this widespread use of the rod explains the large number of fractured left forearms found on skeletons, for it is a natural gesture to raise one's arm and cover one's head in order to ward off blows.

However, the use of X-rays to detect this type of injury without unwrapping the mummy has its limitations. Many skulls have been wrongly reported as fractured because any scratch on the skin of the scalp was likely to be filled with resin which is not transparent to X-rays and so shows up like a fissure in the dome of the skull. Thus the presence of these fractures can only usually be ascertained accurately when the mummy is unbandaged. Sometimes the circumstances of the case provide confirmation of the injury, as in the instance of a little boy of twelve years of age called Panechates, who was found at Thebes with his skull broken, his left eye torn from its socket and his knee dislocated. It can be deduced from a reconstruction of the crime that he had been held by the feet and thrown with great force against a wall or rock. The deed is so horrifying that some experts have tried to find a political motive for it, such as the need to eliminate a pretender to the throne, but this is pure conjecture.

We are equally ignorant of the reasons for the assassination of a Nubian woman who was found by Smith with her brain-pan smashed and clotted blood, brain matter and hair still clinging to her skull. Naturally soldiers suffered a greater number of fractures than civilians, due to the violent hand-to-hand nature of the fighting. The "Satire on the Professions" gives a vivid description of the soldier's life and the dangers to which he was exposed: "A slashing blow lands on his stomach, a brutal thrust batters his eye and another opens up a wound over his eyebrows. There is a gaping hole in his head . . . He is like a bird with its wings fettered, for he has no strength left in his limbs. If he does succeed in making his way back to Egypt, he will feel like a piece of wood eaten away by worms, and will have to keep to his bed with the pain." Later on we shall see the terrible kind of wounds which were inflicted by the weapons in use at this time.

The Royal Institute of Anthropology in London possesses a very odd item which dates from the Ninth Dynasty, and consists of a radius and an ulna, that is to say the bones of the forearm, which had been cut off a third of the way up. Their edges had united in a bony callosity, which proved that the victim must have survived his wound. Gray X-rayed another mummy of a man who had died at the age of fifty, which was even more curious. His left forearm had been severed cleanly just above his wrist a long time before his death, and an artificial forearm and hand had been fixed to the stump. The prosthesis however had nothing in common with sophisticated modern ones which enable the person to pick up objects, and it would not even have been usable during the individual's lifetime. It looked like a sort of gauntlet and was made of rolled up pieces of linen, without any kind of wood or metal framework; the fingers were crudely made from little rolls of cloth, and the whole thing was fastened on to the forearm and had retracted into it after resin had been applied, forming a single solid block. Of course the operation had in fact been carried out by a conscientious embalmer who thereby intended to make the limb whole again for use in eternity. Another surprise can be found in the National Museum of Hungary, where there is a mummy who had lost his nose when he was alive, and when he died had a new one made by the embalmer from a little piece of carved wood held in place by leather thongs.

None of these three cases could possibly be cited as evidence of any knowledge of surgery. There are only two possible explanations as to how the injuries occurred, one being a sabre blow during a battle, and the other being a punishment. The forearm seems to have been so cleanly amputated at right angles that the second explanation seems more likely.

Diodorous of Sicily recounts that "the law lays down that those who betray State secrets to the enemy shall have their tongues cut off; those who forge coins and change inscriptions on seals shall have their hands cut off; and so shall scribes who draw up false documents, deface records, or produce fraudulent contracts." A relatively mild penalty was "amputation of the nose and banishment to Zel," a garrison town on the borders of north eastern Egypt. Under Ramesses III, when a great plot in the harem was discovered the conspirators were brought before a tribunal which was specially set up to deal with such a grave

crime. However two of the judges chosen by the Pharaoh were
bribed by the women of the harem. They too were discovered
and indicted in their turn and in the words of the time "their
crime was apprehended and the penalty carried out on them by
cutting off their nose and ears." The penalties were severe and it
was dangerous to stray from the right path then.

It is also said, but without any proof, that the ancient Egyptians used to cut off their prisoners' hands at the wrist. The
pharaoh is sometimes shown in pictures holding a group of cap-
tives by the hair and striking them on the skull with his huge
club; no doubt this is a purely symbolic image, for there is no
mention of such a thing in any of the written texts. Egypt had
too great a demand for workers to deprive the country of such a
useful source of forced labour by producing sick and broken men
who would then have become a burden in themselves. Prisoners
were brought in long convoys walking in Indian file, to work on
the fields, hew out blocks from the quarries, carry huge loads,
and erect monuments; in short, defeated enemy soldiers who survived were reduced to slavery. It was on the battlefield itself that
the mania of the scribes to record everything accurately, including the precise number of dead, led to the practice of cutting off
a hand from each fallen adversary and counting them so that
there could be no possibility of error. The number of hands
counted and heaped up in piles showed the extent of the victory.
It was not always hands which were counted. There is a picture
on the walls of the temple at Medinet Habu which illustrates a
battle fought under Ramesses II against an army including men
from Libya; and as they were the only neighbouring people not
to be circumcised, it was their phalluses which were cut off and
piled in heaps so that they could be counted separately.

Marks of debauchery

Of all the mummies which have been exhumed in Egypt, there
are only four who can be said with certainty to have tattoos on
their bodies: Amunet, priestess of Hathor, found in an Eleventh
Dynasty tomb; two Theban dancers from a later epoch, and a
Nubian woman. They were not satisfied to have a discreet sign
like a blue dot at the corner of their lips but were literally cov-

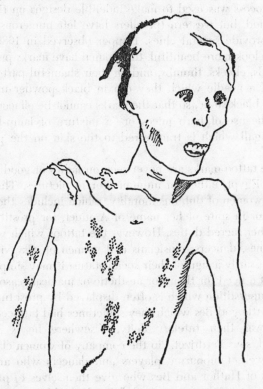

Fig. 11. Lozenge-shaped tattooing on the torso of the mummy
of a Theban dancer.

ered with indelible bluish marks in the shape of dots or dashes
arranged in parallel lines or in lozenges (Fig. 11). The priestess,
for example, was tattooed on her left shoulder, right arm, thigh
and the fold of her right groin; her stomach was sprinkled with
dots in the shape of a rectangle above her navel and in the shape
of a wide ellipse above her pubis.

A good number of statuettes and figurines of women decorated in this way have been discovered, dating from the Middle
Kingdom onwards. In the New Kingdom women dancers and
musicians have been discovered in the tombs with Bes, their
guardian goddess, tattooed on their upper thighs. It is not known

50   THE EGYPTIAN WAY OF DEATH

what process was used to make indelible designs on the skin at this period, but western travellers have left numerous accounts which provide several clues. Dapper observed in 1686 that "in order to look more beautiful, the women have marks put on their foreheads, cheeks, thumbs, and on their shameful parts with the point of a needle which they dip in black powder made from crushed black stone, so that the marks cannot be effaced." Others noted the use of herb juices or "a mixture of lamp-black and mutton gall which is transferred to the skin on the point of a needle."

These tattoo marks are never seen on ladies of good society in ancient Egypt, either on mummies or in pictures. They always involve women of dubious morality, which includes the priestess of Hathor in spite of her name of Amunet, for prostitution was part of her sacred duties. However the tattoos which we find on concubines, dancers, musicians and women of easy virtue were not necessarily a sign of their social status; it may simply be that they felt a need for them for aesthetic or magical reasons, or out of the superstition which is often displayed by prostitutes.

The little god Bes which they sometimes had tattooed on their thighs was their tutelary deity. Elsewhere he is sometimes depicted, says Perdrizet, "in the company of women clad only in their jewels, tambourine players and dancers who are harlots, servants of Hathor and Bes who give themselves to prostitution in the sanctuaries of these gods." Bes looks like a grotesque deformed dwarf with crooked legs, a large belly, hairy body and shaggy locks, an enormous head, with a grimace on his face and his tongue sticking out (Fig. 12).

Whether the tattoos took the form of abstract patterns or a god, they certainly did not signify virtue in ancient Egypt.

II HISTORICAL CONNECTIONS

Royal mummies

Some royal mummies have survived down to the present day sufficiently well preserved to be exhibited in Cairo Museum in a

Fig. 12. The god Bes.

special hall. There for the time being they rest behind glass, but no-one knows how long this state of affairs can last. For three thousand years they lay safely wrapped in their bandages in tombs where the temperature remained constant, whereas now they no longer enjoy the particular conditions which promised them eternal life. When they were brought out into the fresh air and unbandaged the delicate balance between decay and preservation was disturbed, and today they are beginning slowly but surely to disintegrate. Contact with the air produces chemical reactions which we do not yet properly understand and which profoundly alter the cohesiveness of the tissues; as the days pass microscopic mushrooms grow and destroy the outer skin and muscles. Soon if effective measures are not taken the most powerful lords that the ancient world ever knew will be reduced to dust.

The problem is an important one, especially in relation to mummies from the Old Kingdom because so few of them are still in existence today. The earliest known remains were discovered in 1832 by a French Egyptologist called Lauer, who was responsible for repairing the funerary monuments constructed at Saqqara by the famous architect Imhotep, a genius who is credited with having replaced brick with chipped stone and who is also said to be the father of medicine. He immortalised the name of his master King Zoser, founder of the Third Dynasty, by building the famous step pyramid for him, which Lauer was restoring to its original magnificence. One day Lauer decided to go into the pyramid vault to inspect the work. This vault had already been visited several times by explorers and archaeologists, but it contained no sarcophagus and was thought to be empty. Perhaps they had not really gone inside it, or perhaps they had been content with a quick glance around, for access was difficult and had to be effected through an entrance obstructed by an enormous granite block weighing four tons, which robbers had succeeded in moving only a little. By raising his arms, a thin man like Lauer could just squeeze through the opening and let himself fall to the ground, which he did. Once inside the room in the dust, he found two or three fragments of ribs and sternum and a left foot: the oldest surviving evidence of mummification in Egypt. The foot was wrapped in a cloth which had been impregnated with resin and had gone completely hard; indeed when the outer layers of bandaging were removed, the imprint of the tendons on the back of the toes could be clearly seen in the cloth. This was in fact the usual process in ancient Egypt at that time: embalming methods were still at a primitive stage, and so cloth soaked in hot resin was pressed on to the body and took as it were a mould of the corpse. The material clung so closely to the contours of the face that the discoverers of a Sixth Dynasty mummy did not realise that it was in fact bandages, and thought it was the body itself. The breasts and nipples and the genital organs were moulded equally carefully.

There was one man who had succeeded in entering the vault before Lauer, a man called Battiscombe Gunn who in 1926 had removed part of a spine as well as a piece of pelvis which he left with Cairo Museum. He had hesitated to attribute them to Zoser, but when they were compared with the more recent discovery it was apparent that they all came from a single body, which belonged to a man of robust constitution who had lived to an advanced age.

There is still a mystery over the missing pieces of the pharaoh. One explanation may be that the original robbers who had entered the tomb broke up Zoser's corpse and dragged it outside into a corridor in order to strip it at their leisure. In 1821 Von Minutoli and Segato had found the remains of a rich mummy, not in the funerary chamber but in an access passage; they removed it and put it on board a ship, but the ship was wrecked and the remains lost. It must be unique for a mummy to have three such final resting-places, one in the sea, one in a museum, and one still in the original tomb.

Dedkare-Isesi, the last but one pharaoh of the Fifth Dynasty, was another whose body has been recovered, though in a very poor state. Little is known of his history apart from the fact that he led an expedition to Nubia. When he was found in the funerary chamber built in the heart of his pyramid at Saqqara, only the left half of his body and face remained, and several bones were missing from that too. However the strips of skin and muscles clinging to the skeleton showed that an attempt had been made to embalm him. In addition, a packet of viscera was found in a little trench dug in the room, though the canopic vases which originally contained them had been broken. The tomb appeared at first to be intact, for the entrance was secured with a granite block weighing several tons, but looters had forced a way through into the vault by means of a narrow winding tunnel which brought them into the heart of the pyramid.

Dedkare-Isesi was followed by Unas, the last Pharaoh of the Fifth Dynasty, who was also buried in a small pyramid at Saqqara. He was not spared by robbers either, for all that remained of him when he was discovered was his left forearm and hand, which were in excellent condition, and two bones from his skull that were still covered with hair.

After that there is no trace of any royal mummy until the Eleventh Dynasty, when two bodies have come to light, those of the two great wives of Mentuhotep, Aashayt and Henhenet, who were embalmed by injecting oil of cedar through their rectum.

The next royal mummy belonged to the end of the Seventeenth Dynasty, and was that of Sequenenre-Taa, surnamed The Brave. He reigned at a time when his country was undergoing one of the most critical periods of its history, and was still suffering from the cruel blow to national pride which had been inflicted a century and a half earlier by the Hyksos invaders. These foreign aggressors were probably Semites who had themselves been pushed back to the west by the Aryan invasion of the Middle East in the second millenium, and by this time they were firmly settled in the Delta with their own kings. A dynasty of Theban kings continued to reign in Upper Egypt, where they united the southern provinces. It is very probable that Sequenenre-Taa began the reconquest of Egypt, which was carried on by his son Kames and completed by the latter's brother and successor, Ahmosis, who was the first of the Eighteenth Dynasty. Sequenenre died a violent death when he was only forty, killed in combat against the Hyksos according to most authorities or assassinated in a palace plot according to others. If he did die on the battlefield this would explain the negligent way in which he was mummified. The treatment must have been carried out on the spot in haste with whatever materials were available, for his brain was not removed and his body may not even have been treated with natron, a preserving salt; certainly if it was the treatment was inadequate. The body had already begun to decompose when it was embalmed, and everyone who has examined the mummy has remarked on its revolting smell. Its ribs and vertebrae were fractured and dislocated through being squeezed into bandages that were too tight, and its limbs were pulled apart at the joints. Sequenenre had been a handsome man, tall and slim, with powerful muscles; he had curly black hair which framed a small elongated face, and his teeth were in good condition, though his skull and face are disfigured now with six deep wounds.

The first wound, in the middle of his forehead, pushed in a splinter of bone as far as the meninges; the skin and hair pushed back round the edges of the injury indicate that the blow was struck when he was still alive. A second blow fractured the rim of his right eye socket, and a third broke his right cheekbone. All these three blows were inflicted with a battle axe. The fourth one, which broke the king's nose, may have been struck by a stick or the handle of an axe, while a fifth broke the skin on his left cheek and damaged the bone. The sixth was dealt by a pointed instrument, such as a pike, lance or javelin which penetrated below the left ear, shattered the mastoid bone and finished in the first vertebra of the neck. All the evidence proves that Sequenenre must have died in battle, and it seems that at least two attackers must have set on him, one with a pointed weapon and one with a blunt one. The fact that there is no damage to his arms or the rest of his body shows that he put up no resistance, and though there is a faint possibility that he was assassinated in his sleep it is much more likely that the first blow struck by a pointed spear or javelin under his left ear wounded him so badly that he fell, and his enemies then flung themselves at him and finished him off with axe blows (Plate V). In spite of the death of their leader, it seems that the Egyptian army must have won the day because they were able to retrieve and embalm Sequenenre's corpse.

Sequenenre-Taa's son, Uadjkeperre-Kames, also called Kamose, continued the struggle against the invaders, and an account has come down to us of an incident in which he complained in front of his courtesans of having to share his kingdom with an African king who was ruling Nubia in the south and an Asian king who was master of the Delta. Memphis too, the ancient royal city, was in the hands of foreigners, as well as the holy city of Hermopolis. Soon therefore he decided to lead his army into battle against the Hyksos, whom he defeated after he had pushed them back as far as Neferusi, north of Hermopolis. A little while later he disappeared in mysterious circumstances which archaeologists have been unable to clarify, for his mummy fell to pieces as soon as it was taken out of its hiding-place. It had been even less well embalmed than his father's.

His brother Ahmosis carried on the war and finally succeeded in getting rid of the Hyksos after he had seized possession of their capital, Avaris. This was a major turning-point in Egypt's history, and it also marks the coming of the Eighteenth Dynasty and the beginning of the New Kingdom. It was followed by the reconquest of Nubia. Finally, after two hundred years of occupation, the kingdoms of Upper and Lower Egypt were reunited.

Ahmosis married his sister Nefertari, who played an important role in politics, so much so that an extensive cult grew up around her after her death. Some of the characteristics she inherited from her family can be detected in her mummy, such as her teeth which are arranged in the same way as her grandmother Tetisheri's: the upper row juts out, especially the incisors, and the lower wisdom teeth never emerged. This last characteristic is a feature of the Eighteenth Dynasty which Sequenenre-Taa's mother Tetisheri founded, and is common to many of her descendants.

The mummy of Ahmosis himself has an interesting peculiarity, for the king had never been circumcised. Many explanations of this have been offered, including the suggestions that the founders of the dynasty were foreigners, or that he suffered from an illness like haemophilia which would have made surgery dangerous, but there is no factual proof or document which supports any of them. X-rays of his body also show that he suffered from degenerative rheumatism of the spine and fairly advanced arthrosis of the knees which must have caused him intense pain towards the end of his life and would undoubtedly have made it almost impossible for him to take part directly in battles. When he was mummified, his brain was extracted by an unusual method which consisted of making an incision in the side of the neck and cutting a passage to the brain by taking out the first vertebra. This left his nose quite untouched.

Ahmosis, Nefertari and their sister Sit-Amon were all buried in the same cachette at Deir el-Bahri, but Sit-Amon's mummy was less fortunate and was damaged by robbers. Later generations made an attempt to restore it, but all they could do was to gather up the few scattered bones that remained and assemble them as best they could round a bundle of reeds on which they placed her head, and then they bandaged up everything together.

Ahmosis and Nefertari had one son, Amenophis, who succeeded to the throne and was responsible for restoring order to Nubia by pushing back its borders even farther than his father had done, from Palestine right up to the Euphrates. His mummy had to be restored by the priests of Amun in the Twenty-first Dynasty, and it was so well bandaged up that Smith did not dare undo it, and to this day it is still the only one of the royal mummies to remain unwrapped. It was x-rayed in 1943 by Derry, who concluded that the pharaoh must have been fifty to sixty years old at the time he died. His right hand was pulled off by robbers and was put back on his stomach, and both his feet had also been detached. The body was re-examined by the Michigan Expedition in 1974, when they noted that there was still a faint scent from the little spray of delphiniums which the priests had piously placed on the mummy.

Amenophis I also married one of his sisters, Ahmosis-Meryet-Amun, in accordance with tradition. She was an unfortunate young woman who suffered from a badly deformed spine, bore only daughters, and died young. Of course her daughters could not aspire to ascend the throne, so it was a bastard son who succeeded under the name of Thutmosis I, by right of his marriage to Amenophis' legitimate daughter, his half-sister Ahmose. During his lifetime he had to put down two rebellions in the lands his forebears had recently reconquered, one in Nubia and one on the borders of the Euphrates. He was also responsible for the vast extension of the temple at Karnak. There is some controversy about his mummy, for he reigned from 1530 to 1520 B.C. and according to the records must have lived for about fifty years, yet the body supposed to be his is that of a young man. Harris and Weeks established this conclusively when they took X-rays which showed that the mummy discovered at Deir el-Bahri belonged to an unknown youth less than eighteen years old who had not yet finished growing. This body had been rebandaged by priests in the Twenty-first Dynasty, who labelled it Thutmosis I, but this is clearly wrong and the whereabouts of the true pharaoh remain a mystery.

Thutmosis also left only daughters who were legitimate, one of whom, Hatshepsut, married Thutmosis' illegitimate son who succeeded to the throne and took the name Thutmosis II. He too had to defend Egypt's frontiers and quell the troubles which arose in Nubia and Syria during his reign, which lasted from 1520 to 1505. His mummy, like his father's, showed him to have been uncircumcised, and it had the emaciated face of someone who had endured a long illness before dying around the age of thirty (Plate VI). It was also badly damaged by robbers who used knives and hatchets in their frantic search for treasure.

Thutmosis II had a legitimate son who should have succeeded him as Thutmosis III, but he was too young at the time of his father's death so Hatshepsut had herself appointed regent. A contemporary text leaves no doubts about her position: "Thutmosis II ascended to heaven in triumph and became a god. His son took his place as king of the Double Kingdom and became ruler on the throne of him who begat him. His sister (in fact his aunt), the divine wife Hatshepsut, conducted the affairs of the country as she wished." Indeed after one or two years the name of Thutmosis III disappeared from all official decrees and was replaced by Hatshepsut, who proclaimed herself the pharaoh. This extraordinary woman dressed as a man, insisted that her portraits depict her with a beard, and arrogated to herself all the royal titles that belonged to her position with the sole exception of the name of "powerful bull." She discontinued the warlike habits of her predecessors and instead organised trade expeditions, and reigned successfully over Egypt for twenty-two years until her death in 1483. Today she is best known to the modern tourist for the magnificent funerary temple which she had built at Deir el-Bahri. Her mummy has not yet been formally identified, but it is very likely that it is the one of a forty-year-old woman found in Amenophis II's tomb with the remains of other pharaohs. Her left hand is folded on her breast as if it were holding the royal sceptre, and her face, according to Harris and Weeks, bears a strong resemblance to Thutmosis. Originally the mummy was catalogued as belonging to "an old woman" but in fact its long brown hair, prominent forehead and slender nose lend it a certain royal dignity which belies its former attribution (Plate VII).

When Thutmosis III finally ascended the throne, he hastened to avenge his humiliation by erasing all trace of the usurper, and he had the name of Hatshepsut stamped out from all the monuments and replaced by his own and that of his father and grandfather. His early setback proved no disadvantage to him during his reign, which was one of the most glorious that Egypt knew, and lasted until 1450. He was both a great warrior abroad and a great builder at home. He led seventeen campaigns beyond Egypt's frontiers, almost one a year, first to ensure the complete pacification of Nubia and then mainly in Asia Minor against the Mitanni kingdom. When he died in 1450 he left his country larger and stronger than it was ever to be again. His own greatness however did not save him from the depredations of thieves, who soon despoiled his mummy and broke it into three pieces which had to be repaired. Evidently the fragments were difficult to put together securely, so the priests added four splints in the guise of four little oars painted white, three inside and one outside the bandaging. Fortunately the damage did not destroy the earliest evidence we have of a new technique of evisceration, in which the embalmers made a cut in his side parallel to the fold of his groin, rather than vertical. The mummy also shows that Thutmosis III was rather short and of solid build.

Thutmosis III was evidently determined to ensure that his own legitimate son did not have to suffer the same early disappointment as he had, so two years before he died he elevated him to be co-regent. Amenophis II succeeded to the throne without any problems, and reigned from 1450 to 1425. He was unusually strong physically, and an expert at handling weapons, a powerful archer, a skilled horseman, and he even took the oars in his own boat. He was proud of his strength and used to boast about his athletic prowess to all who would listen. He followed his father in carrying out most of his armed expeditions in Syria, but unlike his father he was cruel by nature and gloried in killing prisoners, especially the seven rebel Syrian chiefs whom he struck down with his own hand with a club and then dragged behind his chariot. When he died he was hardly more than forty-five years old. His skull and jawbone are exactly like his father's, but he had been circumcised, and his neck, shoulders, chest and abdomen are disfigured with little nodules whose precise cause has not yet been established because they have not been examined under a microscope.

There was no difficulty over his successor, though it is not certain that the next pharaoh was in fact his eldest son, or even his son at all. If he was not, this would explain why Thutmosis IV felt the need to publicise a dream he had in which he was resting in the shadow of the great Sphinx after he had been hunting for lion in the desert, when the sun god appeared before him and promised him the royal crown if he took on the task of clearing away the sand which was engulfing the Sphinx. He actually did carry out the task as soon as he was crowned, as the engraving on the stela between the beast's paws testifies to this day, and it seems likely that the story was used as a convenient piece of propaganda to advance his own cause and assert his right to the throne.

The style of his reign differed from his ancestors, for he conducted no further punitive expeditions. The eastern world had been pacified and the kingdom of the Mitanni which lay to the east of the Euphrates was at this time actively seeking an alliance with Egypt against the Hittites of the Anatolian plain who were threatening belligerence. A treaty was eventually concluded and sealed with the marriage of Thutmosis IV to a Mitannian princess who may have become the mother of Amenophis III, an uncharacteristically indolent pharaoh of this dynasty. Thutmosis IV's mummy is more shrunken than the process of dehydration alone would warrant, and it may be that some serious illness brought on his death between the ages of thirty and forty years. His arms were carefully folded on his chest, his fingers bent in the position of holding the royal sceptres, and his nails immaculate, but the actual process of embalming was not carried out as conscientiously as the outward signs indicate. The incision in his side is very long and crudely done, and looks as if it had been made in a hurry (Plate VIII).

When Amenophis III came to power in 1408, the alliances contracted by his father began to disintegrate, the Hittites formed a coalition in Syria in their greed to make conquests and annex the Mitanni, and the situation on the eastern borders began to look dangerous. The first cracks in the great empire created by the founders of the Eighteenth Dynasty were starting to appear. It was also the time when the seeds of the religious heresy which was to flourish under his son began to take root.

Amenophis himself seems to have been a weak man, not really capable of coping with the situation. He was an ostentatious sovereign who enjoyed his reputation for lion hunting, though it is true that he also did a great deal to foster the arts during his reign. The monuments that he had constructed are notable both for their gigantic size, best illustrated in the colossi of Memnon, and for their sophisticated reliefs. He was also well known for his taste for foreign princesses, whose hands he sought in marriage as far afield as the Mitanni and Babylon.

However in the end Amenophis III married a commoner, against all tradition. It was apparently the one time in his life that he asserted himself, and afterwards he became completely dominated by his wife, Tiy. The marriage caused considerable problems because it contravened the established rule that the senior royal wife must herself always be the daughter of a pharaoh, which meant that the pharaoh had to marry his sister. It was believed that when the couple were about to conceive, the god Amun intervened and fertilised the wife through the intermediary of the pharaoh, so that the resulting offspring received the imprint of divinity. Now controversy raged as to whether Amun would condescend to be joined with a mere daughter of gentry and if not whether Amenophis' children could have the status they would normally expect as the pharaoh's offspring. The clergy complained but Amenophis refused to listen and Tiy's hold over her husband grew ever greater.

Neither Amenophis' mummy nor Tiy's have ever been found, though a coffin bearing his name as well as another's was discovered in the Deir el-Bahri cachette. However when the coffin was opened it was quickly apparent that the body inside could not

belong to him, for the mummy's limbs had been given a more
lifelike appearance by inserting packets of mud underneath the
skin, a process which was not used in embalming before the
Twenty-first Dynasty. Tiy's father and mother, Yuia and Tjuia,
have been discovered, and indeed their mummies are among the
best preserved that we know. Tjuia's body is rather gaunt and
her nose is flattened by the bandages, but Yuia's is so lifelike that
with his eyes closed he looks as if he is simply sleeping. He has a
strong hooked nose, a slightly disdainful expression to his mouth,
and long fair curly hair which certainly did not belong to a man
of low birth. He was not only a high official of Amun, but also
"prophet of Min," "responsible for Min's oxen," and "lieutenant-
general of the charioteers." When his daughter married the
pharaoh he was also given the title of "Divine Father." Both
Tjuia and Yuia were of Nubian origin.

Amenophis III and Tiy had several children, who included
Amenophis IV, Smenkhkare and Tutankhamun. Amenophis IV
was an extraordinary character who, partly through mysticism
and partly for political reasons, replaced the worship of Amun
and the local gods by a new cult devoted to one god alone, the
sun god Aten, after whom he took the name Akhenaten. He was
so preoccupied by his religious reforms that he neglected the
Egyptian empire in Asia, which gradually crumbled; the Phoeni-
cian ports were lost, the Bedouin revolted in Palestine, the Hittites crushed the kingdom of Mitanni and won themselves the
most important position in the Middle East, but Akhenaten was
not concerned. He was busy building himself a new capital
called Akhetaten, and he also provided great encouragement to
the arts. During all this time however the clergy of Amun were
preparing a secret revolt, and the greatness of Egypt was finally
coming to an end. A whole book could be devoted to Akhenaten
and the various fascinating aspects of his character, but as his
mummy has not been discovered suffice it to add that he was
married to Nefertiti and that there are no more charming products of Egyptian art than the pictures of the royal couple danc-
ing the young princesses on their knees.

It was however Akhenaten's brother or half-brother, Smenkhkare, whom he elevated to be co-regent with him towards the
end of his life. The two enjoyed a close but uneasy friendship.

Smenkhkare only reigned for one year after Akhenaten's death, and his mummy was placed in a coffin bearing Tiy's name. This gave rise to considerable confusion, and indeed the body was for long attributed to Queen Tiy herself, especially since the wide pelvic bones seemed to belong to a woman and the attitude of the body, with its left arm folded across its breast and its right arm straight down the side of the body, was the one the embalmers used for royal spouses. No explanation has yet been offered for this intriguing departure from convention. A later examination concluded that the remains belonged to the heretical Akhenaten himself, but this attribution was proved wrong when it was found that the age of twenty to twenty-five at which the mummy had died was not compatible with the length of Akhenaten's reign. Finally an attempt was made to sculpt a reconstruction of the face, using the bones as a guide, and this resulted in a head which bore a striking resemblance to the gold mask of Tutankhamun, Smenkhkare's brother. There is no doubt too that the structure of the jaw is typical of the Thutmosis family.

If the body did indeed belong to Smenkhkare, we are left with a mystery as to the whereabouts of Akhenaten himself. It may very well be that a few years after his death when the cult of Amun was reestablished, the priests of Amun took their revenge by destroying the body. They had been cruelly humiliated, and it is known that they erased all traces of his name wherever they could, removed it from every monument they could reach, and pulled down the new city he had created stone by stone in the middle of the desert.

Power next passed to Tutankhamun, who at that time was still known as Tutankhaten, and who was married to one of Akhenaten's daughters, Ankhesenpaaten. He was then only ten years old. Three years later he returned to the ancient capital of Thebes, reestablished the worship of Amun as the official state religion, and changed his own name to Tutankhamun. He reigned for nine years, though he probably died too young to have any great influence in the affairs of state, and his chief claim to fame lies in the magnificence of his funerary equipment which survived intact down to the present day. His mummy still rests in its sepulchre in the Valley of the Kings, where it is visited every year by thousands of tourists and archaeologists. It is one of the most desiccated mummies known, not more than three millimetres thick between the skin and thighbone. His skull was shaved after his death in the fashion not of the pharaohs, who were always embalmed with their hair uncut, but of the high priests. No explanation for this has yet come to light, nor is it known whether he died of illness or at the hand of assassins, for he is wounded in the left cheek. His body looks frail and, taking his early death in conjunction with the premature demise of his two brothers Akhenaten and Smenkhkare, it would appear that he may have suffered from some congenital disease, though there is no definite evidence of this. He probably died in 1343, but it is easier to be certain of the time of year because of the bluets and mandragora plants which had been placed in his tomb and which in Egypt bloom in March and April; so if he underwent the ritual seventy days prescribed for embalming, he must have breathed his last in January 1343 B.C.

His widow Ankhesenamun can hardly have completed her period of mourning when she sent an ambassador to the Hittites with the mission of bringing her back a prince of the kingdom as a new husband. King Shuppiluliumash was hesitant at first, and then decided to send one of his own sons to take over the Egyptian throne. However the prince was assassinated on his way by the senior general, Horemheb, who had ambitions of his own, and this naturally revived the quarrel between the Hittites and Egypt.

In the end it was Ay, Ankhesenamun's grandfather and the father of Nefertiti, who married her, and he who became regent for the next four years. After he died, Horemheb took power and proclaimed himself pharaoh. He stamped out every trace of the Aten heresy, gave back the priests of Amun all the privileges of which they had been deprived, and undertook a complete reorganisation of the country to take back the powers which every petty official had appropriated for himself. The Thutmosis line finally faded out, and the new usurper took control and began to rebuild Egypt's former greatness. This was the beginning of the Nineteenth Dynasty, which made an even more brilliant debut than the preceding one but which ended deplorably.

No trace has yet been found of the mummies of Ankhesenamun, Ay and Horemheb. The next incumbent of the throne after them was Paramses, better known under the name of Ramesses I, who shared power with Horemheb during the latter's last years. He too had been a military man before he was crowned, with the titles of "head of the archers, head of the charioteers, head of the fortress, head of the mouths of the Nile, horseman to the king, the king's messenger in all foreign countries, royal scribe in charge of recruiting archers, head of the Double Kingdom's foot-soldiers, head of the prophets of all the gods, lieutenant of Upper and Lower Egypt, head of the judges, vizir and head of the royal households." He was not of royal blood, but the honours heaped on him gave him a claim which could not easily be set aside—though in the end he reigned for only a year and four months and accomplished nothing remarkable in that time. His mummy showed that he was quite old when he died and that he was a man of considerable height, short hair, and power-ful muscles. The features of his face were damaged, but the body itself was well mummified.

In fact his chief contribution to his country was his son Seti I, who ascended the throne in 1312. As usual the change in ruler was accompanied by rebellions on the borders, this time on the part of the Asian Bedouin, but Seti I proved a competent ruler who succeeded in pacifying the Eastern provinces after nu-merous campaigns. He never though managed to win back Syria from Hittite domination. When his mummy was found and unwrapped by Maspéro in 1886, it was completely intact and ad-mirably preserved. Only the area around his navel was damaged during embalming, and though his neck was broken his face looks astonishingly lifelike and has retained an awe-inspiring ex-pression of greatness and serenity. His hair and beard were closely shaved, and he had one ear-lobe pierced, though the pendant was stolen by robbers. He was less than five and a half foot tall. His arms are folded on his breast in the classical posi-tion, though curiously his hands are open and rest on his shoul-ders in such a way that they could not have held the sceptres which were the royal emblems (Plate IX). His genital organs were cut off and mummified separately.

Seti I was succeeded by his son Ramesses II in 1298, after they had shared the throne together for a few years. He had a very long reign of sixty-seven years, which gave him ample time to immortalise his name by inscribing it on the many monuments and buildings he had constructed, not to mention the edifices of his predecessors whose names he erased in order to substitute his own. He was also active militarily, and after he had conducted expeditions to the Sudan and Libya he carried the war to Palestine, and then had to face up to the problem of the Hittites. While Ramesses II had been busy fighting elsewhere, the new king of the Hittites, Muwatallis, had broken the treaty of alliance concluded with Egypt previously and had persuaded twenty other peoples to join a coalition with him. The Pharaoh decided that he would have to destroy this bloc, but he had not reckoned with the strong united army that faced him, and the Egyptian troops nearly came to grief in the main battle near Kadesh, a Syrian town situated on the banks of the river Orontes. It was the personal courage of Ramesses himself, and perhaps a bit of luck sent by the god Amun, which enabled the army to regroup and win a limited victory. An account of the victory was engraved and illustrated on a column of the temple at Luxor, though there is some doubt as to the historical accuracy of this epic poem which tells how the pharaoh put to flight twenty-five thousand enemy chariots by his own unaided efforts. As often happens in history, yesterday's enemy soon became today's friend, for when the Hittites found themselves threatened in their turn by the Assyrians they signed a peace treaty with Egypt and concluded a new pact of mutual assistance in 1278. To seal the friendship, a Hittite princess joined Ramesses II's extensive harem.

Ramesses II made a very impressive mummy which fortunately survived and which has already been described in a previous chapter (Plate X). His jawbone is very similar to his father's, though as might be expected in a man of his age and at that period, his teeth are badly worn and the bone near the roots is badly pitted from abscesses. Towards the end of his life he also suffered from a painful limp caused by arthrosis in his right hip.

Ramesses II had one hundred sons by his twenty wives, but only twenty survived him and it was the thirtieth son in order of birth, Merneptah, who became pharaoh in his turn in 1235. Merneptah inherited a rather precarious state of affairs inside the country, exacerbated by lack of finance which prevented the construction of many monuments, while those which were built were mostly made of blocks taken from Amenophis III's buildings. Abroad, Egypt's standing was little better. Merneptah had to take up arms against an invasion of Libyans who eagerly coveted the rich lands of the Delta because of the poverty of their own country, and he finally succeeded in repulsing them at the battle of Per-ir where he took nine thousand prisoners. Legend favours Merneptah as the pharaoh who makes an appearance in Exodus chasing the Israelites led by Moses out of Egypt. There is little evidence for this theory, which is really supported by only one document, the so-called stela of Israel, where it is written: "Canaan is devastated, Askalon is stripped bare, Gezer is ruined, Yenoam is reduced to nothing, Israel is laid waste and its people are no more, and the region of Kharu is widowed for Egypt; all these lands are united and pacified." No mention is made in the text of any pursuit of the Hebrews, rather the impression is given that they had already returned to their own country when the Egyptians undertook an expedition against them to punish them for their revolt. This would mean that the Jewish people embarked on their exodus before Merneptah came to the throne, under Ramesses II or perhaps even Seti I.

Merneptah was already fifty when he became pharaoh, and he reigned until he was seventy. Once again there is some controversy over whether he died of natural causes or whether he was assassinated, because the experts cannot agree on whether a hole in the nape of his neck was caused by a blow which killed him, or whether it was inflicted after death. In life the man was fat and bald, and suffered from a serious arthrosis of the cervical vertebrae, as well as from arteriosclerosis of the aorta and thigh arteries. In death he was castrated by the embalmers, and large whitish spots appear on his face which were said by some to be salt deposits. This baseless idea gave rise to a highly fanciful reconstruction of historical events, in which the spots were explained as having occurred when the pharaoh was engulfed in the Red Sea as the Bible relates. Unfortunately neither the historical documents we possess nor the chemical analyses which

have been carried out support this idea. There is no salt on Merneptah's skin, and the whitish spots derive from materials used in
the embalming process (Plate XI).

There then followed an interregnum of several years, during
which Egypt was ruled by two usurpers, Amenmes and Merneptah-
Siptah. Seti II, a legitimate successor, finally managed to win
back the crown and reigned uneventfully for six years. He is
chiefly remembered today for his mummy, of which the head and
arms were broken by robbers. His teeth were in good order but
his right hip had incurred an arthrosis.

Little more is known about his successor, Ramesses-Siptah,
who was probably his legitimate son, and who succeeded to the
throne in 1205 and died after a few years when still quite young,
probably between twenty and thirty years old. His mummy had
one arm broken by robbers, and, as we have described earlier, he
had obviously had polioriyelitis.

Egypt was in a bad state by the end of his reign, so much so
that a Syrian, Arsu, managed to seize power for some years. Soon
however a national upheaval put an Egyptian back on the
throne, and Setnakht reestablished order in the land and gave
the priests of Amun back the property of which they had been
deprived. Setnakht, who was the first of the Twentieth Dynasty,
ruled for only two years until 1198, when he was succeeded by
his son Ramesses III who continued the task of reorganisation.
Ramesses III proved to be a brilliant success, and once again
Egypt enjoyed a measure of prosperity, though evidently not to
the extent it knew in the past for the monuments that were
erected at this period were neither as numerous, large nor as
well constructed as the ones built by Ramesses II. Arrogance
seems to have become the besetting sin of pharaohs after
Amenophis II, and Ramesses III never tired of uttering his own
praises. "I planted the whole country with trees and vegetation,"
he boasted, "so that the people may rest in shade; I brought it
about that Egyptian women can travel safely where they wish
without being molested by strangers or anyone else on the way.
The foot-soldiers and chariots have been at peace during my
reign. . . ." The last phrase is exaggerated and could only apply
to the last years of his rule, for the first eleven years saw a succession of campaigns against the Indo-Europeans who threat-

ened Egypt from the west and from Libya. Egypt also had to repulse an invading fleet from the "Peoples of the Sea" which attacked the Delta coast. Ramesses' other boasts may also be misleading, for it is known that there were numerous strikes at this time which must mean that the people were less content with their lot than his self-congratulatory phrases imply.

Ramesses III was assassinated, though this is not clear from an examination of his body. An account of the trial of those involved in the conspiracy in the harem which brought about his death has survived, and informs the reader: "And now I say to you in truth, concerning those who committed the crime, that the crime of which they are guilty should rebound on to their own heads. As for myself, I am protected and guarded for ever for I am among the kings who are vindicated and stand before Amun-Re, lord of the gods, and Osiris, lord of eternity." These words can only have been pronounced before the tribunal in the name of the deceased king.

Ramesses III's mummy belongs to a man of about sixty to sixty-five years, and like his predecessors' has been emasculated. His genitals were embalmed separately and would probably have been preserved in a small wooden box in the shape of Osiris. When his face emerged from the bandages it looked like a mask in a nightmare on account of the thick layer of resin which covered it. Most of his hair has disappeared, apart from a few straight smooth locks which fall on to the nape of his neck, and he has a low forehead and flattish cheekbones. His eyelids have been removed and his eyes stuffed with cloth, while his thin lips are drawn back to reveal white rather protruding teeth in a wide drooping mouth. According to Maspéro, the mummy's features give the impression that in life the king had "an expression that was not very intelligent, perhaps even slightly bestial, coupled with pride, stubbornness, and an air of sovereign majesty" (Plate XII).

In the course of the eighty-three years following his death, there were eight pharaohs who were all content to take the name of Ramesses, from IV to XI. Difficulties in Egypt increased as the central power grew weaker, famine took its toll, and in turn the royal splendour began to dim and could no longer command the old respect. The pharaohs resorted to increased taxation in order to maintain their position, though as religious faith was also on the wane this only meant that no sepulchre was safe from thieves. At the same time the priesthood of Amun increased their temporal power to such an extent that Ramesses XI finally dismissed the high priest and after a few months interval replaced him by a military man, Herihor.

Not all the mummies of these pharaohs are still in existence, and of those that have survived some are in a very bad state. Harris and Weeks X-rayed them, without making any significant discoveries. The body of Ramesses IV was only remarkable for the fact that the incision in its side had been crudely fastened up with a strip of twisted cloth after the abdomen had been stuffed with lichen, while for Ramesses V sawdust was used to stuff the cavities. Ramesses IV had good teeth, and a prominent nose which resembles that of his predecessors and suggests some relationship with them. Ramesses V's face, as has been mentioned already, was disfigured with the marks of smallpox, and he also had an enormous unguinal hernia which had deformed his scrotum. The mummy of Ramesses VI was so badly damaged by robbers that the priests who were responsible for re-wrapping it in the Twentieth Dynasty could only gather whatever pieces of human remains they could salvage, including a woman's hand, and put the bits together as best they could on a piece of wood. There was not much information that this macabre puzzle could yield up to the experts, especially as the face itself had been so badly damaged by knife slashes that it was completely unrecognisable, but it was possible to deduce from the teeth, which were only moderately worn, that the deceased had died between the ages of forty and fifty (Plate XIII). The mummy of Ramesses IX, which was so badly decomposed that it could not be completely unwrapped, brought the somewhat inglorious Twentieth Dynasty to an end.

Once again Egypt was split into two parts, with the high priest of Amun, Herihor, controlling the South with the title of Viceroy of Nubia and Vizir. Although Herihor was in theory the vassal of the legitimate king, Smendes, and acknowledged himself to be so, in fact his position as the highest general provided him with the key to real power. On the monuments the name of Ramesses XI gradually began to become smaller in proportion to

Herihor's name, and then to disappear, until it was completely wiped out. Herihor married Nedjmet, Ramesses XI's sister, in order to legitimise his rule, but little is known about her. In death her oval face framed by plaits of hair took on a strange doll-like appearance because the artificial eyes that were inserted had vertical irises like cats' eyes and her lips were very fleshy. It was not long before Herihor died, leaving Upper Egypt, the pontificate of Amun, to his son Piankhi.

Meanwhile Smendes, who had had one daughter, princess Henattaui, by his first wife Tentamon, married again to Munedjem and had a son called Psusennes. Psusennes was by rights the legitimate ruler of the whole of Egypt, but in reality he inherited authority only over Lower Egypt. He married his half-sister and produced a daughter, Makare, who met Piankhi's son Pinedjem and as in a fairy story they were married, so that once again Egypt was reunited and happy. At any rate this was the accepted version of events up until recently, but the history of this period is so tangled that it is extremely difficult to be sure, and it would seem that the true family relationship of Pinedjem and Makare was rather different, as we shall see later on.

A new technique of mummification was tried on Henattaui, which should have made the body more lifelike but on this occasion led to disaster. Her mouth was stuffed with tampons of natron which swelled when they came into contact with fat, and too much mud was injected under her skin with the result that, instead of reproducing the natural contours of the body, it literally burst through the skin, splitting it at the corners of her lips and tearing it from the eyes down around the cheeks so that it came off in strips as if it were a cardboard mask. The grotesque effect was completed by a wig of twisted black string which had come off and fallen round her neck.

Psusennes I left only a skeleton which was examined in 1940 by Dr. Derry, who found that its teeth were very worn and housed several abscesses, of which one had opened up in the palate. The bones of his dorsal and lumbar vertebrae had grown over and joined up, which would indicate that he suffered from a particularly painful kind of rheumatism known as spondyloarthritis. If so, Psusennes must have suffered excruciating pain every day.

A few dozen years and several reigns were to pass after Psusennes until there came a king whose mummy survived. Very little is known about this pharaoh, whose name was Sheshonq-Heqa-Kheperre, except that he ruled for only a short period. He was buried at Tanis, in the Delta of Lower Egypt where the damp climate and the fact that water was able to penetrate into his tomb and even inside the coffin caused his mummy to deteriorate. Even those who made the discovery found the conditions atrocious, for the tomb was dark and cramped, as well as suffocatingly hot. None of the mummies found in Lower Egypt are as well preserved as the best of those found in Upper Egypt, not because they were less well embalmed but because of the humidity which not even the best embalmed mummy could survive. In Sheshonq's case his coffin had rotted and was reduced to brownish dust, mould and minute plant growths had attacked his mummy so that all that remained was a fragile crumbling skeleton, and only a few last scraps of mouldy linen showed that the corpse had at one time been properly wrapped. Nevertheless there was enough to tell us that Sheshonq was a man of about five and a half foot, and that he had died when he was about fifty of a bone disease in his skull, probably followed by a septic infection and meningitis. The opening at the base of his nose showed how his brain had been removed.

Many more centuries were to pass before the history of ancient Egypt was brought to a close, but the royal mummies who might provide a guide to the course of events have either disappeared or are in such a bad state that they can yield no information. Some, of course, may yet be discovered.

Sixty unknown soldiers

It is not only the royal mummies, however, who can provide us with valuable clues to Egypt's history. The Deir el-Bahri site has yielded exciting discoveries apart from the pharaohs, not least one made by Wilkinson, a famous American archaeologist, in 1923. He was directing excavations in March of that year, when he found his curiosity aroused by an irregularity in the side of the hill which overlooked Hatshepsut's tomb. The entrances to the gigantic tombs were arranged in orderly rows in the hillside, but at one point there was a gap which caught his attention. If a tomb had existed there, it was hidden by a rock fall down the cliff.

This was just at the time when Howard Carter had discovered Tutankhamun's hypogeum and researchers were flocking to the site to marvel at the incredible treasures which Carter was bringing to light. No doubt Wilkinson also dreamt of making a find which would astonish the world, and so he determined to make an effort to solve the mystery of the tomb in the hillside which other archaeologists had failed to recognise. One afternoon he set off, with only a few Arab workers as companions, to make his way with difficulty up the steep slope and across the mass of fallen earth and rocks. He managed to clear away the blocks of stone which obstructed the entrance, but when he reached the interior his hopes were disappointed. No treasure, no untouched tomb awaited his eager gaze, but only an evil-smelling charnel house of bodies. The way in which they had been heaped up in untidy piles, and the disarray of the bodies, showed clearly that thieves had already reached the spot. Wilkinson cast a quick glance around and decided that the bodies must have belonged to some monks from a monastery of early Christian times, so the tomb was closed up again and Wilkinson departed to seek his sensational discovery elsewhere.

This cavalier attitude was hardly worthy of a serious archaeologist, and indeed Wilkinson himself soon realised that his hasty examination was inadequate. Three years later he returned to the tomb intending to explore it more thoroughly, and hoping that if he searched through the torn linen wrappings he might at least find one or two marked with an inscription which would enable him to date the burials accurately. Early one morning he set out again. This time he promised each of his workers a bonus of five piastres for each inscription they discovered, though his hopes were so slim that he hardly thought it would cost him anything. Yet the search proved incredibly fruitful, whether because his workers were imbued with professional conscientiousness or whether they were inspired by the anticipated reward; sixty bandages with inscriptions were found. Twenty-nine of these bore a mark which had previously been noted on the bandages of Queen Aashayt and the concubines belonging to Nebhepetre

Mentuhotep, which was a diagrammatic picture of Mentuhotep's palace accompanied by the hieroglyph for cloth, repeated twice (Fig. 13). The tomb, far from being a Coptic burial-place, contained some sixty corpses from the Eleventh Dynasty.

The tomb itself consisted of a central corridor and two side passages; each of the side passages ended in a little room which was only about three feet high, and which only allowed the bodies to be piled up in threes. They had all been buried at the same time, with the result that the ones underneath had been squashed and their limbs displaced by the weight of the ones above. Their brains and viscera were still in place, and there was no sign of any incision having been made for the purpose of removing them, so the fact that the bodies were comparatively well preserved must be put down to the absence of moisture and the extreme dryness of the place. Their faces were mostly intact, with the skin still whole, while the tendons in their limbs and their solid thick muscles were also in good condition. On the other hand, the fact that their arms and legs were swollen showed that they must have started to decompose at one stage. Many of them had sand on their skin and in their hair, eyes and mouth, and as this was not the kind of fine sand that the wind blows across the deserts, but rather the coarse kind with different-sized irregular grains such as is found at the entrance to valleys, it may be supposed that the bodies had been buried in the ground for a while and dried out partially by the heat. It is

Fig. 13. Marks on the linen in the tomb of the sixty soldiers. The upper sign represents the façade of Mentuhotep's palace; the two lower signs represent rolls of bandaging.

also possible, as Wilkinson thought, that sand had been used to clean the bodies instead of natron.

Most of the mummies were only wrapped in some twenty layers of material, less than half an inch thick, which were made up as follows: six or seven inner layers of cloth, then three layers of bandages, three or four layers of cloth, three more layers of bandages, and then finally three or four of cloth on the outside. Two of the mummies belonged to more important people and had been given eighty layers of linen to a thickness of two inches, and no doubt the two coffins in the tomb belonged to them, but the robbers had taken the bodies out. All the bodies had been dragged into the central corridor where they had been viciously gashed from face to knees as the robbers conducted a furious search for jewels. Most of them were so damaged that only ten could be put together again with any accuracy. It was during the Fifteenth Dynasty that these depredations had taken place, in the troubled period of Hyksos domination, and then later around 1600 B.C. the entrance to the tomb was lost and its inhabitants forgotten when a landslide covered everything up. At one time a stairway had been hacked out of the rock to make access easier, but this too was destroyed when other tombs were built and it was no longer needed.

The bodies which were buried there all proved to belong to men from the army of Nebhepetre Mentuhotep, which accounts for the fact that their bandages bore the royal insignia. Fifty-eight of them were ordinary soldiers, and two of them officers who received special treatment in death, and all of them were solidly built men around five and a half foot tall and between thirty and forty years old, with physical characteristics which were typically Egyptian. Four of them must have taken part in previous battles, to judge from the scars on their foreheads and cheek-bones, and the signs of fractures which had healed. They must have been brave men, for their wounds were all in front, but their valour had not saved them on this occasion. Four soldiers had a little piece of leather two inches long tied around their wrists, which showed that they were archers, and was used to protect the skin as the arrows were loosed (Fig. 14).

Today, four thousand years later, it is still possible to reconstruct the battle from a careful examination of the remains. In a

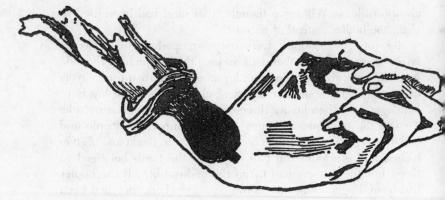

Fig. 14. Little piece of leather worn by the archer to protect his wrist, on a mummified arm.

dozen or so bodies, ebony arrow-heads have been found embedded in a limb, trunk or skull. This type of arrow-head was common in the Eleventh Dynasty, and the fact that more were not found is only due to the practice of retrieving intact arrows from the bodies after battle; no doubt many more died from arrow wounds. Other wounds were made by javelins, and these are found only on the skull and face; while fourteen soldiers had their skulls crushed from the top as if they had been hit by stones falling from a great height. Others died from arrows which struck them in the back of the neck from above, and many more have wounds in their skulls and shoulders. Putting this evidence together, we can reconstruct a scene where the soldiers were endeavouring to scale the walls of a fortress, but were struck down by a hail of stones and arrows launched at them from the top.

The most horrible wounds were received by fifteen soldiers whose skulls and faces were completely crushed. They may have been killed by direct axe blows in the course of hand to hand fighting, but it is perhaps more likely that at some stage in the struggle the attackers were momentarily put to flight, leaving some of their number wounded on the ground, who were then brutally massacred by the fortress defenders. The blows mostly

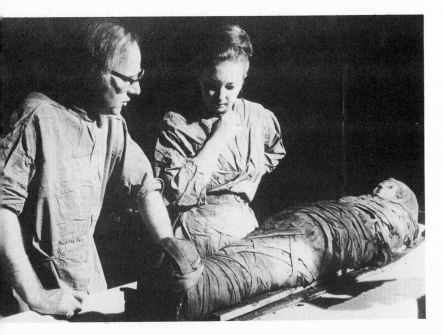

I   Dr. A. R. David and Dr. E. Tapp discuss the unwrapping of
Mummy 1770

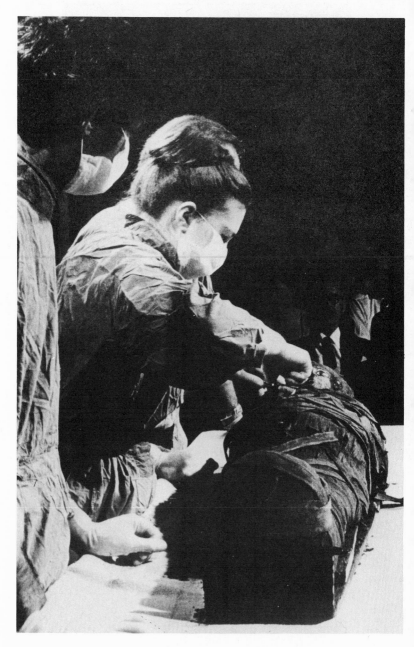

II   Dr. David unwraps Mummy 1770

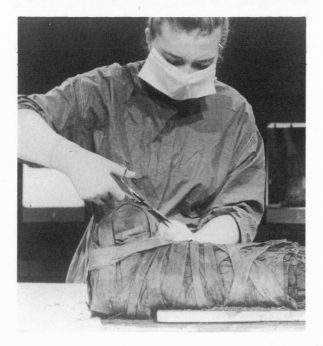

III Dr. David cuts the wrapping over the mummy's feet

IV Analysing the bandages

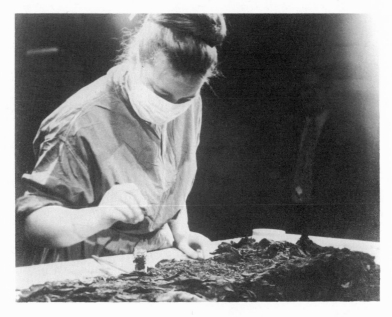

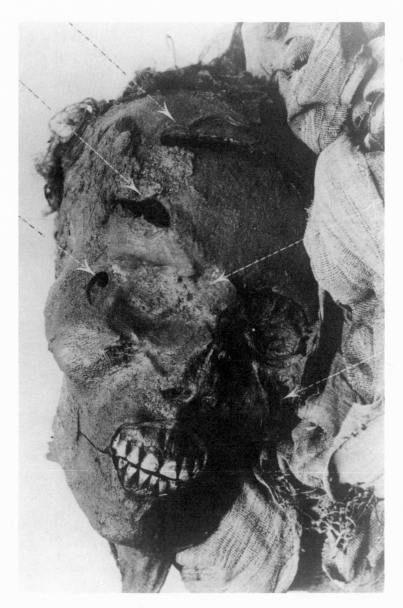

V The Mummy of Sequenenre-Taa (end of the XVII Dynasty)

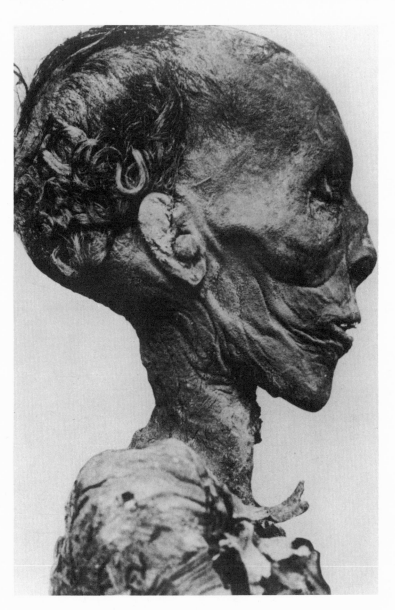

VI   Thutmosis II (1520–1484 B.C.)

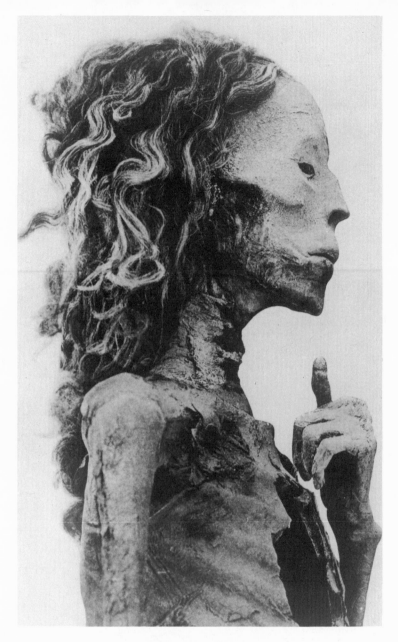

VII   Hatchepsut (1520–1484 B.C.)

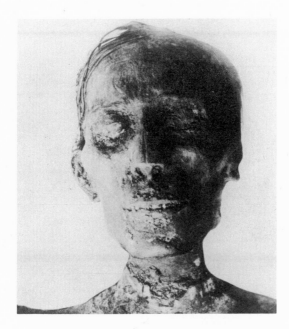

VIII   Thutmosis IV (1425–1408 B.C.)

IX   Seti I (1312–1298 B.C.)

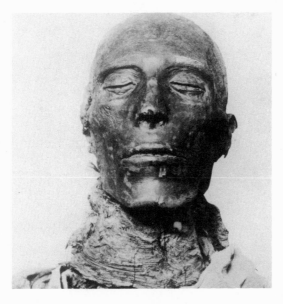

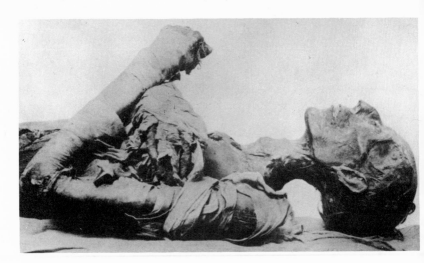

X   Ramesses II (1298–1235 B.C.)

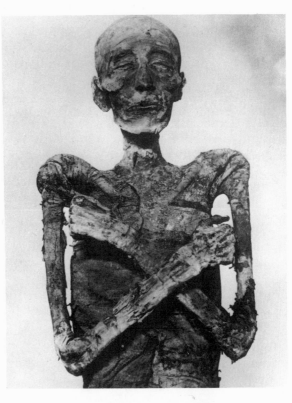

XI   Mineptah (1235–1224 B.C.)

landed on the left cheek or left side of the skull, which argues that they were aimed with some deliberation; it all calls to mind most unpleasantly those pictures where the pharaoh has seized a prisoner by the hair and is threatening him with his massive club (Fig. 15).

It seems quite likely on the basis of the evidence that there was a respite in the fighting, for six of the soldiers must certainly have been left on the battlefield for a while, because there are little holes in their stomachs which could only have been made by vultures in search of their favourite delicacy, entrails. The birds also tore off the skin in order to gorge themselves on the flesh, leaving some bones completely bare except for the tendons.

Even the attitude of the corpses provides clues as to how the battle went. Most of them are correctly laid out, with their arms and legs straight, but a few are curled up with their forearms bent and their hands on their shoulders. The first ones were either wrapped immediately after death before rigor mortis set in, or later when the stiffening had worn off, while the rest must have been treated while they were still stiff. This looks as if there were indeed two phases in the battle. Circumstances only allowed time for a hasty preparation for burial, but nevertheless care was taken to wrap them, and they had the honour of being laid to rest in a tomb sited just beneath their pharaoh's.

Unfortunately, there is no documentary evidence to substantiate Wilkinson's theories, though of course there is no doubt that the tomb contains the bodies of soldiers killed in battle. Some authorities like Drioton and Vandier regret the lack of confirmation, but it is remarkable how much it is possible to establish from the remains we possess. There must indeed have been two assaults before Mentuhotep's troops finally succeeded in storming the citadel and winning the battle, and those who did not survive died heroically facing the enemy from below. At the time of the battle, Egypt was divided in two with Herakleopolis as the capital of the Northern Kingdom and Thebes, where Mentuhotep reigned, the capital of the South, and it is very probable that these sixty soldiers were killed in the course of the war between the two kingdoms, which only came to an end when Mentuhotep reconquered Herakleopolis and united Egypt once more.

Fig. 15. Narmer's palette representing the victorious Pharaoh seizing a prisoner by the hair and threatening him with his mace.

Mass execution

A little earlier than Wilkinson another archaeologist, the late Professor Reisner, was excavating the relics of an ancient Roman camp at Shellal, in Upper Nubia, when in 1908 he came across a trench inside the north-east angle of the ramparts near the remains of an old tower. The trench proved to be four feet deep and contained sixty-two bodies arranged in an orderly way in three layers, one on top of another. A little distance away he found a second and much shallower trench, which contained around forty bodies; these had been covered with a layer of bricks and stones.

None of the bodies had been mummified, but they had all been crudely wrapped in poor quality cloth, and each skeleton still had a rope tied in a slip-knot around its neck. At the base of nearly every skull was the mark of a fracture, which Dr. Wood-Jones considered was caused by hanging, though the method used must have been rather different from the one in use in England for example up until recently, which would not have produced the same injuries.

In some cases, a long clean cut had slashed into the bones of the forehead, made by some such instrument as a sabre, while in others a blow from an axe or sabre had either cut the skull completely through or if the weapon slipped on the bone had split the sternum in two.

It was quite clear that these men, who came originally from Nubia, had been condemned to death and brutally executed en masse. The precise date of the massacre has not been ascertained yet, but a few coins and a copper arrow-head that were found show that it must have been in the Roman period, and very probably took place to make an example of men who were involved in one of the local rebellions which were disturbing the Pax Romana in the region.

The virgin and child

Another puzzle was posed by the mummy of a princess who has already been mentioned earlier, and whose history was for long the subject of great controversy. Princess Makare was originally thought to be the wife of the first prophet Pinedjem I, with the title of Divine Wife and Worshipper of Amun which gave her a very important role in the government of Thebes. However although at one time, certainly up to the Eighteenth Dynasty, royal wives had not been precluded from taking on the office of Worshipper, by the time of the Twenty-first Dynasty this was no longer possible, for only priestesses of Amun who were virgins dedicated to the one god were entitled to become Worshippers.

Nevertheless Makare's coffin bore the inscription "Daughter of the King and Great Wife of the King," which gave her a status incompatible with the virginity required of a Worshipper. Another interpretation of the inscription was proposed by Daressy, "Daughter of the King and Daughter of the Great Wife of the King," which would indeed have allowed her to become a Worshipper but seemed totally at variance with the presence in her coffin of a little bundle containing the mummified body of a baby. It was even thought that one of the names on the coffin, Muthemat, belonged to the baby, though in fact it was Makare's first name.

All sorts of theories were put forward to resolve the baby's identity. Perhaps Makare had really been married to Pinedjem and had died in childbirth, which would explain why the baby was buried with her, or perhaps she had been the Worshipper and had transgressed her vows of celibacy and so been condemned to death with her baby. Arguments raged until 1968, when the bodies were X-rayed. The little baby turned out in fact to be a monkey, an Arabian baboon, and Makare's honour was safe. Obviously she had been buried with her favorite pet, like her half-sister Esemkheb who took a mummified gazelle with her into the grave. As J. Yoyotte concluded: "It is clear that Makare, conferred as she was with a cartouche praenomen and described as a virgin like the preceding Worshippers, had never been married to anyone but the one god of Thebes."

CHAPTER 4

ANIMAL MUMMIES

MUMMIFICATION BY THE MILLION

One of the most extraordinary features of ancient Egyptian civilisation was the veneration they accorded to animals. The Egyptians firmly believed that animals were incarnations of their gods, and so for them it became as natural to embalm a cat or a bird as it was to mummify their closest relative; the little mummies of a monkey and a gazelle in the graves of the two Theban princesses who have just been mentioned in the previous chapter were only the forerunners of an immense religious enterprise which was to grow up in the Greco-Roman period and which not only is amazing to us today but also provided a source of endless astonishment and amusement to the Persian invaders of Egypt and later to the Greeks and Romans.

However, the Theban monkey which turned out to have been a favorite pet buried with its mistress to keep her company in the afterlife was not the only beast to have puzzled researchers, and many queries remain to be solved. For example, there are the cattle and pig bones found in the little rooms next to Dedkare's funerary chamber in the heart of his pyramid, whose purpose is still the subject of argument. Perhaps they formed part of a sacred rite, perhaps the bull itself was sacred, or perhaps they were there simply as provisions to nourish the pharaoh during his long rest in the tomb.

Clearly, it was not religious veneration which led to the mummification of all the animals that have been found, and even where religious factors are involved there is a distinction between the worship which was accorded to one particular animal and the homage which was paid to every member of the species in death. Certain animals were singled out as sacred because of a special mark which distinguished them from the rest of their kind, and these had the right to special treatment while they were alive and to burial in a superior tomb when they died. Ordinary animals of the same variety were embalmed when they died and were buried in thousands in vast necropolises, but no grandiose ceremonies accompanied them to the grave.

From the very earliest times, animals were involved in religious practices. Cattle and sheep have been found from the Badarian period, buried like human beings in oval trenches and rolled up in mats, and gazelles wrapped in mats or even cloth were discovered in a few tombs of the Gerzean (late neolithic) period in the course of Debono's excavations in 1950 at Heliopolis, near the Cairo racecourse. Not every animal embalmed was buried in fulfilment of a religious obligation, and certainly the dogs who lie with their masters in the Thinite cemeteries were interred there as a mark of the affection they were held in. However, where an animal was accorded the same funerary rites as the men who buried it, this argues strongly for a religious explanation.

Outsiders mocked at the strange masquerade, but if we go back to the dawn of Egyptian civilisation we can trace its gradual development quite logically from the totem held sacred by the nomadic tribes. This was often in the shape of an animal, so that later when the tribes settled down within set boundaries and adopted a different and more organized way of life they often chose an animal as the guardian deity of their territory. Their choice was based on particular qualities such as strength in the bull, cleverness in the monkey, and so on, and each animal was seen as the earthly incarnation of a superior being.

Gradually, perhaps as the art of statuary developed, worship of an animal was superseded by worship of its effigy, and this in turn gave way to the more metaphysical concept of a god represented by the figure of a man with an animal's head. However the animal itself was still revered as the receptacle of divine power, kin to or the same as Ra or Osiris. During the Twenty-second dynasty the philosopher Ani wrote that "the god Nuter of this country is in reality the Sun on the horizon, but his images are present on earth," which can be understood as meaning that divine power resides in a large number of earthly creatures. St. Francis of Assisi, whose thought is closer to ours than to the Egyptian philosopher's, nonetheless knew a similar inspiration when he proclaimed:

> And praise be yours, my Lord, through all that you have made,
> And first my lord Brother Sun,
> Who brings the day; and light you give to us through him.
> How beautiful he is, how radiant in all his splendour!
> Of you, Most High, he bears the likeness.°

There were many different kinds of sacred animal, and no less than forty species were honoured by their own religious cult. One of each, or sometimes more than one, had its temple and tomb in the chosen city. The most celebrated of all was the bull Apis, which incarnated the god Ptah Memphis, though elsewhere other bulls symbolised other gods. The ram was worshipped as the living symbol of Amun at Thebes, of Khnum at Elephantine, and of Arsaphes at Herakleopolis, while Busiris and Mendes paid tribute to the billy-goat of Osiris, Faiyum to the crocodile of Suchos, and Bubastis to the cat of the goddess Bastet. Some towns worshipped several gods and so had several sacred animals, while later on towards the end of Egyptian civilisation different popular traditions or different theological strands fused together and resulted in one animal symbolising several gods. It was also possible for one god to impart his qualities to different species, as did Thoth, incarnated in both the ibis and the baboon. A few gods had sanctuaries housing the animals sacred to them in several places, or like Horus the falcon-god, Hathor the cow-god and Anubis the jackal-god were worshipped throughout

° *The Writings of St. Francis of Assisi,* translated by Benen Fahy, Burns and Oates, London, 1964.

Egypt. There is a whole labyrinth of different beliefs and cults which developed and intertwined over centuries following the fortunes of different groups of priests, and even the Egyptians themselves were not always clear on the details.

Eventually animal worship declined, but not before it had reached spectacular heights. Great temples were built, like the one which was initially sacred to the bull of the god Montu at Medamut, north-east of Karnak, and was then reconstructed in the Ptolemaic period so that inside it was divided into two completely separate parts, one of which was the temple proper where the priests officiated, and the other the bull's pavilion, surrounded by a little garden, where the faithful could come to consult the oracles. As the priests became more and more isolated from their flock, and their flock were in effect cut off from the gods in the temple, so the people transferred their devotion to the animals themselves. The events of the Persian invasion further confirmed them in their views.

On this occasion the priests disgraced themselves by their cowardice. They allowed the Persian soldiers to extract all the valuables they could from the temples and to carry away the statues and all the precious furnishings, while they did nothing to prevent injury to their gods. The sacred animals were not spared either, but the outrages inflicted on them served to reinforce the piety of the common people who associated worship of the living animals with their ancestor worship. As Drioton rightly remarked, "these animals became to some extent the gods of resistance."

From then on the cult grew to encompass not just the one unique animal but the whole species, which was considered divine. One animal, chosen for its particular characteristics, still enjoyed special privileges, but all its kind were also venerated in an incredible zoolatry which reached its height in the Greek and Roman periods, when it really knew no limits. This was the people's reaction to the sacrileges perpetrated by the invaders, and their adoration so impressed the Greeks that the latter rebaptised some cities with the name of the animal worshipped there: for instance Asyut became Lycopolis, town of the wolf, and Shedit where the god Sobek was worshipped became Crocodilopolis.

Such curious beliefs, so strongly held, did not make life any easier for their adherents. Sacred animals demanded care, which was rewarded in the afterlife when someone who was appearing before the tribunal of the shades could sway the judges in his favour by saying: "I gave bread to the hungry, water to the thirsty, and clothes to those who had none. I took care of the ibis, the falcons and the holy cats, and I buried them ritually, anointed with oil and wrapped in cloth." In its own town the sacred animal was inviolate, and anyone who injured it was liable to reap a terrible penalty. Diodorus witnessed the lengths to which believers were prepared to go, and recorded that he saw a Roman who had accidentally killed a cat besieged in his house by the people, although he denied any malicious intent; he was finally lynched in spite of the intervention of the magistrates who were hastily sent to the scene by the king in the hope of calming down the crowd. This was not an isolated case, for it was also recorded that if a passer-by saw a sacred animal dying of natural causes he would take care to remove himself from the spot as quickly as possible, lamenting and protesting his innocence.

Further complications arose when an animal was considered sacred in one province and not in another. A fish that was happily consumed at any meal in one place could be held in veneration a few miles away, and this easily led to conflict between neighbouring localities with different religious allegiances.

If anything more is needed to show the inordinate lengths to which animal worshippers went, we need only look at the immense cemeteries where every kind of animal was embalmed and buried in millions. Mummification, which was originally reserved for the pharaoh alone and then became obligatory for every citizen, spread first of all to one chosen animal of its kind and then by the Late Middle Kingdom to all members of its species.

SACRED BULLS

Apis

The most famous of all the animals who were held in special veneration was Apis the bull. We are fortunate to possess a good deal of information about his cult, starting in the First Dynasty when he was proclaimed a deity and continuing right through Egyptian history. Memphis was always the centre of his worship, and there is a reference to his sanctuary there in the Fifth Dynasty, when it was visited by King Neuserre during a jubilee festival, as well as brief inscriptions in the pyramid corridors which show that a cemetery existed solely for dead Apis bulls, though its site has never been discovered. The most ancient tomb known dates only from the time of Amenophis III in the Eighteenth Dynasty. Each Apis had his own private tomb surmounted by a chapel until the reign of Ramesses II, who embarked on the construction of a funerary complex for all the sacred bulls of Memphis, known as the Serapeum.

It was a happy combination of chance and intuition joined to a great deal of knowledge and a reliable memory which led to the discovery of this unique building. The man who embodied all these qualities, Auguste Mariette, was a young Egyptologist of twenty-nine years who in fact arrived in Cairo in 1850 with the intention of carrying out research into Coptic manuscripts. However, he changed his mind when he stumbled across the head of a sphinx one day when he was taking a walk across the Saqqara sands. He remembered at once that he had seen some fifteen lions with human heads bought by individuals who had all been told that they originated from Saqqara, and he also remembered a passage from Strabo where the latter describes the Serapeum as being surrounded by sphinxes which were three quarters buried in sand. Mariette was convinced that the bulls' graveyard could not be far away, so he abandoned his search for manuscripts and hired a small team of Egyptian labourers to help him clear away the sand from what he hoped would be an avenue of sphinxes leading to the Serapeum. The statues were each twenty feet apart, and many of them were buried as deep as forty feet under the accumulated sand of centuries, making the work both arduous and dangerous. However the threat of falls of sand did not deter him, and he eventually arrived at the one hundred and thirty-fourth sphinx. On the way he had experienced the excitement of discovering a most beautiful example of Egyptian statuary, the famous "Squatting Scribe," but at this point the trail seemed to disappear and he was on the verge of despairing when he finally found another sphinx at right angles to the line of the rest, where the avenue made a turn. Once again he was disappointed to find twenty feet further on, not the long-awaited entrance to the tomb but a statue of Pindarus, followed by ones of Plato, Protagoras, Homer and seven other Greek poets and philosophers, arranged in a half-moon shape. He had already spent two months without reaching his goal, yet he pressed on with his excavations towards the east and next came to two large sphinxes and a little temple built by Nekhthoreb-Nectanebo II in honour of Apis. His hopes revived, and he felt sure he was near the Serapeum. Unfortunately by this time the funds the government had allowed him to purchase manuscripts were exhausted, and he had to wait many long months before he could again resume his search at the beginning of 1851.

He soon discovered an alley a hundred yards long and bordered with more Greek statues, and began methodically lifting every slab along it, in case the entrance to the tomb should lie beneath. At first there was no trace of it, but he did uncover some hundreds of bronze statuettes, many of them effigies of the sacred bull. His finds excited a great deal of jealousy among the local traders, who were not anxious to allow such treasures to pass directly to museums without any profit to themselves, and so they caused a great deal of trouble for Mariette who very foolishly had never obtained government authorisation for his excavations. After many delays, work finally started again. At last, after clearing the surrounding wall of the funerary complex, Mariette succeeded in reaching his goal on 12 November 1851 when he arrived at the gateway to the Serapeum and then penetrated underground to the great tunnel dug in the Saite, Persian and Ptolemaic periods.

The plan of the sepulchre was simple, and consisted of a central passage which could be lengthened if necessary, with chambers leading off from both sides where each succeeding Apis was buried in his own huge sarcophagus. Mariette discovered twenty-eight rooms in all, of which twenty-four still held stone sarcophaguses, though every single one had been broken open and emptied of its mummy. By February 1852 he had reached other and older galleries which were not so big and where the chambers were more crudely hollowed out. Here he found

wooden sarcophaguses belonging to bulls buried between the
thirtieth year of the reign of Ramesses II and the twenty-first
year of Psammeticus I's reign. These mummies had escaped the
robbers. Then from March to September of the same year he
found a third series of tombs which had been dug out separately
from each other in no particular order in the period between
Amenophis III and Ramesses II. In one room which was still
walled up, the excavators even found the imprint of a foot in the
sand, just as it had been left by the last Egyptian to leave the
tomb three thousand years before.

At this point Mariette again came up against the hostility of
clandestine operators who were eager to conduct their own excavations, including the Mayor of Saqqara who even tried to stop
the workers Mariette had hired from going to work. In April
events became more heated when Bedouins armed with guns attacked him, but he succeeded in beating them off on horseback
with a rifle. Archaeology in the last century was not always the
peaceful pursuit it is now, and it had some thrilling moments!
Apart from this, Mariette lived quietly on the site of the excavations in a mud house without furniture, doors or windows,
though when he received a foreign visitor he liked to put on a
show for them. One of those who came to see the Serapeum was
Théodule Deveria, who was the son of Achille Deveria, a famous painter of the time, and who was himself to become an
Egyptologist. Complete darkness reigned when Mariette and his
guest entered the tomb. They stopped for a minute and then
continued into the main tunnel, which was illuminated by two
hundred children "sitting in an Egyptian pose, as still as statues,"
each holding a candle. More children were posted with candles
on top of the tombs in the depths of the chambers which held
the biggest sarcophaguses, and the extraordinary spectacle cannot have failed to impress the visitor. Today, the Serapeum is lit
by electricity.

The history of Apis is a long one. Originally he was a god of
fertility and physical strength, the incarnation of Ptah, god of
Memphis, who is represented in pictures as a man with a shaven
head, clad in close-fitting mummy's apparel, and holding a long
sceptre in his hand. Soon his association with fertility drew him
into a closer relationship with Osiris, the god of renascent vege-

tation, and then, in spite of the fact that he was mortal and subject to death and burial like other living creatures, he in some way took on the qualities of Osiris as god of the dead. Thus Apis and Osiris became doubly linked. They had also been connected for a long time in what was called "the race of Apis" in which a sacred bull ran from town to town and from province to province bearing on its back a sack containing the bones of Osiris whom his brother Seth had put to death.

By extension, Apis in the Saite epoch came to be shown carrying other mummies in the same way as he carried Osiris. At first the living bull, Osiris-Apis, was distinguished from Apis-Osiris, the dead bull, and the Greeks retained this duality when they referred to the living beast as Apis and the dead one as Serapis (from which the name of Serapeion or Serapeum derives for the sepulchre); they even went further and recognised one Serapis as the symbol of all dead sacred bulls, and one Osorapis as the representative of each living bull. Elsewhere Apis was also linked with the god Horus, who appears as a falcon or a man with the head of a falcon, and is the guardian of the monarchy; because the king was assimilated to Horus when he was alive and to Osiris when he was dead, it was natural to associate Apis and Horus, and consequently for the sacred bull to play a role in royal ceremonies and in particular to participate in the king's jubilee festival, the sed-festival, which was celebrated at Memphis. Apis still further increased his prestige when in the Eighteenth Dynasty he was allied with Atum, god of Heliopolis, who was the evening sun-god and so had some association too with death. The fact that Memphis and Heliopolis were quite close also helped to bring about the association, for the priests from each city decided it would be better to unite their different religious practices rather than fight over them. In the end therefore, Apis embodied a whole complex of religious concepts, from his own identity as the sacred bull of Memphis, to Horus, the pharaoh's guardian, Osiris, god of fertility and death, and Atum, god of the setting sun.

When one sacred bull died, it was a question of "Apis is dead, long live Apis!", for Memphis needed a new reincarnation of its god as soon as possible, and so the priests immediately ran to the fields to seek a successor with the right characteristics. The beast

did not necessarily have to come from Memphis but could origi-
nate anywhere in Egypt, provided it satisfied various physical
criteria: it had to be black, with a white triangle on its forehead,
a crescent moon on its chest and another on its flanks, and double hairs in its tail, alternately black and white. The moon shape
is clearly an allusion to Osiris, god of the moon, but to show that
the bull is allied with the sun too he is shown in pictures as
wearing a disc between his horns surmounted by an enraged
cobra, the uraeus or symbol of royalty. One stela in the Serapeum referred to Apis as "You who have no father," which
clearly indicates that he was miraculously conceived, through
the intervention of the god Ptah who came down from heaven in
the shape of a flame and impregnated the chosen mother cow.
Plutarch talks of a "moonbeam touching a cow on heat," and the
Apis' mother was held in high regard in Memphis and brought to
live with her sacred son. When she died she was buried only a
short distance from the Serapeum, in a graveyard for sacred
cows where Mariette discovered the undamaged tomb of a
strange personage called Unennefer, son of Petosiris, and
prophet of the mothers of Apis.

Once the right animal was found, the priests brought him back
to Memphis and the celebrations began. A priest of Ptah presided over the rites which marked the enthronement of a new
living god on the earth. After the ceremonies in the temple of
Ptah (in Greek, Hephaestus, god of blacksmiths), which had to
take place at the full moon, the bull left from the east door
which was the side of the rising sun, and the people were allowed to enter and make their devotions. Meanwhile the bull
was brought to his own sanctuary the Apieion, which from now
on would be his permanent abode except when he left to take
part in various religious observances, royal feasts or processions.
Diodorus states that for forty days after his installation only
women were admitted to his presence, and that they stood facing
him, raised their skirts and revealed their genital organs. When
the time came for Apis to participate in his first official ceremony, he was embarked on board ship with great pomp and
then sailed over a hundred miles down the Nile to visit Hapy,
spirit of the floods in his sanctuary on the little island of Roda.
There he had to wait until the moon began to wax to come back

to Memphis, when the people could once more gather at the windows of his temple to watch him. Every day at a certain time the priests let him out into the courtyard, which was a magnificent place surrounded by a portico supported by statues twenty feet high serving as pillars to hold up the roof. It was here that the faithful came to worship their reincarnated god, and here that his oracles were issued, while his mother was housed in a nearby sanctuary. He had numerous attendants to look after him, provide his food, and keep his temple in good order, and every year he was presented with a cow specially selected for the sacred markings she bore. It is not known whether this had some special religious significance or whether it was simply to fulfil the bull's needs, but in any event the cow was put to death immediately after the coupling.

When the current Apis came to die in his turn, the whole city of Memphis went into mourning to show its grief; some people shaved their heads, and it was considered sacrilegious to eat any solid food other than vegetables. It has been claimed that the age of twenty-eight, at which Osiris died, was fateful for the bull, and that if it reached it it was drowned, but there is no serious proof of this legend and in fact no Apis is known to have attained this number of years. On the contrary, those whose length of life can be established died before they were twenty-eight, like the one which succumbed to old age during the crowning of Ptolemy I. Their fate after death was radically different in the classical Egyptian period from later times, for up to the Nineteenth Dynasty and perhaps later they were eaten. The oldest sarcophaguses, the wooden ones that robbers did not discover, contained only pieces of broken bones in an evil-smelling bituminous mess, with a number of funerary statuettes with a bull's head to symbolise the dead Apis, jewels, and amulets made from semi-precious stones. Obviously there had been no attempt to mummify the body, though from the presence of four canopic jars in the most ancient tombs it did seem that evisceration had taken place. The bones simply lay in a shallow depression, covered by a sarcophagus with no floor. It is not unlikely that the bull was ceremonially devoured, in a rite similar to the one described in a pyramid text as the "cannibal hymn," in which the dead pharaoh consumes the flesh of the gods and so becomes their equal. "He crushed the vertebrae and the vertebral marrow," the hymn says, "he took the gods' hearts . . . Uenis fed on the lungs of the wise . . . His food was more nourishing than gods' food, for it was cooked by the wise men from their bones." Through this sympathetic magic, the deceased king could acquire the force and power of the gods, and one can easily imagine a similar rite in which the pharaoh ate the Apis' flesh and marrow in order to take on his strength and virility. The inedible remains would then have been buried, enclosed in a wooden coffin.

The outlines of another strange ceremony can be guessed at from the contents of another very old tomb which Mariette investigated. He found a wooden sarcophagus whose lid had been partly crushed by falls from the chamber roof, and which contained a mummy in human shape. The mummy's face was covered with a thick gold mask, and it wore a small gold chain round its neck containing two amulets in the name of Kha-em-Uas, one of the sons of Ramesses II, prince of Memphis. A gold sparrow-hawk decorated with mosaic patterns lay on his chest, and round him were eighteen porcelain statuettes with human heads bearing the inscription "Apis-Osiris, great god, lord of eternity." For a long time it was thought that this was the mummy of a prince who had dedicated himself to the worship of Apis to such a degree that he was buried in the same grave, but when Mond and Myers decided to make a closer examination of the body they discovered that the shrouds and bandages contained nothing but a mass of pitch mixed with minute fragments of bone. At this period the technique of mummification was at its height, and it is inconceivable that a prince could have been treated so badly that his body disintegrated completely. It seems reasonable therefore to conclude that the amalgam consists in reality of the remains of a sacred bull. Perhaps the prince was sick, so after he had feasted on the bull he arranged its bones to look like a human body and decorated it with his own jewellery, hoping to transfer his sickness to the god's bones.

As animal worship grew in importance, so the animals' treatment in death changed radically. From the time of Apries and Amasis in the Twenty-sixth Dynasty the Apis came to be treated like a human being and was embalmed in the traditional fashion with special rites. On his death, two chapels had to be decorated, one with red linen where priests clothed in "seshed" were to officiate, and one with "seshed" cloth where only priests clothed in red could enter. After highly elaborate ceremonies the priests dragged the coffin containing the Apis all the way from the chapels to the embalming kiosk, the "place of purity," which was set up on the edge of the Nile. As the bull arrived, all the people burst into loud lamentations, and bewailed the death of their god continously for a considerable period. Then when the rites in the kiosk were over the officiating priests emerged to embark on a reed barque which was floating on the Nile, on which they had to read out another ritual which was written on nine rolls of papyrus. Next they returned to the kiosk to perform the ceremony of the opening of the mouth for the first time, and then the "Priests of the Lake and the way and Priest in charge of the rites collected everything they would need from the dissection chamber."

The ceremony was in fact a good deal more complicated than this indicates, and there were more precise instructions which had to be followed before the actual embalming began. A special technician attached to the temple had the honour of beginning mummification, with some assistance. The bull's huge body was laid on a plank on an alabaster or limestone table, which could be from three to five yards long to judge by the eight surviving examples found at Memphis, and then the long delicate task began. The bull had to be put stretched out, not in the usual position he would sleep in, that is to say with his legs folded, but like a dog with his legs straight in front of him, and to do this it was necessary to cut the tendons. His tail was slipped under his right thigh, his nose raised up on a wooden support placed under his jaw, and then he was firmly held in place with straps. To mummify him, the embalmers used the second technique described by Herodotus, which was to dissolve the viscera by means of injecting oil of cedar through the anus.

There is an Apis papyrus which lays down the correct procedures and accompanying rites at this stage, and recommends that the stuffing should be pushed in as far as possible. "A reader stands before the god," says the text. "He must reach out as far as his arm can stretch and gather up the linen and everything he finds there. He must wash the god with water and stuff him properly with cloth. He must wash the stuffing and the wrappings with that which the five priests in the boat have brought and which contains the things of the anus. He must anoint them with oil and wrap them in linen. Another reader stands in front of the wrappings . . ." The text makes no mention of evisceration through the flank, and it would seem that this was not practised because there are no canopic jars in tombs of this type of mummy, and also because a little brownish matter containing bits of vegetable issued from the anus has been found under some bulls. When this stage was completed, the animal was covered with a layer of dry natron which was left to work until it was fully dehydrated, and then all that remained to do was to wrap it in the required length of bandaging, thousands of yards in all. Plaster covered in gold leaf was spread on its head, and a disc of gilded wood was secured between its horns as a symbol of Apis' relation to the sun. Finally, eyes of white glass decorated with a black spot for the pupil were set in position, sometimes more delicately worked in glass of different colours or made of precious stones set in bronze. The cost of such a burial must have been enormous, and was a source of amazement to Diodorus when he learnt that the guardian of the bull who died at Memphis during the coronation of Ptolemy I used up all his own fortune and still had to borrow fifty silver talents from the pharaoh to pay for the funeral. Even later when expenses were cut down, each bull still cost its guardian a hundred talents, which was a considerable sum given that one talent represented the value of twenty to twenty-seven kilos of silver.

When all was ready the mummy of the Apis was transported with great pomp along the avenue bordered with sphinxes to the Serapeum, and was then brought through the long underground passage to be placed in its sarcophagus which was waiting in a newly-excavated chamber. At first this was a simple wooden chest, but from the Twenty-sixth Dynasty enormous monolithic troughs were used which weighed anything up to sixty-nine tons. There was room for forty people to stand on top of them, and they were so high that a ladder was necessary to climb them. It seems incredible that the Egyptians could hew out these enormous blocks and hollow them inside without any of the steel instruments that we possess today, then polish them beautifully, and finally transport them from the quarries of upper Egypt hundreds of miles to Memphis in the Delta, but so they did. When the bull was placed in position, the opening to the room was sealed off by a wall which was built right up to the roof, and no further access was possible. Pilgrims who visited the Serapeum could only walk up and down the central passage and read the dates of birth and death of each Apis on stelae embedded in the wall in front of each tomb. These stelae have furnished researchers with invaluable information on the chronology of the last pharaohs. The most recent tomb dates from the time of Ptolemy VII, but it is known that bulls were being ceremonially buried much later, right up to A.D. 362 in the reign of Julian the Apostate, so somewhere a Roman necropolis containing more Apis bulls remains to be found.

The Serapeum very quickly became one of the great religious centres of Egypt, and many gods had their own sanctuaries inside the grounds. The sick used to come in search of a miraculous cure. They stayed in special rest-houses called sanatoria, though these were not quite what one would expect today but instead were buildings with a central corridor off which opened rooms decorated with white plaster where those who sought to restore their physical or moral health could repair. A niche was built high up in the wall to house the god's statue, which in this case was Serapis, who would appear to the patient in a dream in order to cure him. A sanatorium of this type has been discovered at Dendera.

Mnevis

Less well-known than Apis was Mnevis, though he too had a long history to his worship. His name was originally Merour, but the Greeks changed this to Mnevis, and he was sacred to Heliopolis, the city of the sun-god Atum-Re. Indeed his full title was "herald of Re, he who brings the truth to Atum" and it was because he incarnated the sun god that Akhenaten, the monotheistic pharaoh, instated his cult in the new town of Amarna.

No complete burial-ground for Mnevis has ever been found, only two tombs which show that his funeral rites were much the same as those for Apis, and closely connected with Osiris. He was mummified in the same way, and we know he was bandaged because there is a letter from the priests of the temple of Re and Mnevis-Atum at Heliopolis which acknowledges the receipt of twenty cubits of fine linen sent by the priests of the temple at Tebtynis for the burial of Mnevis.

Mnevis was a black bull without markings, who needed tufts of hair all over his body and on his tail as the sign by which the priests could recognise his divinity. He lived in his sanctuary surrounded by sacred cows and calves, which were not reverenced to the same degree as he was but which nonetheless had the right to a proper burial.

Buchis

Yet a third bull cult was discovered by Sir Robert Mond, an English Egyptologist, when he was working at Thebes to uncover the tomb of Vizir Ramose, which has some of the most exquisite bas-reliefs found in Egyptian statuary. When therefore it was reported to him in 1926 that a little bronze ox had been discovered at Armant, it would not have been surprising if he had decided to ignore it. The area scarcely looks promising, and indeed today tourists hardly visit it for little but the foundations are left of the town and great temple of the god Montu, while the small temple built by Cleopatra entirely disappeared in the last century when its stones were removed by Khedive Said to build a sugar factory. However, for an Egyptologist it is a fascinating part of the country because Armant is in fact the ancient Hermonthis which Egyptians called the southern On, as opposed to the northern On which was Heliopolis. Mond recognised that if Heliopolis had a cult of Mnevis, then it was likely that Hermonthis-Armant also had a sacred bull, and this in fact was mentioned in Greek texts. Its name was Buchis.

The little bronze ox find therefore persuaded Mond that he should take on the task of looking for the Bucheum, which was the name of the burial-ground of the bulls of Hermonthis. His excavations soon led him to the graveyard of the mother-cows, six miles west of Armant, where he succeeded in finding the sar-

cophaguses and opening them up—a difficult undertaking because the lids alone weighed almost fifteen tons. He was disappointed by the first fruits of his labours, for inside the mummies
were almost entirely destroyed by mould. Soon afterwards however he came on a ramp which led downwards under the earth
to the entrance to the Bucheum, and then proceeded along an
underground gallery with corridors opening off it at right-angles
to each side. As in the Serapeum, tombs had been dug in the
walls of these corridors for the sacred bulls, and Mond found
thirty-five of them, all unfortunately rifled by thieves in search of
treasure. Nevertheless some mummies were still there in their
wrappings, and the vital stelae had survived with their inscriptions, which are often of more value to archaeologists than any
gold or precious stones.

The cult of Buchis undoubtedly goes back very far, but it only
became important under Nectanebo II when the Bucheum was
built. It lasted until the Roman era under Diocletian.

The theology which lay behind the cult of the sacred bulls is
not easy to comprehend today, and the worship of Buchis presents particular difficulties, though a brief summary may serve to
show how Buchis became allied with other deities. When the
cult was established, Hermonthis was the capital of the district,
which was known as the province of the Sceptre, and the god of
both the town and the province was Montu, who symbolised war
and was represented in the shape of a man with a falcon's head
and armed with a bow and arrow. Montu was incarnated on
earth only in the bull Buchis, but when the nearby town of
Thebes became the capital of the whole kingdom it was natural
that its own god, Amun, should very soon supplant Montu.
Buchis therefore took on Amun's qualities as well as his own,
and because Amun was associated with Re, the sun-god, so was
Buchis, who was thereafter represented with a disc between his
horns surmounted by two long plumes which are the insignia of
Amun (Fig. 16). In the Late New Kingdom other gods became
more prominent with the increasing influence of particular castes
of priests, and this resulted in Buchis acquiring the characteristics of many more gods, though the development did not really benefit his ordinary followers who remained unaffected by
such theological subtleties.

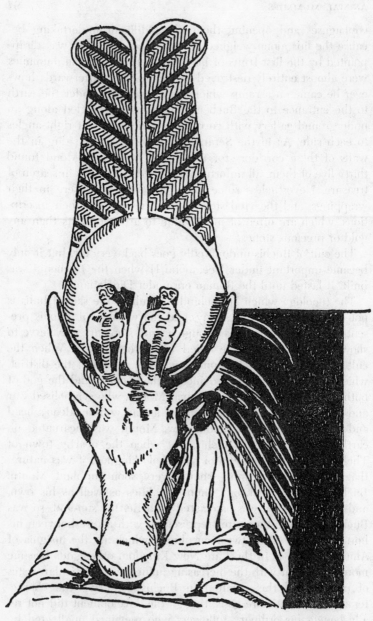

Fig. 16. Reconstruction of the mummified bull Buchis.

The bull himself resembled the bulls of Mesopotamia and Asia Minor, with short horns and a bump at the base of his neck. He had to be white with a black head, and born of a virgin mother, and it may be that the god Montu was himself the father. Once he had been found he was visited by a panel of experts, which we are informed by a stela commemorating Ptolemy VI's second bull was composed of "priests, royal inspectors, and soldiers from the Great Houses." This panel may have been responsible for authenticating all sacred animals, and was charged with verifying the characteristic markings and, probably, obtaining from the animal's owner a declaration certifying that the honour of its virgin mother was intact. No doubt the owner shared in the glory attaching to his beast, and very likely he also benefited materially.

The first two bulls which belonged to Nectanebo II and Ptolemy IV and the third which belonged to Ptolemy V were installed in Armant-Hermonthis by the king himself, accompanied by notables from the surrounding towns and prophets. Then every ten days they were visited by the god Amun, or at least by his statue, which came from Thebes with offerings. Later the bulls moved to Thebes, but subsidiary sanctuaries were maintained in the neighbourhood at Medamut to the north, Tod to the south, and Armant to the south-west, to receive the bull when he journeyed about to issue his oracles.

His death caused great scenes of grief among the people, who embarked on a period of mourning much as they did elsewhere for Apis. He was embalmed in exactly the same way. Two kinds of bronze objects which were used for mummification have been found in the Bucheum. One, a retractor, was a kind of flat-bladed instrument with a short handle which was used to keep the anus open so that the embalmer could inject liquid inside the animal to dissolve or clean his entrails by means of the other, a vessel with a nozzle (Fig. 17). Once the bull had been arranged on a plank and wrapped, he was buried in a sarcophagus. Widely different types were used over the years. They started as a single enormous block of granite which was hollowed out in the centre, then changed to sandstone which was easier to work, and finally under Ptolemy V developed into a much more ordi-

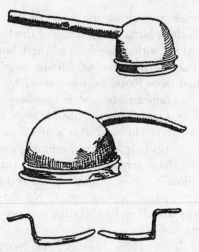

Fig. 17. Implements used during the mummification of the
bull Buchis, found in the Bucheum. Retractors and
holders with nozzles for dealing with the entrails.

nary chest constructed from several pieces. Monolithic sarcophaguses came back into fashion from Tiberius until Caracalla, and
then were abandoned altogether with the bulls simply being
buried in chambers without any protection. The two last ones
were deprived of even this courtesy, and were interred directly
in the corridor.

RUMINANTS

The sacred bull was one animal which personified the gods and
enjoyed its own special form of worship. Another was the cow,
which incarnated Hathor, the goddess of joy and music, who is
represented joyfully shaking her sistrum either in the shape of a
cow or as a woman with a cow's head, or even more simply as a
human head with cow's ears; in all cases two long horns on her
head clasped a solar disc. Hathor was particularly venerated at
Dendera, but also had numerous sanctuaries all over Egypt, and

one sacred cow was chosen as the object of worship in each temple.

At that time there were two varieties of cow in Egypt, and both were represented in bas-reliefs. One had short horns and probably came from the Sudan, while the other had long horns and was the oldest variety, which produced the sacred bulls. Today the African ox has been decimated by epidemics of disease and has largely been supplanted by the buffalo (gamoose) imported from Asia during the Middle Ages.

While many oxen were killed during sacrificial ceremonies and their flesh dedicated to the god, this did not prevent meat from the carcases being served to the officiating priests and the public. Milch-cows however were never sacrificed, and were regarded with particular respect in their capacity as foster-mothers to the sun and to the king. Whole herds of cows accompanied the sacred bulls and the goddess Hathor, and this led to a problem. Should cattle be slaughtered for food if they were in some way connected with the deity? Some provinces ignored the issue and continued to permit the consumption of beef, while others resolved to stop the slaughter altogether and let the animals die peacefully of old age. In the latter case cows and bullocks were mummified en masse, sometimes with care but usually hastily. Two French specialists in this field, Lortet and Gaillard, made a study of cattle from the great cemetery at Abusir, and found that the magnificent exterior of the mummies was utterly belied by the mess they discovered inside. One mummy which appeared to be a bull just over eight feet long and three feet wide was superbly wrapped in fine linen and bandages which crossed over each other with a marvellous sense of the artistic; some palm fibre string held everything in place, while the head jutted out from the end of the package crowned by two impressive horns. However, inside the mummy were only a few odd bones bundled carelessly together, which proved to have come from seven male animals, four of them with ancient toothless jaws showing that they had been very old and had probably died of old age. Inside a second seeming bull, the embalmer had mixed the bones of seven animals of which one was a two-year-old calf and one an enormous old male. A third held two skulls.

It seems strange that the priests treated such mixed-up collections of remains with such great care, when it might have been easier to mummify each animal as soon as it died. However, it is likely that the owners were not sufficiently wealthy to do this, especially if they lived far away from the embalming workshops. Instead, they buried the bodies in the vicinity of their home villages, leaving the horns sticking up out of the ground so that they could find them again easily. Each year more bodies accumulated, until the responsible officials came round the villages digging them all up, whether or not they had decomposed, and collected them together by the boat-load to bring them by river to Memphis, where they were sent to the embalmers. These then had the unenviable task of sorting out the half-rotten, dismembered and broken bodies and reconstructing them in the shape of a bull as best they could, and keeping the skull with the best horns to finish off their work. It seems that the corpses came from a considerable distance and, to judge by the size of the cattle necropolis situated between Abusir and Saqqara, the workshops can never have been short of work. In modern times the cemetery proved a considerable source of profit to European industrialists who imported millions of mummies to be converted into fertiliser for the soil. They were not at all deterred by the sacred character of the animals.

The range of animals domesticated by the Egyptians was amazingly wide, and besides cattle included antelopes, gazelles, bubals, onyx, wild mountain sheep, and ibex. Their flesh was considered a delicacy, and funerary offerings always included a haunch in a prominent position. However, they were not really tame and as we see from mural paintings each one always had to be accompanied by a man, whereas the same person could shepherd a whole flock of cows or sheep on his own. From the time of the Middle Kingdom therefore antelopes were no longer raised domestically. Some varieties were considered divine, and gazelles, which are found in private prehistoric tombs, were mummified during the Late New Kingdom, though not in such large numbers as the big ruminants. The British Museum has a mummy of one of them.

The ram was always considered sacred, and numerous temples were dedicated to him during the Late New Kingdom. Two types were to be found along the banks of the Nile, the *Ovis*

Longipes, which was tall and chiefly distinguished by its long twisted horns which jutted out at right-angles from each side of the top of its head and the *Ovis Platyra* which supplanted it around the second millenium and which was smaller, with thick horns laid back against its head and curled round its ears. Sheep had many uses in ancient Egypt, although the fleece itself was not greatly valued because priests and mummies were prohibited from using wool in their apparel, and linen was generally preferred. Their chief usefulness lay in farming for it was the custom to let flocks of sheep loose on the light soil of the fields after they had been sown with grain, in order to firm in the seeds, and they were also employed on the threshing-floor. Their flesh was excluded from ritual banquets in honour of the gods and the dead, and probably also from the diet of priests, but the common people were allowed to eat it.

Among the places where the ram was worshipped and mummified on its death was Mendes, which was the capital of the Delta province of the Dolphin and one of the greatest cities in Egypt in its latter days. Nothing now remains of its glory except a hillock surmounted by the great chapel of the sacred ram which legend says was the place where the spirits of Osiris and Re met, and united so closely that they became one. They were incarnated in the ram, which symbolised fertility. No doubt a union involving the two principal gods of Egypt was highly beneficial to the priests of the city, though in fact the place had always been held in high regard by the faithful and in predynastic times the kings of Buto always made a major stop at Mendes to visit its ram when they were going on their pilgrimage around the holy cities of the Delta. At that time it would have been the long-horned beast which was worshipped, but later on when this variety had disappeared an ordinary he-goat was substituted which made the Greeks associate it with their god Pan.

A second long-horned ram was worshipped at Herakleopolis under the name of Arsaphes. A special order of priests was attached to its temple, and it was such a great honour to be allowed to become a member that even a close relative of Sheshonq I was happy to accept an invitation to become its head or "divine father."

The holiest ram was probably Khnum, who lived in a sanctuary at Elephantine. He was the incarnation of the creator god who made the earth and modelled each human being to be born on his potter's wheel.

Later on the ram became associated with Amun and was worshipped as the incarnation of the god at Thebes. Amun's statues were given sheep heads, of the short-horned variety, and at Karnak there is an avenue of sphinxes all bearing ram's heads which leads to the great temple of Amun (Fig. 18).

Thousands of rams and sheep passed through the embalmers' hands.

CATS, DOGS AND MONGOOSES

The cat family was well represented in Egypt, both domestically and in the pantheon of the gods. Petrie found two kinds of skulls at Giza, of which the oldest belonged to a species of big wild cat, and were poorly embalmed. The others were domestic cats of a variety which first made an appearance about 2100 B.C. and which was imported into Egypt by the Greeks; this was the Libyan cat, often shown in pictures in the company of its owners, and which had orange fur, long ears, long paws and a waving tail. Of the two hundred mummified cats exhumed at Giza, it was the most common and was the ancestor of our ordinary cat. The Egyptians simply called it a "myeu," and used it as we do to catch rats and mice. The Ebers papyrus attributed magic powers to its remains, and advised on "another remedy to keep away mice: cat fat. Spread it everywhere." The Egyptians also employed cats to flush out waterbirds from thickets of reeds.

The cat became important in Egyptian religion when the sun god Re was rejected, and Ptah sent down on earth the lionness Sekhmet, goddess of war and plagues, mother of epidemics, whom the priests had great difficulty in appeasing when they were required to act as healers. Sekhmet was a bloodthirsty monster, but she also had another side to her character which was the complete reverse and in this aspect she was known as Bastet, a benevolent goddess who finally won the upper hand. Bastet had a woman's form with a cat's head, and she became a major

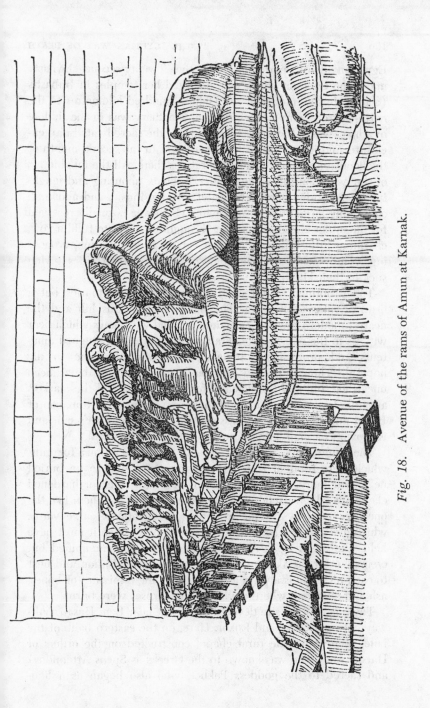

Fig. 18. Avenue of the rams of Amun at Karnak.

Egyptian deity, particularly in the Twenty-second Dynasty under the Osorkon kings, who enlarged her temples in Bubastis (a town in the middle of the Delta a hundred kilometres to the north-east of Cairo). Her principal sanctuary was in the middle of a lake, where the priests looked after the sacred cats in an enclosure, and it was the custom every year in the second month of the floods to organise great celebrations there. All the inhabitants of the neighbouring villages came in boats, shouting and laughing to each other across the water, playing music, and above all consuming large quantities of wine which was normally reserved for the upper classes only. Some brought offerings to fulfil a vow, charming little bronze statues of cats in every position, crouching, voluptuously stretched out, or lying on their sides giving suck to their kittens.

Today nothing is left of Bubastis and its sanctuaries but a heap of ruins, Tell Basta. The plain between this hill and the nearest modern town of Zagazig is riddled with holes which bear witness to the efforts of generations of thieves, enlightened amateurs and professional archaeologists, who all came to dig hopeful. Thousands and thousands of statuettes have been unearthed, but still the demand for them grows and the markets are full of fakes. Some of the bronzes represent Nefertum, son of Bastet and Ptah, who was associated with his mother's cult and is shown as a man with a lotus leaf on top of his head.

The same place was also the site of a necropolis for cats, which were brought from every corner of Egypt to be buried near their deity. They were put in pits with brick or hardened clay walls which stretch in every direction, some of them like the one excavated by Naville extending to twenty-six cubic yards, which gives some idea of the number of cats which it must have held. Unusually in Egypt, the bodies were not mummified but cremated, for the skeletons show signs of carbonisation and next to each pit there is always a place containing a mixture of bones, ash and charcoal, where obviously the corpses were burnt.

There is another site devoted to the cat near Beni Hasan, halfway between Cairo and Luxor. Here, on the eastern bank of the Nile, there is a little rural chapel constructed on the orders of Hatshepsut (who was known to the Greeks as Speos Artemidos) and sacred to the goddess Pakhet, who also began as a lion-goddess but was transformed into a cat-goddess. In 1859 a fellah discovered a cat graveyard near the sanctuary while he was digging up land which had not previously been cultivated. Three hundred thousand animals were eventually disinterred from the site, not without profit to British farmers for most of them were transported to England and converted into fertiliser. Fortunately a number of them were preserved as they were found, neatly wrapped in cloth of two colours (Fig. 19). The mummies were usually placed in little bronze or wooden sarcophaguses in the shape of a cat, with eyes of inlaid coloured glass, obsidian or rock crystal, or sometimes when there was no coffin the head alone was covered with a bronze mask of a cat with its ears

Fig. 19. Bandaged mummy of a cat.

decorated with a gold ring. Kittens and foetuses were placed inside the stomach of a statue which represented their mother, or in a wooden or bronze box surmounted by a statue of the animal.

It is easy to see that the cat played an important role in Egyptian daily life. When it died, we are told, the family went into mourning, shaved off their eyebrows, and watched over it until it was time to take it to the embalmer. Normally it was considered a heinous crime to kill a cat, but there were circumstances in which its death could be hastened with beneficial results, provided the correct magic formulae were applied. An account of these strange proceedings appears in a Greek papyrus, which Capart tells us described how to take revenge against an enemy by drowning a cat and, while it is still struggling under the water, reciting the following prayer:

> Come to me, you to whom the appearance of Helios, the cat-headed god, belongs, and see how your adversaries X and Y have maltreated you; take vengeance on them and accomplish such and such a task, for I appeal to you, o sacred demon; gather up your forces against your enemies, for I conjure you in your name. . . . Rise up for me, o cat-headed god, and carry out such and such a thing.

This formula ingeniously throws the responsibility for the murder on one's enemies with the result that the tutelary god of the animal and the divine animal itself both direct their vengeance at them. Once the animal was dead, it was necessary to put inside its body some little pieces of papyrus on which was written in red ink the request to the goddess Bastet. The corpse had to be wrapped in a sheet of papyrus previously decorated with ritual images, and then it could be buried. Next the tomb was sprinkled with water in which the cat had been drowned, and the following words were uttered: "I conjure you, o demon summoned to this spot, and you, demon of this cat now become spirit, come to me today at once and execute such and such a thing for me." Finally, the owner shook the cat's whiskers in the air while walking towards the sun, and affirmed aloud that it was indeed his enemies who had put the poor beast to death.

The papyrus testified to the excellence of the spell in these words: "Such is the magic working of the cat, suitable for every purpose, good for causing harm to a chariot-driver in the races, for bringing dreams, for winning the love of a woman, for arousing divisions or hatred." This explains all the inscriptions on the base of statuettes of the cat, which read: "Goddess Bastet, give life, health and a happy existence to so-and-so, son of so-and-so," and it also accounts for the size of the graves at Bubastis and the enormous numbers of cats buried at Beni Hasan.

Their popularity was rivalled by man's other favourite companion, the dog, which in fact had been domesticated earlier than the cat. At the same time hordes of wild dogs still roamed about the deserts and hills, and some authorities believe that it is wrong to describe the god Anubis as jackal-headed, when really he took his shape from these dogs. Keimer for example, who is both an Egyptologist and a zoologist, states firmly that there are not and never have been jackals in Egypt, but only wandering dogs with tapering noses, big pointed ears and a long shaggy tail, which look rather like wolves. A troop of them was described by an official who was besieged by them in his lonely frontier post: "If ever I open a pot of beer and take it outside to drink, two hundred big dogs and three hundred wolf-dogs appear, five hundred in all. Every day they are there in front of the door, every time I go out, because of the smell from the pot when it is opened. What would happen to me if I did not have here the young wolf-dog belonging to Nahiho the royal scribe? He is the only one to save me from them whenever I go out, and he guides me along the way."

Many gods were incarnated in the dog. The most famous was Anubis, who was specially venerated in his town of Cynopolis, city of dogs, in Middle Egypt; he was the funerary god who had invented mummification when he embalmed Osiris. He also watched over the necropolises and protected the dead against thieves and prowling dogs. He was represented as a black dog (or jackal, according to tradition) lying on a plinth, or as a man with a dog's head (Fig. 20). He had to be black because bodies were black after they had been mummified, so as to signify his connection with death, while the special shape and colour of his spots were recognised by the priests as the signs of his sa-

Fig. 20. Anubis, in the shape of a black dog, stretched out on his pedestal.

credness. Another god to be personified in a dog was Khentamentiu, chief of the people of the west, that is to say of the dead, at Abydos; he was confused with Osiris in the Late Middle Kingdom. Finally there was Upuaout, another god who watched over the deceased, who presided over Asyut and was drawn as a dog standing on its hindlegs. His name meant "opener of paths,"

and he used to precede Osiris into battle, while on earth a stand-
ard-bearer carrying his portrait was traditionally supposed to
go in front of the pharaoh clearing a way through his enemies.
All these animals belonged to the canine species, although today
it is no longer possible to establish whether they were dogs,
jackals or wolves.

Dogs were buried with due cermony from the predynastic
period onwards. Debono found them in the graveyard at Heliopolis with the gazelles, placed on their sides with their legs
folded under them, but not facing in any particular direction, in
shallow graves. They lay in rows all round the edge of the
necropolis, rather as if they were still acting as guards, which
suggests some connection with a cult of Anubis that predated
historical times.

In later periods some regions accorded every dog, tame or
wild, the same honours as the sacred ones, and as with the cat all
members of a household went into mourning on the death of
their pet, shaved their hair and were forbidden to eat any food
that was in the house. There were several cemeteries especially
for dogs in Egypt, one at Thebes where the bodies were
wrapped in brown and ochre bandages which made a pattern of
interlocking rectangles, and the biggest one excavated by Peet at
Abydos at the beginning of this century. Here a shaft faced with
stone led down to underground galleries opening into the mortu-
ary chambers, all of which were filled with dog mummies
heaped up in rows, eight to ten on top of each other, reaching a
height of up to five feet. There were literally thousands of them,
poorly embalmed, hastily wrapped in white cloth, and untidily
deposited facing in every direction, with the result that when an
attempt was made to move them most of them disintegrated into
dust. The Roman lamps dating from the 1st century B.C. that
were left on the sand and subsequently covered with a layer of
corpses gave some indication of the date of the burials. Even
here robbers had been busy, leaving a pile of broken bones
mixed with skeletons and cloth near the entrance.

Besides providing a cemetery for dogs and gazelles, Heliopolis
was also a centre for the worship of Atum, who was represented
by the lion, the serpent, and above all the ichneumon or North
African mongoose. Mongooses were reared in all Atum's temples,

but specially at Bubastis. Here they were fed on a diet of bread soaked in milk, though whether they enjoyed this may be doubted since in the wild they like snakes, which they attack with great skill. Egyptian theology relates how Atum transformed himself into a mongoose in order to defeat the huge serpent Apopis, god of evil and enemy of the sun, who is always being defeated but always rises again. Sympathetic magic, like that practised with cats, compelled the god to avenge the death of a mongoose if it was drowned, but in return the mongoose had the right to be buried in a beautiful bronze box adorned with its own effigy.

Another animal which was mummified, though more rarely, was the shrew. They are sometimes found squeezed in among the birds in collections arranged in a spindle shape, and sometimes curiously their skeletons are bandaged in such a way as to look like ibises from the outside. Usually they are preserved separately, wrapped and safely placed in a little coffin of sycamore wood carved in their likeness; the lid of these boxes slips into position along grooves, just like an old-fashioned child's pencil-box.

IBISES, BABOONS AND FALCONS

Thoth was the intellectual among the gods. He was credited with having invented writing, introduced record-keeping, created laws, and devised the calendar. He was at once the patron of scribes and the secretary of the gods, a writer, historian and mathematician. He also had an unrivalled command of language which enabled him to exercise magic powers like those attributed to the Greek Hermes Trismegistos, the triply great, with whom he was associated in the Hellenic period. Rumour had it that he had himself written the "hermetic books" which were jealously guarded in a secret recess of the temple of Hermopolis. It is somewhat strange therefore that such a brilliant personage should be represented on earth by a humble bird like the ibis, which the Egyptians called *hib;* this was neither the bronze plumaged glossy ibis nor the tufted ibis with its rather dull

brown feathers, but the great white ibis with a black head, the
sacred ibis which used to destroy reptiles and come back to
Egypt every year just before the Nile started to rise in flood. In
those days it must have been a much bigger bird than it is now,
for its descendants in the Sudan never reach the dimensions of
the mummified ones that have been discovered.

There was no lack of sanctuaries devoted to Thoth in Egypt,
but his favourite town soon became Khmunu, better known
today under its Greco-Egyptian name of Hermopolis, in Hare
Province. Khmunu was already a centre for the worship of a
number of animals, including the hare, the frog, and especially
the dog-headed baboon which was not actually a native of
Egypt but had to be imported from Ethiopia and the Sudan. Another way in which it was obtained was in part payment of the
tribute which Egypt exacted from the subject peoples of Nubia,
who were required to capture a certain number of the animals in
their forests every year. The male animal had dog-like jaws,
prominent scarlet buttocks and a thick mane, and his lubricious
temperament and frequently erect penis were not always easy to
deal with; his sporadic outbursts of aggression led the scribes to
use a hieroglyph of an angry baboon standing on all four legs to
signify "to be angry" (Fig. 21). On occasions however when he
was sitting calmly on his hindquarters, with his forepaws on his
knees, he took on a more regal air, and this was how he was usually represented in sculpture. He was soon adopted by the god
Thoth, who was thus doubly insured on earth by his incarnation
in two animals, once in the ibis which was brought to Hermopolis for the purpose and once in the dog-headed baboon
which was already there.

Fig. 21. Hieroglyph for "to be angry," followed by the determinative sign of an infuriated baboon, standing up.

The religious centre and necropolis were situated north of Hermopolis, at Tuna el-Gebel, where Samuel Gabra directed the University of Egypt's excavations. These laid bare a vast funerary complex testifying to the tremendous importance accorded to animal cults in the era of Egypt's decline. Pilgrims who had gone in huge numbers to Hermopolis to pay homage to Thoth in his temple there on feast days would then cover the seven miles to the animal sanctuary on foot under the exhausting rays of the sun. Fortunately the sanctuary itself was situated in an oasis of palm-trees which well merited its description of "place of silence and freshness." Monkeys skipped from tree to tree, and the ibises found shelter in a vast lake which had been specially constructed for them, and which was fed by an ingenious hoisting apparatus from a well which descended in two stages to a depth of one hundred and twelve feet. On the edge of the desert, this animal enclosure was a real haven of rest and hospitality, and visitors were even provided with lodging if they wished to stay on. At the same time traders, never far away from any holy place, made the most of their advantage and sold offerings which the pilgrims were obliged to buy in fulfilment of their vows if they wanted their pilgrimage to bear fruit; or perhaps it was the priests themselves who profited from the shops around the temple.

The great temple was called the "Temple of the Higher Spirits," and though it is in ruins it has now been uncovered from the sand which had buried it nearly forty feet deep before. It is inscribed with the name of Petosiris, high priest of Thoth, and with a plea to passers-by that they should spell out his name so that he might live for ever.

The huge area in which the sacred animals were interred covers an area of thirty-seven acres, and right from antiquity was considered to be a marvel. Naturally such a famous place could not hope to escape the attentions of looters, and the University of Egypt team was preceded by many other clandestine excavators. A stone balustrade three feet high, six hundred and forty yards long and two hundred and twenty yards wide marked the boundaries of the funerary area for animals where the entrances to the underground passages were found. There were three galleries, each with a chapel at its entrance, which extended for several hundred yards. Human remains were buried outside the confines of the balustrade.

The most recent gallery, gallery A, housed only ibises, and opened out into a complete underground town, with streets giving on to a series of dark badly ventilated rooms in which thousands of bird mummies were piled up. Most of them were ibises, but a few were falcons or flamingoes, perhaps because the priests in the Late New Kingdom were less scrupulous about the type of bird they admitted. They were poorly embalmed, some of them inside little jars, but most of them lying on the ground in layers on top of each other.

Gallery B dates from the Ptolemaic era and is the biggest. It is reached by a monumental stairway, and consists of a labyrinth of corridors which cross and recross each other without any plan, forced to change direction from time to time when the rock was too hard to tunnel through. There are very few rooms here, but instead the walls are lined with niches cut out of the stone and extending from top to bottom of the corridor as far as the eye can see, in orderly rows which the shadows they cast make even more impressive. All the cachettes are empty, some because they had been looted, as the presence of a large number of broken jars shows, but in many cases because they had been hollowed out in advance to provide for the future needs of the ibis cult, and had never been occupied.

The oldest gallery is gallery C, which has also given us the most information about the precise rites used by the worshippers of Thoth. It had an open-air chapel, last restored by the son of Alexander the Great and Roxana, to welcome those who were to officiate in the funerary ceremony prior to the burial, and next to this in another building was the "Archive Office" where some of the original documents concerning the running of the temple were found in sealed jars. One of these was a letter carried by a messenger from Faiyum who was bringing an ibis to be mummified; it bore the seal of Psammeticus I so it served both as a safe-conduct during the journey and an introduction to the priests. It seems that Hermopolis was also used as a stopping-place for travellers, certainly during the difficult times of the Persian occupation, for in a piece of pottery seven letters were dis-

covered carefully hidden among the ibis bodies, written in
Aramaic. Apparently the Jews of Elephantine were conveying secret messages to their co-religionists at Memphis.

Inside the gallery, a small room two by three yards led off
from the right, and was used as the embalming workshop. To
judge from the numbers of birds; it must have been in constant
use by relays of embalmers: four million mummified birds were
found in the underground corridors of the necropolis. The embalming table stood in the middle of the room, its surface on a
slight incline so that the liquids could run down into a gutter; it
was still covered with resin or bitumen, and surrounded by jars
set in the ground from which the embalmers took their materials.
Chemical analysis of one large container showed that the usual
natron, salt and oil of turpentine were used. The ibises were
treated with natron and resin, though they were not eviscerated
and the embalmers seem to have worked very hurriedly. On the
other hand the man in charge of the bandaging took immense
care and the patterns he produced by crossing the bandages over
each other were often very elegant. The finished package was
sometimes given a human shape but was generally conical, with
the bird's head and long beak emerging from one end (Fig. 22),

Fig. 22.   Bandaged ibis.

and it was often decorated by a picture of the goddess Isis cut out of pieces of cloth and glued to its chest. Finally, the mummified bird was put in the gallery. Birds which were brought in by the faithful from the outside to be mummified in homage to Thoth had to be paid for by the donor, and they were piled into jars and placed directly on the sandy floor of the rooms, which were filled right up to the ceiling, whereas sacred birds which had been reared within the temple had a right to be placed in the niches hollowed out of the passage walls.

From time to time, priests conducted services. A limestone statue which was discovered shows us a priest dressed in linen, carrying a table of offerings, and going backwards down the great stairway to the underground tunnels. He was followed by a procession of the faithful who had stopped to rest in one of the chapels which had been set up inside, decorated with zodiacs and provided with stone benches.

Besides ibises, the galleries also contained the mummified bodies of the sacred baboons, though in much smaller numbers, presumably because there were far fewer of them. Their brains were left inside their bodies, though again the exterior was carefully treated and Gabra found one specimen in Gallery C which was covered in gold jewels and amulets.

Only one human being was buried in the cemetery. He was Ankhor, high priest of Thoth, who had spent all his life in the service of the sacred birds, and at the end of it decided to remain with them. It is an impressive sight to walk along the long corridor to his sepulchre, past rooms fifty foot square and twenty foot high filled with rows of wooden coffins containing the baboons, on top of which again were placed thousands of jars each with four ibises inside.

It is hard to envisage four million mummified ibises. The incredible number shows the inordinate lengths to which animal worship was pushed in ancient Egypt, and makes it likely too that like cats ibises were killed for magic purposes, especially as both here and in other cemeteries they do not always appear to have died from sickness or old age.

One of these other cemeteries was situated at Abydos, the sacred town of Osiris, not far from the dog cemetery. Here too the birds were buried in their thousands, enclosed singly or in num-

bers of up to a hundred in pottery jars. These were made of clay
baked in ovens or dried in the sun, and in order to get the birds
inside them the bulge of the jar had to be cut out and then replaced and sealed with mud (Fig. 23). A few of the jars held ibis
eggs, anything from forty to a hundred of them, each carefully
wrapped in cloth so as not to damage the shell. The ibises themselves were wrapped in two ways, according to whether the
wrapping was done before or after rigor mortis had set in, either
compactly with their heads lowered and their beaks down on
their chests, or with their heads held upright. In either case the
legs were always bent, and where there was a gap between the
corpse and the bandaging it was filled with linen stuffing. The
last bandages were skilfully wrapped around so as to make a variety of geometric patterns, and as at Hermopolis the embalmer
occasionally gave a human shape to the final package, leaving
the bird's head outside which he finished off with a crown.

The ibis birds were also considered sacred to Imhotep, who
was translated into a god of medicine in the year 170 B.C. This
was odd in view of the fact that during his lifetime in the Third
Dynasty he had been vizir to King Zoser and was famous both
for his political role and also as an architect of genius, who as we

Fig. 23.   Ibis in its operculated jar.

know had built the famous step pyramid, but not as far as can be discovered for anything connected with medicine. Perhaps in the course of his work as sage, scribe, chief reader-priest, astrologist and musician he had effected some miraculous cures whose fame increased after his death. In any event his name became increasingly honoured, and even by the time of Amenophis III it was the custom for a scribe who was about to start drawing hieroglyphs on to a sheet of papyrus to let a drop of ink fall from his pen in tribute to Imhotep. It was under Ptolemy-Euergetes II that he was deified, sanctuaries were raised to him, and his worship established. In many ways he resembled the god Thoth because of his wide knowledge in numerous areas and his outstanding intellectual qualities, so perhaps it is not surprising that he took on many of Thoth's attributes, and became known as "principal chief of the ibises."

Imhotep's tomb has never been found, though it is very likely that he was buried near the step pyramid which he built for his pharaoh at Saqqara. There is a large ibis necropolis just to the north which must have posed considerable difficulties for its builders, and would probably not have been put there unless Imhotep's tomb was somewhere in the vicinity. There were plenty of more suitable places but these presumably would not have had the attraction of being so near the grave of a man closely linked with the ibis cult. The chosen site was very large, and already contained human tombs from the Old and Middle Kingdoms, with the result that the tunnels often met with obstacles such as an ancient funerary shaft which had to be strengthened, or the floor of a tomb which needed support, and all in all considerable work in shoring up the tunnels was needed. The labyrinth of passages has never been fully explored, even by Emery who made extensive excavations in 1965, though it has been known to exist for a very long time and attracted tourist visits as far back as the time of Napoleon, when no stay in Egypt was complete without a trip to the "tomb of the bird mummies." Hundreds of thousands of ibises inside sealed jars line the corridors and fill the rooms on each side, walled off from the main passage by a mixture of mud and plaster. The immensity of the task involved in slaughtering and preparing these unfortunate birds for their preservation in tribute both to Imhotep

at Saqqara and to Thoth at Hermopolis and Abydos almost
passes belief.

They were not the only representatives of the feathered tribes
to be perserved. Thirty-eight different kinds from all parts of
Egypt were distinguished by Lortet and Gaillard, including owls,
swallows, various sparrows, and in greater numbers the diurnal
birds of prey, buzzards, sparrow-hawks, kites, small eagles and
so on. Most prized of all was the royal falcon, which was often
represented as the incarnation of the great Horus, tutelary god of
the monarchy, either in the shape of the bird itself or as a man
with a falcon's head (Fig. 24). It also appeared as Re, with the
disc of the sun on its head, Montu the god of war whose head
was crowned with two long plumes, Sokaris, a primitive funerary
deity, in the shape of a mummified falcon, Horus in his capacity

Fig. 24. Re-Horakhty.

of son of Isis, dressed in the double royal crown, Horus of Behedet, represented by a sun disc flanked with two outspread wings, and many others. Consequently it was worshipped in many places and had many graveyards. The sacred falcons were reared in temples and enjoyed a life of ease in which their guardians called them every day to receive their scraps of meat, which they caught on the wing, and no doubt it was these special birds which were embalmed and put into bronze or cardboard boxes. Their dainty sarcophaguses were often shaped like a man, and were barely twenty inches long. Ordinary birds were collected into large spindle-shaped arrangements five foot long which included other kinds of birds and even, if a sufficiently large number of birds of prey was not to hand, just piles of bones and feathers. No doubt, as with cows, the birds were gathered together over a period of time and so decomposition would often have set in before they arrived at the temple, and in any case the priests did not accord them the same attention and care as they did the sacred birds which they themselves had reared.

CROCODILES, SNAKES, AND OTHER REPULSIVE CREATURES

One of the most curious gods was Sobek, who became Suchos under the Greeks, and who was worshipped in the form of a crocodile in many temples all along the Nile. Religious art shows him either as a recumbent crocodile or as a man with a crocodile's head, on top of which was a pair of ram's horns and two plumes of Amun, sometimes flanked by two erect cobras, but always with the sun disc between its horns to show the animal's religious significance, emphasised by the fact that, like the sun, he emerged from the water. Sobek was god of the water, and symbolised life and resurrection, and it was in this capacity that he was worshipped at Kom Ombo, where every year they celebrated the life-giving Nile floods. Here, fifty miles north of Aswan, one can still see a unique Egyptian building, a double temple in which the courtyard, the two pillared halls, the three vestibules, and all its rooms are common to both parts yet have two different entrances, except for the two chapels at the end of the sanctuary which are separate. Each chapel was dedicated to a divine triad: the first consisted of Haroeris, Horus the Great with his sparrow-hawk's head, and his two companions, the goddess Senetnofret, "the good sister" and Panebtaui, the "lord of the double country"; the second was composed of Sobek, the crocodile god, accompanied by his mother, the goddess Hathor with a cow's head, and his son, the god Khonsu, a man with a falcon's head. Near the north-western wall of the temple, a complex of wells had been dug in order to supply the lakes in which the young crocodiles were bred.

However the principal centre was the ancient town of Shedit, which the Greeks called Crocodilopolis and which took the name of Arsinoë in the Ptolemaic period. Today there is still a town sixty miles to the south of Cairo, but even with its seventy thousand inhabitants the present-day Medinet el-Faiyum cannot rival the bustling life of earlier times when it welcomed thousands of visitors to pay homage to the crocodile and, in Greco-Roman times, to visit the thermal springs whose vestiges can still be detected. The worship of Sobek dates from the Twelfth Dynasty, when a temple was built to him which was later restored by Ramesses II, but it was in the era of the Ptolemies with the expansion of animal worship that the town reached the height of its fame. The huge crocodiles there, which were cared for by a whole college of priests, excited universal admiration. They took their ease in the sun on the edges of a sacred lake, without ever having to stir in search of a meal, for the priests brought them everything. Assistants held them down firmly at dinnertime, while others opened their jaws and one shovelled in cooked and slightly burnt meat and bread, and poured in drink from a pitcher of hydromel, which was a mixture of honey and water. When the beast had received his ration, he plunged into the lake to a place of refuge on the far side, though if a stranger arrived with offerings the priests would immediately rush round the lake and recommence the proceedings all over again. It can easily be imagined that the monsters did not survive long on such an unsuitable diet. They were popularly considered to be as holy as the gods themselves, so they were accorded tremendous veneration, and according to Herodotus were adorned with bracelets

around their forelegs. This does not seem improbable in view of
the lengths to which their worshippers went, but what is impossible is that they should also have had ear-rings dangling from
their non-existent ears! Clearly the temple and lake were a
sufficient attraction on their own to merit a special visit, quite
apart from their religious significance, and so the temple officials
were well equipped to provide every contemporary convenience
for travellers. When a Roman senator called Mummius was plan-
ning a visit, an official letter was sent in advance urging that no
effort should be spared to make his trip an enjoyable and com-
fortable one; but at the same time the religious aspect was not
ignored, and one item on the list of extra expenses was "additional food for Petesuchos and the crocodiles."

When a crocodile died, it was sent to the embalmers and then
buried with the customary pomp in the sacred crocodile cemetery. Unfortunately no trace of this Sucheion has ever come to
light, though we do know of other graveyards where ordinary
crocodiles were interred. Presumably these had been brought as
offerings to the gods, but they would not have been treated with
the same care as the sacred ones. Twelve miles to the south of
Crocodilopolis, for example, there is the Tebtynis cemetery from
which some two thousand mummified crocodiles have been
disinterred, and more remain. Here there were no stelae or
funerary buildings to indicate the site, and the tombs were simply dug out of the sand and the mummies buried in family
groups consisting of the father, mother, five or six young, and
sometimes a few eggs. Again, it is striking how much care was
taken with the outside of the creatures, when so little of the actual animal remained inside the meticulously concocted pack-
ages, usually just one crocodile bone, the rest being made of
straw stuffing and palm branches, with the head fashioned from
long strips of papyrus which incidentally have provided Egyptologists with very interesting material. It looks as if the priests
had found a good way of producing some extra revenue for
themselves through the production of crocodile mummies for
sale. Not all the mummies were fake however. One extraordinary
one was discovered in 1901 by Gorostarzu, with a crocodile six
feet long inside the package, and on top of it the pieces of a
larger beast which had been carefully placed on the corre-

sponding parts of the small one; between the pieces lay an army
of some fifty tiny crocodiles which can only just have emerged
from their eggs, looking as if they are about to advance on the
beholder.

There is another sanctuary in Upper Egypt, near Armant,
which is also called Crocodilopolis, and here in a cave Arabs discovered a quantity of crocodile mummies of all sizes, heaped up
quite carelessly and mixed up with human remains. The finders
realised that the cartonnage packaging would be valuable because it was made of Greek papyrus glued together, but unfortunately in their eagerness to explore the cave they neglected to
take the proper precautions and by mistake set it on fire. Tragically, everything was lost.

Apart from crocodiles, Egypt was infested with snakes, from
the cobra which glided through the vegetation in the Delta
marshes, suddenly rising up and puffing out its neck in anger as
it appears in the uraeus on the pharaoh's headdress, to the little
black-tailed viper and the horned adder slipping through the desert sands. Their bite was fatal, and not even the water which
was poured over statues bearing magic inscriptions supposed to
effect a miraculous cure could do much to help. The only solution therefore was to make allies out of the creatures by elevat-
ing them to the rank of tutelary deities. Thus the lady cobra,
"Renenutet, mistress of the granary," represented by a woman
with a cobra's head, seated and holding her son Neper on her
knees, was the goddess of the harvest. Her statue kept watch
over the granaries and every year when the time came to bring
in the grain and the grapes a portion of the fruits of the earth
was consecrated to her. She was honoured all over the country,
but especially in Medinet Madi where Amenemhat III and
Amenemhat IV erected a temple to her, though it was so small
that Seti II, Ramesses III and Osorkon added a monumental avenue to it in recognition of her services, along which processions
in her honour could pass.

Another serpent-goddess called Meret-Seger, "she who loves
silence," was worshipped at Deir el-Medina, where the workers
from the Theban necropolis lived, and she was supposed to protect and watch over the city of the dead. A sanctuary was built
for her, sometimes referred to "the Summit," half-way up the

slopes of the mountain which dominates the valley to the west of Thebes. These lesser divinities were evidently not as important as the primordial gods, but nevertheless they too, in their guise as snakes, had the right to be embalmed like other sacred animals, and they are found wrapped in bandages and lying in graves dug out of the sand, or more often enclosed in little wooden or bronze sarcophaguses decorated with a coiled serpent with a human head. It is not unusual to find these boxes hanging in human dwellings.

Bronze was also the metal favoured for the small caskets which held mummified bodies of the frogs who were the embodiment of the goddess Heket, a frog-headed matron whose function it was to look after women in child-birth and breathe life into their newly-born babies.

Once he had survived infancy, the average Egyptian depended a great deal on fish for his daily nourishment. The Nile was full of fish of all varieties, mostly edible except for the tasteless cat-fish and the globe-fish which puffs out its spines at the first sign of danger, so a peasant only had to cast a line or set up a net at the edge of the river or in the marshes in order to catch an adequate supply. If he formed part of a team of labourers, he would get a ration of fish as part of his wages. It seems simple, but in reality numerous religious prohibitions complicated the situation. Some fish were sacred to a particular region and could never be eaten there, on some feast-days it was considered sacrilegious to eat fish, and there were a whole array of local beliefs which changed from place to place. Priests and pharaohs were never allowed to eat fish.

Two examples will illustrate the variety of beliefs. In Pimasi, the Delta town which the Greeks later called Oxyrynchus, the people worshipped the god Seth in the form of the oxyrynchus fish, a kind of electric fish with a long curving snout, which was supposed to have swallowed Osiris' penis when the fragments of his body were scattered and lost. Seth was the sworn enemy of Osiris, so it is not surprising that the privilege of being embalmed was bestowed on this creature which was at once an embodiment of Seth and a living reliquary for the remains of Seth's brother Osiris.

Another important deity to be incarnated in a fish was Neith, a primordial goddess who was the androgynous creator of the world, said to have drifted through the waters before hurling the sun into the air to start it on its eternal path through the skies. It was therefore appropriate to choose the Nile perch or lates, from which the Greeks derived the name Latopolis that they gave to Esna, to incarnate her in the flesh. An incredible number of these fish were found mummified and bandaged six miles to the west of the city in the sandy plain which stretches as far as the foothills of the Libyan mountains. They had been buried directly in the sand and were of all sizes, from the tiniest which were only a few inches long to the biggest which reached six and a half feet. As a sign of the people's piety, hundreds of their fry were incorporated into balls made of reeds wound together and then wrapped up with cloth. Poor pilgrims who could not afford the services of an embalmer made their own balls into which they slipped a few fish scales. The best specimens, however, were beautifully preserved, and though they were not eviscerated they had been sliced down the side to allow the natron to penetrate properly. They were covered with a layer of very highly salted mud to finish the process, and then buried in hot dry sand to accelerate the process of dehydration. The scales of some of them are still amazingly bright, and the bronze glint in their eyes is very striking.

Insects were not neglected in this pantheon of the gods, and indeed one of the most important was the scarab beetle which replaced the man's head in representations of Khepri, the rising sun. In hieroglyphics the scarab stood for Kheper, which according to Yoyotte means "to come into existence by assuming a given shape," that is to say to be and to become at one and the same time. Thus the scarab beetle pushing his mud-ball backwards was a good choice to represent the god Khepri, "who came into existence by himself." Mummies of scarabs are rare though. There are two specimens in the British Museum, one in a wooden box and the other in a little stone sarcophagus, and the same type of instructions for drowning scarabs as for cats in order to achieve a specific purpose is to be found in the magic papyrus, which prescribes plunging the insect into a mixture of myrrh and wine from Mendes, and then wrapping it in fine linen cloth before burying it. The writer evidently found it a useful prescription, for he states: "In the whole world I know of no more efficacious recipe; ask the god for what you want and he will grant it to you."

Another notorious Egyptian creature was the scorpion, which had its lair among warm stones and stung the unwary person who trod on it barefoot, with agonising results. The sting, according to the Chester Beattie papyrus VII, is "hotter than fire, more burning than flames, sharper than needles," and many stelae bear the names of those whom the poison killed, such as "Appolonius, son of Eusebius and Tanis, killed by a scorpion on the island of Apolinaris"; "Aurelius Amonicus lost his life from a scorpion's sting." The victims might die in less than twenty-four hours, as one stela in Abydos tells us: "You who perished without glory and obscurely, from a violent death unworthy of your generous nature, for you were stung by a scorpion in the sanctuary of Thripis on the tenth day of Thoth, in the third year, at five o'clock, and died on the eleventh day." It seems that the lustral water sprinkled on the miraculous statues was not very effective. The scorpion, as befitted its formidable nature, represented a deity called Selket, who was depicted either as a scorpion with a woman's head or as a woman with a scorpion on top of her head. Selket was a benevolent goddess, patron of healers to whom pleas for help were addressed when a sting had been inflicted. The few mummies of scorpions that have been found are enclosed in rectangular boxes decorated with a bronze effigy of the goddess wearing a sun disc and horns.

One rather gruesome object of mummification was found in a Roman tomb next to two mummies in sarcophaguses with covers in the form of plaster masks, that were the mode at the time. This was the larder beetle, which feeds on dead flesh. A number of them were found inside a little glass phial sealed with wax into which the embalmer had carefully inserted them one by one through the narrow neck after he had either cooked or soaked them in wine. Today it is impossible to guess the motives which led to such a curious practice, but by now we have met so many extraordinary aspects of mummification that the extraordinary should no longer astonish us.

So the practice of mummification entered its final stages in Egypt. We have traced its development and its spread down the ages, starting with the pharaoh alone whom mummification assimilated to Osiris, then being extended to his family and all the high dignitaries, until finally it covered people from every station in life who wished to avail themselves of the same privileges when they died. In the same way mummification of animals started with one sacred animal of each chosen kind, which was the living representation of a god on earth, and then spread to cover the embalming of all animals of the same kind, and extended to the humblest representatives of the species. Even the grain of corn placed in some tombs may possibly have been intended to incarnate the little god Neper, son of Renenutet and symbol of rebirth; the principle of mummification of living things could hardly have been carried any further.

In any case there was no opportunity to do so, for soon with the coming of Coptic civilisation and the end of ancient Egypt, mummification and the urge to perpetuate the appearance of life died out.

CHAPTER 5

MUMMIES AND
THEIR MAKERS

As we have seen Egypt is full of burial grounds, known as necropolises. Indeed it is estimated that about five hundred million bodies were mummified up to the Roman period, more than in any other civilisation in antiquity. These incredible numbers combined with the widespread and elaborate cult of the dead gave rise to a profusion of tombs which have often lasted down to the present day because they were built to last, unlike ordinary buildings which were constructed from more perishable materials. The funerary buildings, their decoration and furnishings, have all bequeathed us an abundant legacy of material which can be used to study Egyptian civilisation.

The best place to examine the workings of a necropolis lies in the Theban region, for it was Thebes which during the period of the Middle Kingdom superseded Memphis and became the great political and religious capital of Egypt. Unfortunately the most important and complete documents on the subject date only from Greek and Roman times, but nevertheless if they are interpreted in the light of a few earlier texts of Egyptian origin they give some idea of how these vast funerary enterprises functioned. I owe a great deal to Bataille, whose *Recherches de papyrologie grecque sur la Nécropole de Thèbes* provided the basis for this chapter, and to Bruyère's excavations in Deir el-Medina.

The first examples of mummification go back to the Fourth Dynasty; they involve only people of royal rank. A little later, the pharaoh authorised a few high dignitaries to have themselves mummified, which was a particularly important privilege because mummification was supposed to endow the pharaoh with the divine nature of the god Osiris, so that he in fact became the equal of the gods. This signal mark of royal favour was especially appreciated and referred to as the "King's gift." The number of people who were honoured in this fashion constantly increased, and the pharaoh made them presents of funerary chests, beds, viscera jars, and stelae with false doors. In the end it was accepted that the whole of the wealthy classes should have themselves mummified, though the numbers at this peroid were still few in comparison with the numbers in the era of Persian domination, when every person from peasant to trader to official, whatever his rank, wanted to attain immortality in this way. Embalming was no longer a privilege but was open to everyone, so the necropolises had to be progressively expanded and their functioning carefully organised.

For religious reasons, burial grounds were most often situated on the western bank of the Nile, where the sun sets, and when Alexandria was founded the first necropolis was established to the west of the town too. They were built at a distance from the cities for obvious reasons of hygiene, but even so some citizens complained of the nauseating stench which issued from the embalming establishments. However, let us first describe the scene and introduce the actors, before we go on to raise the curtain on the strange activities that took place in the city of the dead.

PURIFICATION IN THE TENT

The corpse did not go straight to the embalmer after it had crossed the Nile. It was first brought into the purification tent, the *ibu*, where it was washed in lustral water. The word *ibu* initially referred to a simple fisherman's wattle hut; the Egyptians then applied it to this temporary structure which was made of flimsy materials, canvas and rush matting, so that it could easily be taken down and re-erected. At the top of the landing-stage where the corpse arrived was a kind of terrace from which ran two ramps giving access to the so-called tent; the latter was rectangular in shape and had two doors, one at each side of its façade, which opened on to the ramps. This was the most common form of purification tent (Fig. 25). Its modest design was copied from some of the temples built for the kings.

The royal pyramids of the Old Kingdom had in fact been accompanied by two temples: the funerary or valley temple, on the edge of the Nile, and the upper temple situated next to the pyramid, which were connected by a causeway which was sometimes covered (Fig. 26). A brief historical reminder will explain the reason for this arrangement. Egypt had originally been divided into the Northern Kingdom and the Southern Kingdom, and was united in the reign of Narmer, who was the first pharaoh of the First Dynasty. The custom grew up of celebrating the union on every possible occasion and so the king, who owed his position to the protection of the goddesses of the North and South, wore a double crown, and took part in ceremonies as the king first of Upper Egypt and then of Lower Egypt. It was for the same symbolic reasons that the early

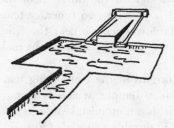

Fig. 25. The purification tent (viewed in perspective and from above). In the foreground is the landing-stage, with two ramps, one on each side, leading up to the two entrance doors to the building.

Fig. 26. Reconstruction of the Abusir pyramids. 1. Pyramid and upper temple; 2. Valley temple.

pharaohs who belonged to the Thinite dynasties constructed both a tomb at Abydos in Upper Egypt and a cenotaph at Saqqara in Lower Egypt. The northern temple was devoted to the care of the dead, and the southern to offerings and sacrifices. From the Fourth Dynasty onwards and for the duration of the Old Kingdom, only one tomb was built with two funerary temples as described, and it was in the lower temple near the Nile, the valley temple, that the embalming rites of the pharaohs took place.

The most striking proof of the origins of the embalming temple is provided by Chephren's Valley temple, which is rectangular, with the longest façade. It is an unmistakeable reproduction of a purification tent, built in durable materials (Fig. 27), and with its roof tiles actually pierced with holes as if for tent-poles. It is now clear that the valley temple housed all the arrangements for mummification, and there is every reason to believe that the sprinkling of the corpse with lustral water took place inside this building which is so similar in shape to the origi-

Fig. 27. Reconstruction of the façade of the lower temple of Chephren (equivalent to the purification tent).

nal purification tent. The actual embalming no doubt took place on the roof, in a temporary edifice.

MAKING MUMMIES

For a long time it was thought that the embalming laboratories or workshops were hidden from the view of the living in buildings where teams of workmen processed the bodies handed into their care as if they were conducting a factory operation. However, while this was probably true of some large animal cemeteries, proof is hard to come by. There is one drawing in existence which shows us an overseer passing from cell to cell to supervise the wrapping of several mummies. Another piece of evidence was discovered by Naville on behalf of the Egypt Exploration Fund between the columns of the central terrace of the Hatshepsut temple, where he found inner walls of unbaked bricks indicating the outline of an unusual building in that particular place; materials used in the course of embalming were strewn over the ground, together with jars containing bags of natron, chopped straw, amulets and broken beds. However, there is no means of telling whether this was a permanent workshop or simply a store for materials. Another building of unbaked bricks was found by Belgian archaeologists in 1972 on the Assassif hill; this contained a coffin bearing the name of Aba, director of civil ad-

ministration in Thebes in the 6th century B.C. The presence of
seven large jars as well as linen and spices shows that this was
probably the place where he was mummified.

In fact, while the pharaohs had their own embalming temples,
the corpses of ordinary people were usually treated in a portable
hut which the embalmers could erect for each tomb as occasion
demanded, though some texts which speak of "your embalming
place" or "his embalming place" make it clear that the place they
are referring to belonged to a particular person. In any event the
"uabit per nefer" or "house of regeneration" was a special place
reserved for embalming, and housed the embalming table where
the operation would be conducted. The embalming table was
usually intended for re-use and was not left in the tomb except
in a few rare instances in private tombs. The oldest one found is
a simple wooden platform, about seven foot long and five foot
wide, which was discovered near the tomb of Vizir Ipy of the
Twelfth Dynasty. It was accompanied by four wooden blocks,
which served to hold the body in place, and everything was impregnated with resin and natron, so there can be no doubt as to
its purpose. A second very similar table made of two sycamore
planks was found in Assassif, with its two front legs sculpted in
the shape of lion heads still intact. No doubt a mat found nearby
was used to cover the table at different stages of the embalming.

Another limestone table from Heliopolis had been reused as a
sarcophagus cover by Reduty, who was a steward of the royal
household, washer of hands and a high officer of the chamber.
The only table that is known to have been a personal possession
is an alabaster one, unfortunately partly damaged, which bears
the name of Amenhotep, administrator of Memphis during the
reign of Amenophis III. At each corner of the table a hole was
drilled, though for what purpose has not yet been established. It
may be that they held candles for use during the death rites, for
along the side of the table runs the following inscription: "May
the king make an offering to Anubis (who presides over
mummification) the highest in the tent of the gods . . . So that
he may give you a candle to light you during the night, and that
the light may shine over your body . . ." Elsewhere there is an
invocation to Osiris on a stela of Ramesses which would appear

to confirm this hypothesis: "O Osiris, I have lit a candle for you on the day of the wrapping of your mummy . . ." It could be too that these small cavities held "ankh" tokens, amulets in the shape of a looped cross which represented the sign of life.

The most impressive embalming table we know was dug up in a good state of preservation in Medinet Habu temple (Fig. 28). Two elongated lions frame its sides. The table itself is built at a slight angle sloping from head to foot and the surface is hollowed out crosswise as in modern dissecting tables. Liquids from the body drained off through a hole pierced in the bottom

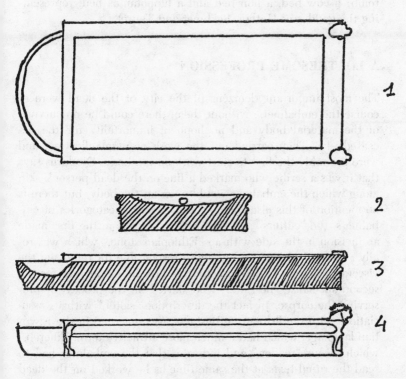

Fig. 28. Embalming table. 1. View from above; 2. Transverse section; 3. Longitudinal section; 4. View from the side.

edge of the table into a semi-circular basin. It can be deduced from the fact that the table is only ten inches high that the embalmers squatted down to work.

It is clear that messy tasks were carried out on tables like these, while a different piece of furniture was reserved for the lying in state of the mummy: the funerary bed. It may be that the mummy was finally wrapped on the lion-shaped ceremonial bed, but certainly it rested there for the fulfilment of the last rites. From the New Kingdom onwards the kings, and the kings alone, possessed three ceremonial beds like those shown on the walls inside the tomb of Seti I or found in Tutankhamun's tomb: a cow bed, a lion bed and a hippopotamus bed, representing the goddesses Hathor, Sekhmet and Tauret.

A LOATHESOME PROFESSION

The most important denizens of the city of the dead were of course the embalmers; without them, there could be no survival of the material body and no hope of immortality for the deceased's ka. They carried out the work of mummification, and were probably the first to start work on the body. Diodorus says that it was a scribe who marked a line on the dead person's skin along which the embalmer would open up the body, but there is no mention of this elsewhere. There were two categories of embalmers, the "cutters" and the "salters," of whom the first made an incision in the side with an "Ethiopian stone," which was really a sharpened flint, and was also responsible for removing the viscera. When he had completed his task he made way for the second specialist, the salter, who started on the process of preserving the corpse. In fact the description "salter," with its associations with the fish-curing business, was not used in the Egyptian language, which had a much more attractive term, "khereb," which means "reader," and indicates that the embalmer had to read the ritual texts at the same time as he worked on the dead person's anatomy. There is no evidence of this distinction between cutter and salter before the Ptolemaic period, and it may be that originally both tasks were performed by the same person.

Each embalmer was limited by contract to a certain geographical area, and took charge of the dead in his allotted villages; it was forbidden to trespass on a colleague's territory. As one can imagine the contracts were not always respected and we even have a record of the friction which arose when an ibis embalmer complained to a high official that he had not received the remuneration due to him. Although he came from Hermopolis, he had been working on an ibis from the temple of Thoth at Memphis, which did not fall within his own area, and so he had infringed the regulations. No doubt the same problem occurred among those who mummified humans.

The embalming profession was a hereditary one, whose practitioners were both held in awe and regarded with disgust. The general population had so little respect for them that they had to be protected from arbitary expulsions, harassment and attacks on their liberty by a special decree passed during the Ptolemaic period. They themselves, as we know from the Rhind papyrus, made desperate efforts to enhance their position by comparing themselves successively to all the gods in the Egyptian pantheon. Of course in their own place of work they were the master practitioners and were treated accordingly, as if they were above the rank of mere mortals. "Anubis, Overseer of the Mysteries," directed operations wearing a jackal-head mask which represented the god who had presided over the embalming of Osiris. The "Chancellor of the gods," who from the Sixth Dynasty onwards was the chief embalmer, assisted him and played the role of Horus, son of Isis and Osiris. They were surrounded by readers, priests whose task it was to recite the liturgies while the different stages of mummification were being carried out. No doubt it also devolved on them to choose the wrappings and draw the ritual figures on the linen.

Finally there were the assistants, who were kept busy around the body washing it and the viscera, and who were responsible for preparing the ointments and were in charge of the bandages.

In the world outside, the embalmers as we have said occupied a comparatively low rank in the social hierarchy, and in view of their functions it is not surprising to read in Diodorus that they inspired considerable repugnance among the public. This was even reflected in the ceremonies themselves, for when the embalmer had finished his unpleasant job of eviscerating the corpse he had to flee from his assistants who were so horrified that he had dared to injure the corpse that they rushed at him throwing stones. This may provide us with some extra testimony to Diodorus' accuracy, or more likely it may simply have been the ritual enactment of a lost custom. Even if the profession of embalmer was lucrative, it was certainly not pleasant, for as we can read in the papyrus Sallier III: "The embalmer's fingers are evil-smelling, for their odour is that of corpses. His eyes burn with the heat. He is too tired to stand up to his own daughter. He passes the day in cutting garments out of old rags for his clothing is an abomination to him."

Elsewhere we can read of an embalmer who was surprised in the act of raping a woman's corpse. It was evidently not an isolated occurrence for the custom grew up of only entrusting the bodies of high-born or particularly beautiful women to the necropolis a few days after their death. This may also be the reason why a later period saw the emergence of women embalmers who alone were responsible for female corpses.

MANAGEMENT AND WORKERS

Although the embalmers were the most important group of people in the city of the dead, they were not the most numerous, and the organisation could not have continued without the assistance of large numbers of priests and subordinates. They were not compelled to live on the same bank of the Nile as the necropolis where they worked, and in principle were entitled to dwell in the town on the eastern bank, but in practice nearly everyone lived near Thebes in a workers' village at Deir el-Medina, on the same side of the river as the dead. The village had its own necropolis where the graveyard employees were buried, as we know from their stelae. For many years the French school of archaeology conducted very fruitful excavations there.

When a family was bereaved, in the Roman period anyway, the first person they had to apply to was a representative of the administration who was entitled to give them permission for the mummification; at the same time, the deceased's name was crossed off the list of taxpayers. Then began the burial proceedings, which involved a whole flock of workers of all kinds. Navvies, quarrymen, masons and labourers directed by foremen and architects were all required to construct the tomb. Gardeners looked after the plants and irrigation channels. Painters, sculptors and carpenters were necessary to decorate the tomb and make the coffins and masks. Shops were set up to distribute wages in kind, and were supplied by hunters, fishermen, herdsmen and honey-collectors. Domestic servants and retainers looked after the tombs and participated in the religious ceremonies for the dead on the prescribed days when the priests officiated. An army of clerks registered incomes and different taxes, checked the equipment coming in and going out, and distributed wages, for the Egyptian administration was prone to red tape and few activities did not require the presence of one or more scribes. Then there were the indispensable hired mourners who had to carry the dead man to his grave; their task must have been a hard one when several heavy coffins were enclosed one inside another, and we can imagine them manoeuvring an unwieldy system of blocks and pulleys, winches and sledges, to convey the deceased into their subterranean resting-place. They too had their disputes on occasion, and one of them was in fact recorded by a scribe. It happened in the town of Oxyrhynchus, when one group of hired mourners accused another of having removed a larger number of dead than they were entitled to do.

A squad of police patrolled the tombs to protect them against the incursions of looters. We know this from a complaint lodged by a Theban priest around the year 127 b.c.; it was a serious matter, for after the tomb had been robbed it was left open, and jackals were able to enter and devour the corpse. The criminals had apparently been able to commit their offence with impunity on that particular day, because the necropolis police had been called in as reinforcements to the eastern bank for a task which did not normally fall to them.

The entire system was crowned by an official body composed of administrators, stewards and managers. At its summit was the "President of the necropolis," who in Thebes was called the Prince of Western Thebes, and who had supreme control over the functioning of the enterprise. He is principally known to us today through the dues which he received.

Within the necropolis, the question of the flow of money and the payment of wages in cash and in kind is extremely complex, for it varied at different periods and the texts to which one can refer are not easy to interpret. The President was paid certain sums of money by a high official, direct from the royal treasury. He also had rights in the production of wine and beer, and was accustomed to receive the taxes not indeed directly into his own hands, which one would hardly expect, but via a strange motley of employees who were responsible for collecting them: people such as the singers of Amon, gardeners, gate keepers, and so on. Burial charges were separate and varied according to the number of mummies and type of embalming chosen. They were remitted to the President by a necropolis official. Unlike the first duties, these depended directly on the workings of the funerary organisation and represented a kind of tax on the mummy, which varied from a half to one kite of money. The charges collected by the official were levied on the family. However, the expense of embalming could be met in another way, for in a papyrus dated the 38th year of Amasis we can read that the President acknowledged receipt of a cow intended to settle a bill for mummification.

WORK AND STRIKES

Conditions for the workers varied in different periods; they were good when the pharaoh succeeded in bringing prosperity to Egypt, and wretched when he failed. Thus under Ramesses II there is no doubt that the population enjoyed a satisfactory standard of living which is well documented. At this time the necropolis had not yet reached the gigantic proportions that it was to attain later under the Ptolemies, and it is thought that around a hundred and twenty families lived in the little village of Deir el-Medina, each one owning a white-washed house that consisted of first the master's room built slightly lower than the street, then the main room, followed by another room and then a kitchen; one stairway led to the terrace, and another to the cellar (Fig. 29). Their food was varied and consisted of fruit, different vegetables, meat and fish of every kind, and beer. Their wages were paid in kind and made up with copper. It was a point of honour with the king that the workers should be well treated, and on one occasion he wrote: "I have had the shops filled for you with all kinds of things for the Red Mountain workers," including "sandals and apparel so that you may be clothed all the year round and have good shoes on your feet every day."

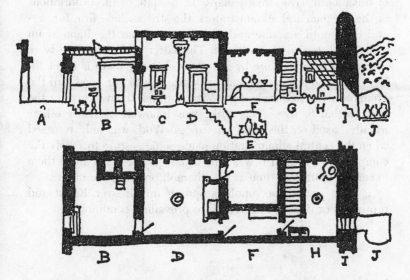

Fig. 29.   Deir el-Medina style house in the necropolis workers' village: A. Street; B. Bedroom with box-bed; C. Room for the household deities; D. Room with couch; E. Cellar; F. Women's rooms; G. Stairway to terrace; H. Kitchen and kneading-trough; I. Oven; J. Cellar.

In spite of all these benefits, the conduct of the recipients was not always everything that could be desired. When an offence was committed the delinquent was brought to justice before a tribunal of workers, unless the case was too serious for them to deal with. This happened during the Nineteenth Dynasty in the case of one citizen, a woman named Heiya, who had a bone to pick with the central authorities on the subject of some copper objects which had been stolen from the city of the dead.

Later under Ramesses III the royal power declined and Egypt underwent years of misery. The necropolis workers went on strike for the first time recorded in history, because they had not been paid: "On that day, a team of workers crossed over the walls of the Royal Tomb, saying: we are hungry; eighteen days of this month have already elapsed." In spite of the exhortations of the foremen and administrators, the strikers held firm for several days until a scribe and some priests from the Ramesseum came "to listen to the workers. The latter told them: we were compelled to come here by hunger and thirst; there is no clothing, no fat, no fish, no vegetables. Write this to our good lord the Pharaoh, write to our chief the Vizir, and tell them to give us the wherewithal to live." This strike was followed by many others usually based on the same grievances. Work was only resumed when the central administration made some gesture to satisfy the complainants, even if it was only a part-payment "to allow them to subsist until such time as the Pharaoh provides the rations."

As time passed, necropolises sprang up all over Egypt and prospered or declined according to prevailing conditions.

CHAPTER 6

PREPARING
THE MUMMY

Mummification in Egypt never reached the pinnacle of perfection it attained in other civilisations. The Chinese, for instance, knew how to keep the body supple and the features lifelike and undistorted, and their knowledge was so advanced that the femoral artery of Prince Li-Chu-Tsang, whose two thousand one hundred years old body has recently been discovered, is said to be still the same colour as it would be if it had just been removed from a newly-dead corpse. Nevertheless the vast scale, far greater than anywhere else, on which mummification was carried out in Egypt cannot fail to impress us, and there is something infinitely touching about the Egyptian attempts to immortalise the human body in order to ensure the survival of the soul. The frailty of the body makes a strange contrast to the elaborate care taken to preserve its outward appearance.

There were roughly three eras of mummification in Egypt. The first lasted up to the Eighteenth Dynasty, when the process was still in the experimental stage, the second up to the Twenty-first Dynasty when it was in full flower, and the third when, with the start of the Persian invasion, it went into decline. All the bodies were treated in workshops in the necropolises by members of the embalming profession, which was divided into two specialist branches, the parischistes and the taricheutes, the cutters and salters. Their work was not always of the same quality, and the methods they used varied from era to era, so it is understandable that the experts frequently disagree on the way in which the detailed points of the mummification process were carried out. I shall endeavour to present their conclusions as accurately as possible, though in some cases where a controversy remains to be settled I too shall have to take sides. Even the order of operations is not fully agreed, but can be reconstructed as follows:

> Removal of the brain
> Evisceration
> First washing of the body
> Treatment of the viscera
> Dehydration of the corpse
> Second washing
> Stuffing of the body
> Special treatment of the nails, eyes and external genital organs
> Anointing and massaging the body after dehydration
> Placing a covering on the side of the body
> Final preparations before wrapping, treating the body with resin
> Wrapping

EXTRACTING THE BRAIN

When the corpse arrived, the embalmers first of all had to remove its brain, which in the eyes of the Egyptians was just another ordinary piece of viscera and had no special significance. It was usually extracted through the nasal canal with the aid of long bronze needles with hooks or spirals on the end. Some writers have made the mistake of thinking that the brain could be removed in one piece which was then dried and buried with the mummy; but this would be anatomically impossible, for the brain is composed of such fragile material that it could only be extracted little by little through the channel they used. Leek actually carried out an experiment on two sheep and found great difficulty in removing their brains at all, and when he did succeed, the result was horribly like porridge in appearance.

Clearly, the operation demanded considerable skill. The bronze shaft penetrated up one nostril, sometimes destroying the nasal partition, and perforated the base of the skull at the root of the nose, where the bone is very thin and riddled with little holes for the olfactory nerves to pass through. Then by pulling and pushing with the needle the brain was broken up and removed. It frequently happened in the process that one of the turbinate bones of the nose was torn off because the task was so awkward. Usually the thmoid bone at the base of the skull is perforated on the right-hand side, from which one can deduce that the embalmer placed himself on the left of the body and if he was right-handed, as is likely, inserted the needle through the left nostril; and as he scraped the instrument would have had a natural tendency to veer to the right.

Sometimes the nose wall was completely or partially removed so that a larger hole could be made at the base of the skull and the brain tissue more easily taken out. This happened to the beautiful mummy of Tausert, priestess of Amun during the Twenty-second Dynasty, who was discovered in the second Deir el-Bahri cache. From the outside the face seems well preserved, but in fact the removal of the brain was carried out so roughly that not only the nose wall was destroyed but also all the bones around the base of the skull. Another little used method consisted in taking out an eye and breaking through the upper wall of the eye socket, which again resulted in a larger opening for extracting the brain. Even more radically, some practitioners decapitated the corpse and were then able to use a spoon to take the brain out through the passage at the back of the skull. Afterwards they set the head on a stick or a bundle of palm tree twigs and fixed it back on to the trunk with the aid of bandages. This method was used for King Ahmosis and is only rarely found prior to the Ptolemaic age. Finally, in a skull dating from the Greek epoch, some instrument had cut an opening barely an inch wide through the side of the skull, leaving hair still clinging today to the edge of the wound. It is possible that this opening was intended simply for ventilation, though on the other hand both it and the perforation made at the base of the skull through the nose root could have been made for the purpose of providing a second orifice through which the brain could be drained off, perhaps by using water.

Not every corpse had its brain removed, for the process was a costly one. However it became more common as the centuries passed, as Nicolaeff demonstrated in his study of four hundred and ninety-two skulls from Saqqara which showed that less than five per cent of Fourth Dynasty cases had had the brains removed, compared to fifty per cent during the Greek period.

CUTTING OUT THE ENTRAILS

Once the brain had been taken out, the embalmers started on the entrails. The parischiste used a flint he had prepared to cut a vertical incision five inches long which extended from the end ribs down to the top of the pelvis on the lefthand side. At any rate, this was the practice up to the reign of Thutmosis II, when a new way of cutting came into fashion. This consisted in making an abdominal incision along the fold of the groin. The slit was not very wide, but nonetheless it sufficed for the embalmer to insert his hand to pull out the intestine, which he then unwound and cut up into sections. Next he removed the stomach, liver and spleen, followed by the periotineum and sometimes the kidneys. The bladder was usually left where it was. Once the abdominal cavity was empty, the embalmer turned to the thoracic cavity. To reach this, he had first to break through the wall of muscles and fibrous tissue which form the diaphragm, and then he plunged his arm up to the armpit into the entrails and cut through the windpipe and oesophagus so that he could extract the lungs. The entrails were always removed, even right at the beginning of the Old Kingdom when mummification was in its infancy. Queen Hetepheres, the mother of Cheops who built the great pyramid, had hers preserved in four compartments of an alabaster jar, immersed in a weak solution of natron.

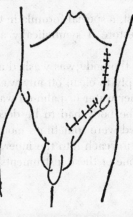

Fig. 30. Evisceration incisions. Vertical, before Thutmosis III; oblique, after Thutmosis III.

Special care was taken with the heart, which always had to be left in place. It is still to be found in most mummies, and though it is sometimes damaged by the embalmer's knife and sometimes grazed or gashed, it is invariably in the normal part of the body. If it did happen that it came out by mistake with the lungs, it was carefully replaced and occasionally sewn up at the back. In the case of one fifty-year old woman discovered at Lisht to whom this happened, the embalmer wrapped up the heart in some cloth and put it back in the thorax.

A text found on the walls of a sarcophagus of the Middle Kingdom proves that the rule was a strict one: ". . . Put my head on my neck . . . keep my limbs together . . . and let not my heart be cut out." The heart was so vital because the Egyptians considered it was the seat of all emotional, intellectual and physical life, and believed that it housed each person's character. When the deceased was brought before the heavenly tribunal, it was his heart which was weighed in the balance because outside the body it could not lie. It was essential for the judgment, and essential later for eternal life, so naturally every precaution was taken with it, and if by any chance the embalmer was negligent and the heart was lost, a special formula in the Book of the Dead could be used to restore it symbolically and so safeguard the body.

After evisceration the body was washed again, not for any ritual purpose but simply to clean off any waste matter which was left on the skin. Either water or palm-oil was used. Both the outside and inside of the body had to be decontaminated and the wads of material used were sometimes mounted on thin wooden rods to make swabs to reach into the inner recesses of the body. Cairo Museum has one of these instruments in its possession.

DISPOSING OF THE ENTRAILS

Once the organs were taken out they were treated separately, washed by the embalmer and then put into natron as the body would be later. After they had dried out they were covered with hot gum resin and carefully wrapped in several yards of linen bandages, making four packets which the embalmer then put into four funerary urns. The "Ritual of Embalming," which makes no mention of the preceding stages, is very explicit on this, and states: "Then, . . . place them in a faience jar containing ointment of the Children of Horus so that the god's ointment may permeate the divine body. For the entrails are regenerated by the fluids which issue from the divine body. You shall recite the same formula over them (the entrails) a second time while you place them to rest in a receptacle until they are needed once more."

The vases which hold the viscera are called canopic jars by archaeologists. Canopus was a port situated at the mouth of the Nile where today we find Abuquir, and during the Greek period the image of Osiris which was worshipped at Canopus took the form of a vase with a stopper shaped like Osiris' head. Hence came the custom of calling these jars "canopic jars." Usually they are made of baked clay, limestone, hard stone or, for the wealthy, alabaster. There are four kinds, each crowned with the head of one of the four sons of Horus, who are the guardian geniuses of the entrails. The small intestine, folded in half into an oblong parcel, was placed in a jar with the head of a dog-faced baboon, the god Hapi; the liver, often rolled up in a tube shape, was placed in a jar with the head of a falcon, the god Qebehsenuf; the stomach was destined for a jar with the head of a man, Amset; while the lungs were under the protection of the jackal-headed god Duamutef (Fig. 31).

When the stoppers had been sealed in position with plaster, the canopic jars accompanied the dead body to its sepulchre, like four small coffins. They were often all put into one chest divided into four compartments that, from the Fifth Dynasty onwards, was placed next to the sarcophagus. Previously during the Third

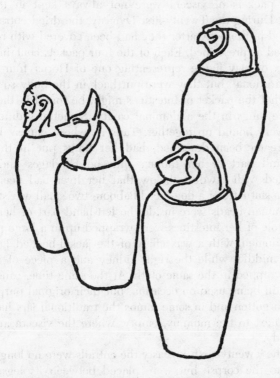

Fig. 31. The four canopic jars. The stoppers are shaped like the heads of the four sons of Horus.

Dynasty they were placed on a ledge hollowed out in the southern end of the tomb's ante-chamber, or sometimes put into a second sarcophagus which stood next to the one containing the
body. There were even occasions when a second burial chamber
was built specially for the canopic jars, as was probably the case
for King Zoser in his step pyramid; the southern tomb could
have sheltered the royal viscera. The earliest example of a
canopic chest known to us contained the traditional four packets
and belonged to Queen Hetepheres, who has already been mentioned. In the royal tombs of the Old Kingdom the chests and
sarcophaguses were often made of the same material such as
quartz, rose quartz and quartzite; later the stone was replaced
by painted and decorated wood.

The packets of viscera were not always kept in the same
places. During the Twenty-first Dynasty, the dried entrails were
replaced in the body after they had been covered with resin and
wrapped as prescribed. Each of the four packets contained a little wax or clay figure representing one of Horus' four sons, as
was traditional, but they were put back in the body so haphaz-
ardly that the packet of intestines might be found in the thorax,
and the lungs in the abdominal cavity. Sometimes different organs were bound up together. Tausert, whose clumsy handling
has already been described, had her lungs put in the upper
righthand part of her thorax, with no bandages and simply
sprinkled with sawdust; below that her liver had been folded
round a statuette of a dog-faced baboon; two small wax statuettes
with human heads were inside the left-hand part of her thorax;
the whole of her intestines were wrapped up in a large parcel in
her abdomen, with a wax effigy of the jackal-headed Duamutef
in the middle; while the right kidney and a piece of intestine
were wrapped in the same cloth. At the same time, canopic jars
were still being used on occasion, but their original purpose had
been forgotten and in some tombs the traditional jars have been
found next to the mummy, empty, where the viscera are inside
the body.

By the Twenty-sixth Dynasty the entrails were no longer being
put into the corpse but were placed between its legs. At the
same time another variation came into fashion in which the

canopic jars were used for the viscera as they had been before, but four dummy packets were put inside the body. The procedure of the Twenty-first Dynasty was reversed, and it was the packets which were simply empty bundles of cloth, soaked in resin.

During the Roman period, mummification degenerated into a sham in which bodies were no longer eviscerated, though they were still accompanied by four canopic jars which served no real purpose and sometimes were false ones, solid with no inside. Embalming was being carried out according to the letter but no longer according to the spirit.

REMOVING THE GENITAL ORGANS

The internal female genital organs, the uterus, tubes and ovaries, were always removed. The perineum was often held in place by cloth wadding, while in the case of the mummies of Nefertari, Ahmosis' wife, and Merytaten, Akhenaten's daughter, the vulva was covered in resinous paste. The lips were either joined together or held apart by a linen tampon which was pushed inside to fill the vaginal cavity.

For the man, the external genital organs were nearly always left in position. In rare cases such as Seti I and Ramesses II, they were cleanly removed with the aid of a sharp instrument, but we have no hint of the meaning of this ritual amputation. The penis and testicles were then separately wrapped and preserved inside a statuette of Osiris in gilded wood which was kept with the body inside the tomb.

DEHYDRATING THE BODY

The most important process in mummification, the one which ensured mummification, was the drying out of the corpse, which has aroused more controversy among researchers than any other stage of mummification. The human body consists of seventy-five per cent water, so it is not an easy matter to remove it. We know that the intense heat of the sun and the scorching sand can spontaneously mummify bodies because dried corpses have been found, but it takes a long time and requires several years in the sand before a body is sufficiently dehydrated to place in a coffin, and this does not fit in with our knowledge of the funerary rites of ancient Egypt.

It has been suggested in some circles that bodies were dehydrated through fire. In the Thebes necropolis for example, Yievin discovered inside one tomb rooms blackened with smoke, one of which contained a heap of dried mummies piled up to the ceiling. Bruyère too found many such rooms in the village of Deir el-Medina. In reality though it seems that tombs were blackened from fires lit either by looters, or perhaps by early Christians zealously burning idols. In any case it is quite unthinkable that this method could have been used on a large scale in Egypt, simply because wood was so rare; we know that the authorities distributed charcoal very sparingly, and so on cool evenings people warmed themselves by burning dried dung.

Another theory is that the bodies were treated with lime, since limestone is plentiful in Egypt. However no chemical analysis of a mummy (of which there have been many) has ever revealed more than slight traces of carbonised lime, which could come from impurities in the natron.

Lucas, an eighteenth century chemist, investigated another popular idea which was that the Egyptians may have used salt because they customarily preserved fish by drying it in salt; but although he conducted numerous examinations of mummies and the instruments used to embalm them, he found only tiny quantities such as would in any case be present in natron.

Finally therefore we come back to natron, which has already been mentioned several times in this book. References can be found to it in antiquity, and it is now certain that it was the essential agent in mummification. Natron is found on the shores of some of the lakes in the Wadi Natrun district between Cairo and Alexandria, in the form of a crystallised deposit left in spring when the waters of the lakes recede, and even today it is still used to whiten linen. It contains, in varying proportions, sodium carbonate (the washing soda used in cleaning), sodium bicarbonate, sodium chloride (ordinary salt), and sodium sulphate, with the addition of small quantities of different mineral salts. It is the sodium carbonate which gives natron its special qualities. Common salt would be equally efficacious as a drying and preserving agent, and would also have been cheaper because it was more easily obtainable than natron which came from one area only and so had to be transported further. However salt lacks the cleansing ingredient contained in natron, sodium carbonate, which dissolved the fats in the body and so was used in religious ceremonies as a purifying agent and held to be sacred. There can be no doubt that natron was the vital chemical agent, for it has been found everywhere in the embalmers' workshops, in sachets and jars, encrusted in the wood of the embalming tables, crystallised on the skin and flesh of the mummies, and soaked into the wads of cloth used to stuff the corpses.

As to how precisely it was used, opinions differ. Dawson held that the bodies were immersed in a solution of natron, because the body hair and outer layer of skin have often disappeared from the mummies. He thought that it was for this reason that the nails were bound on to the corpse by a thin thread. On the other hand, the head usually retains its skin and hair. Dawson, nothing daunted, explained that the corpse must have been curled up in a foetus-like position and placed in a huge jar from which only its head protruded, covered in a thick layer of resinous paste. As the liquid natron evaporated, more would have been poured in to the jar to keep it at the right level. Unfortunately no such huge jar has ever been found, nor even any trace or fragment of one. It is unlikely therefore that one ever existed.

In addition, the fact that the epidermis is missing is not an adequate proof that liquid natron was used. In the normal course of events, as decay sets in the outer layer of skin would come away and fall off or, if still on the body, would stick to the bandages and peel off with them when the mummy was unwrapped. This has not been shown to be the case. The truth is that natron is caustic and even in the dry state is capable of destroying skin and hair.

One more argument is sometimes adduced in favour of the natron bath, and that is the existence of dismembered mummies in
the Late New Kingdom period. It is quite common to find bodies
with a limb missing, bodies with more than four limbs, or bodies
whose limbs have been replaced with sticks. Some writers therefore have dreamed up huge baths in which the bodies were immersed to pickle gradually for the ritual forty days. Since, it is
supposed, they were already starting to decompose when they
arrived, they tended to come to pieces, and without proper surveillance the different parts floated here and there and were in-
evitably mixed up, so that the embalmers had to reassemble
them as best they could. This however does not explain why the
mummies broke up only in the Roman period, if the same process of immersion was used in preceding epochs. Also, even if dry
natron were used, a body that was delivered late to the embalmers might come to pieces because putrefaction would have
set in before the process of dehydration was complete. Perhaps
in the later period they tried to economise by using less natron,
by reusing it to treat more than one body, or even by abandoing
its use altogether.

The precise way in which natron was used was finally clarified
by Lucas, who experimented with four different methods of embalming. He took a number of pigeons, eviscerated them, and
then divided them into four lots: he put the first lot into a solution of three per cent natron, and the second into a solution of
salt; he covered the third lot with dry natron, and buried the
fourth in salt. Then he left them for forty days, during which
time a highly disagreeable odour began to come from the bodies
in the liquid solutions. When he took them out, the pigeon in the
natron solution was in a fairly good state, with its skin intact,
and he could rinse it and place it in the sun to dry for a few
weeks. The pigeon in the salt solution was just a shapeless mass
of skin, bones and fat from which all flesh had disappeared. The
pigeons which had been put into dry natron or salt were the only
ones which were completely intact, dry, hard and shrunken, just
like the mummies we know today.

Thus he had succeeded in showing that dehydration was
carried out through the use of dry natron. Clearly, what hap-

pened was that the corpse was placed on a mat, or more probably on the slightly sloping table that we know from the tombs,
and then covered with natron. As the water drained off the body
it mixed with the natron to form a concentrated solution which
ran along the channels carved out of the table down the slope
and into the semi-circular hollow at the bottom. At the same
time the alkaline solution had the effect of dissolving the fats.
The cavities inside the body, which as has been described had
already been emptied of the viscera, were treated with wads of
cloth or sachets of natron stuffed into the thorax or abdomen in
order to dehydrate the interior. A little sawdust with the addition of some chopped straw, palm-leaf fibre and lichen helped to
absorb the liquids. It may be too that some kind of aromatic
gum resin was added in order to hide the smell of decay which
set in before the body was completely dried. The stuffing served
not only to absorb the blood, bodily liquids and water, but also
to give a more lifelike appearance to the body by holding up the
abdominal wall. These wads have been found in jars and an
analysis of their composition shows that they were indeed used
for temporary stuffing; they contain natron and soaps, in the
chemical sense of the word, that is to say products which result
from a mixture of alkaline matter and fatty acids, in this case
bodily fats.

When the corpse was finally dehydrated, it was taken out of
the natron, and all the wet cloths were removed from the interior
and placed in jars. Next it was thoroughly washed again, both inside and out, and dried with towels. It was important to get the
body properly dry before starting on the bandaging, because
otherwise mould would grow; and indeed traces of it have been
found on some bodies under their wrapping, and sometimes even
fungus has grown on the cloth next to the skin.

We have already noted that before the corpse was put into the
natron, its finger and toe-nails were fastened on with thread so
that they were not lost. Then when the drying process was complete, a small cut was made at the base of each nail so that the
skin of the joint was detached and looked rather like a thimble
on the end of each finger and toe. Sometimes the threads were
removed, sometimes not. The nails were dyed with henna.

STUFFING THE BODY

By this time the mummy was no longer perishable. In the process, however, the flesh had lost its rounded look and appeared shrunken and emaciated, so in the Eighteenth Dynasty the practice developed of filling up the empty hollows in the body, though it did not become general until later. The embalmers began with the gap in the skull left by the removal of the brain, first of all filling the dome with cloths impregnated with resin, or with lichen, or else pouring in hot resin through the hole from which the brain had been extracted. X-rays of the head of some mummies taken in profile show the resin clearly as an opaque shadow with a straight edge marking the level it had reached at the back of the head when the mummy was laid flat. Much later, the occasional use of bitumen may have necessitated making larger holes and perforating the dome of the skull in order to pour it in.

After this the embalmers proceeded to the final stuffing. If the visceral cavities had already been more or less filled with the packets of entrails, the addition of some cloth wadding sufficed. However if the packets had been placed in canopic jars, then a large space was left which would have resulted in the collapse of the thoracic and abdominal walls if it was not filled. The problem was solved in the case of the mummies of Siptah, Ramesses IV and a man from the Twenty-first Dynasty, by literally cramming dry lichen into their abdomens. In others, sawdust was used, either on its own or in the interstices of bundles of cloth dipped in resin. Smith often found onions inside corpses which had been embalmed between the Twentieth and Twenty-second Dynasty. Sometimes resin was poured in through the incision which had been made in the flank; inside one Greco-Roman mummy belonging to a young man of seventeen years called Crates was a fragment of the pottery which had originally been filled with burning resin, and which must have slipped from the embalmer's hands. Another, Sepa, a plain citizen from the Twelfth Dynasty, had had a bowl of baked clay inserted into his thorax in order to hold up his chest. No trick was ruled out if it resulted in a more life-like appearance.

PROVIDING ARTIFICIAL EYES

No attempt was made to preserve the mummy's eyes. In any case it is hard to see what could have been done to keep the eyes' shine and elasticity when the process of dehydration affected them as much as the rest of the bodily tissues. The natron made the eyeballs shrink almost to nothing with the result that the sockets appeared empty. Embalmers in the Middle Kingdom made some attempt to lower the eyelids a little, and that was all, but later in the New Kingdom they began to try to fill the hole with scraps of cloth which were sometimes rolled into a ball and painted with a blob of black paint to simulate the iris; this was done for Ramesses III. An even better effect was achieved for Ramesses IV, whose eye sockets were filled with two little onions realistically painted. The onions served two purposes, for as well as looking more life-like they also had a magical function. Ramesses V had his eyes stuffed with cloth only, but at a later period the royal princesses were provided with white stones inlaid with black ones, representing the pupils and irises. Even more true to life were the artificial eyes of wax and gilded stucco which Bruyère noted on Greco-Roman mummies.

OILING THE BODY

When the mummy emerged from the natron it was dried up and its skin was shrivelled and stiff, so as Diodorus of Sicily tells us it had to be rubbed with precious ointments in order to make it supple enough to be bandaged. It needed several applications, which were specified in the Ritual of Embalming. First of all, the head was rubbed with olibanum oil, and then "perfuming the body all over except for the head" took place, for which, it was laid down, the embalmer had to "take the jar of ointment to anoint it ten times." Next the back was softened by massaging it with oil: "You shall massage his back to soften it with the same precious oil as before. Make sure that his back is as supple as when he was on earth." The next part of the instructions makes it clear that the embalmer was not rubbing the body with his bare hands but was using a piece of cloth impregnated with oil. Then the Ritual goes into very detailed points of technique: "Take care not to turn it over on to its chest or stomach, which are full of medicinal products, for otherwise the gods inside his abdomen will be turned out of the place where they should be." The point was obviously intended to ensure that the visceral packets in the stomach, which were protected by the statuettes of the sons of Horus, the gods, did not fall out of the gaping wound in the side of the body. There followed a "second anointing and covering of the head" and the "last anointings of the head." Perhaps it was at this moment that the sweet-smelling grease which is often found to have penetrated the first shroud was pasted on to the skull.

We are fortunate to have an actual list of the ingredients which were used for the ointment. Among a hoard of jars discovered at Saqqara, a cup was found containing some yellowish matter which had been used for embalming, and bearing an inscription which was noted by Lauer and Iskander: "Cedar oil, liquid oil of gebety [?], cummin oil, oil from Lebanon, wax, rubber, fresh oil of turpentine, incense, natron, and other mineral substances." Chemical analysis pretty well confirmed this list as correct, and so also gave credence to Diodorus' description.

MAKING THE FINAL PREPARATIONS

The incision in the left-hand side which had been used for eviscerating the body was sometimes, though not very often, sewn together and crudely whipped with thread. Usually the edges were drawn together so that the embalmer could pour hot wax over it to make a patch. If the corpse was of royal rank the wound was sealed with bronze or occasionally gold to make an oblong, round or rectangular patch. This covering could be blank or engraved with a motif which was often an "Udjat," the painted

eye of Horus with its little white triangle underneath like the
mark on a falcon's head.

Next the mouth and nose had to be filled with scraps of cloth
to restore their shape. If the nasal cavities had collapsed they
had to be propped up, and sometimes the natural openings of
the nostrils were sealed with wax. During later periods a gold
patch was placed on the tongue, which might be decorated with
the royal cartouche. Gold was used because it symbolised both
the sun's flesh and the "castle of gold," which was another name
for the purification tent through which the deceased passed a
second time to attain immortality and finally become the equal
of the gods; and so the gold patch endowed the mummy's tongue
with a god-like quality. It was for the same reason that, in the
highest grade of embalming, the face, nails and chest were also
gilded. Finally the whole body was covered with red colouring
for men and saffron for women, just as one sees it in wall paintings.

Before the wax covering was poured on to the incision, resin
had also to be poured through it inside the body to protect the
cavities. The body was shaken to ensure that the resin reached
into every crevice, and if it was boiling hot it often burned the
material used for stuffing, as it did in the case of Sit-Amon's
mummy when it flowed right up between the ribs and even into
the medullary cavity inside one bone which had been broken. At
such a high temperature the wax would have acted as a bac-
tericide, and its presence is probably also one of the reasons why
some mummies crumble to dust so easily. All these materials
were no doubt very costly, for conifers do not grow in Egypt and
the resin had to come from Syria where it was extracted from so-
called "ash" wood which has been identified as ordinary or
Cilician pine. The same "ash" was used to make masts for boats,
and the temple pylons or gateways. A little vase found in Tutankhamun's tomb was marked "ash resin."

There is no evidence to show that bitumen was regularly used
by embalmers, though it is found infrequently from the Ptolemaic period onwards. On the contrary, numerous chemical
analyses and spectroscopic examinations have failed to reveal any
trace in the classical epochs. Bitumen was supposed to cause the
black colour of some mummies, as natron caused the whiteness

of others, but it is now certain that this is not the case, and Lucas has explained the dark, almost bluish, hue of the bodies as being due to the spread of mould under the wrappings causing a slow process of organic combustion. It is equally possible that some kinds of gum resin turned black from heat or even from aging.

We do know however that honey was occasionally used as a preservative. History relates that the body of Alexander the Great was embalmed in it, though for a long time there was no evidence that this process ever existed, and it was only confirmed by a story recounted to a Baghdad doctor, Abd-el-Latif, who has already appeared in these pages. An Egyptian friend of his told him that when he and some companions were seeking for treasure in the Giza region they found a sealed jar containing honey, which at first seemed perfectly edible. However, when they dipped their fingers in they found a hair, so they emptied the jar and were amazed to find the corpse of a tiny child, fully clothed, adorned with amulets and very well preserved.

PERFORMING COSMETIC SURGERY

The oils applied to the body to counter the drying effects of the natron succeeded in making the skin more supple, but the mummy still looked emaciated, with its skin limp and the contours of the body sunken. In the Twenty-first Dynasty therefore the embalmers started inventing ways of restoring the body's natural roundness by making a series of special incisions through which they inserted mud, sand and sawdust, and sometimes even pieces of cloth. This material was pushed up between the gums and cheek to the edge of the eye sockets until the cheeks regained their curves, and then down into the chin to recreate the oval shape of the face. Next they plunged a hand up through the incision in the side of the body, and with extraordinary dexterity managed to loosen the skin of the neck and insert mud into the space they made; the mud was then held in place by two strips of cloth wound round the base of the neck. They used the same method to loosen and fill up the skin of the thighs, but were not able to reach further than the knee by hand. So they had recourse to long rods which reached down into the leg and pushed in the stuffing.

They also cut the sole of the foot between the first and second toes to insert sawdust there. The upper limbs were treated through a vertical incision in the arm or a horizontal one under the shoulder. The embalmers used rods again to penetrate through the opening in the side and separate the skin and muscles over the whole area of the back and buttocks, which left a huge space to be filled with quantities of mud that had to be moulded when it started to set so as to reproduce the curve of the buttocks and back. They did the same for the abdomen.

GIVING AN ENEMA

It is a strange fact that some mummies were left intact and never eviscerated at all. They were usually ones which had received the lowest grade of treatment, but not always, for Winlock found two royal mummies at Deir el-Bahri which had been expensively embalmed in every other respect; they were Queen Aashayt, wife of Mentuhotep II, and Mayet, a princess who was buried with her. Other mummies of the New Kingdom which Bruyère found at Deir el-Medina were indeed missing a few viscera, yet they bore no trace of any incision, and it was the same for a Persian mummy examined by Granville and a Nubian mummy which Smith noted had no abdominal organs at all.

According to Herodotus, there were three grades of mummification, which were as follows: "When the corpse is brought to them, the embalmers show their clients models of mummies in painted wood, which look very realistic. They explain that the most costly follows closely the way in which Osiris was embalmed; they then show a second model which is less well finished and less expensive than the first; and then a third, the cheapest of all." We know now that the highest grade of treatment included evisceration through an incision in the side. Herodotus informs us about the other methods: "If you choose the middle grade and wish to avoid any great expense, then they

prepare the body in the following manner. They fill their
syringes with all the oil of cedar and fill the abdomen with it
without making any incision or removing the entrails; they inject
the oil in the buttocks and, having prevented it from flowing out
again, they leave it to do its work for the required number of
days. On the last day, they let the oil of cedar that they had injected flow out of the abdomen, and such is its power that the
entrails and internal organs which it has dissolved come out with
it. . . . The third method of embalming, which is used by the
poorest classes, is the following: after they have cleaned out the
abdomen with a purgative, they treat the corpse for seventy days
and then prepare it to be taken away."

This text resolves the mystery of the missing viscera. It is clear
that in a third grade mummification, they were not destroyed but
were simply washed with some kind of liquid, which might have
been plain water, whereas in a second grade treatment the oil of
cedar inserted through the rectum slowly dissolved the viscera
while the body was undergoing the dehydration process in natron. When the embalmer removed the plug of cloth or perhaps
wax which was stopping up the anus, he had only to let the
resulting horrid mixture of dissolved entrails flow out. The oil of
cedar mentioned probably came not from a Lebanon cedar but
from a juniper whose wood was distilled and mixed with oil of
turpentine and tar to make a corrosive acid.

ARRANGING THE ARMS

Different epochs saw the mummy's arms and hands arranged in
many different ways. At first the arms were stretched down along
the body and bandaged up together with it; the women's straight
fingers rested on the outer thighs, while the men's hands were
crossed over their genitals. From the Eighteenth Dynasty the
arms began to be wrapped separately, and to be folded over the
chest with the hands touching the shoulders: Amenophis I, Thutmosis II, Thutmosis III, Amenophis II and Thutmosis IV were
all given this pose. During the Nineteenth and Twentieth Dynas-

ties it became general, at least for royal mummies such as Seti I,
Ramesses II, Merneptah, Siptah, Seti II, Ramesses III, Ramesses
IV and Ramesses V. Sometimes one arm was folded and the
other straight. Later the custom changed again, and the arms
were once more laid out straight, usually along the thighs for the
women and with the hands over the genitals for the men. During
the Ptolemaic period the arms were folded, and then reverted to
a straight position in the Roman period.

RISE AND FALL OF MUMMIFICATIOIN

Before reaching the degree of perfection that we have observed
between the Eighteenth and Twenty-sixth Dynasties, the method
of mummification developed unevenly through a process of trial
and error.

It was during the Third Dynasty that the Egyptians began to
try to preserve corpses from putrefaction by removing their entrails, which were most liable to decay. The treatment was then
still in its initial stages, and their attempts to produce a sem-
blance of life from the results of their efforts were limited to
placing cloth soaked in resin on the body, and shaping it into
human form. The nose, mouth, external genital organs and, for a
woman, the breasts and nipples, were all faithfully moulded. Little has survived of these early experiments, but we do have a
fragment of the foot of King Zoser of the Third Dynasty, the
same Zoser for whom the famous Imhotep constructed the step
pyramid at Saqqara. Its condition shows that some effort had
been made to preserve the body. The mummy of King Dedkare
Isesi of the Fifth Dynasty has also survived, in a very bad state
but nevertheless still retaining scraps of skin, muscles, tendons,
ligaments, blood-vessels and nerves which can be clearly
identified over many areas of the body. Inside, traces of resin on
the ribs testify to the attentions of the embalmers, as do the
canopic jars near the body.

The technique did not develop greatly during the Middle
Kingdom, and again few examples have survived. The only
mummies from the Eleventh Dynasty which we know come from

the court of Mentuhotep II. Evisceration through an incision in the side seems to have been little practised, and they relied on anal injection of oil of cedar. That and the fact that the bodies may not have been properly dehydrated no doubt contributed to the fragility of the mummies, which developed mould and as a result disintegrate if they are taken out of the tomb. The same is true for the mummies from the Twelfth Dynasty and the second intermediate period.

After mummification had reached its height in the New Kingdom, it then began to decline as the Egyptian empire itself started to fall apart and Egypt lost her possessions in Asia Minor which previously had supplied her with ointments and scented oils. Now she lacked money to pay for them, and the religious faith of her citizens was no longer as firm as before, so through force of circumstances less and less care was taken in treating the body. Instead attention was focussed principally on the bandages. Wrapping became a real work of art during the Roman period, but inside all the magnificent packaging little was left of the being which was supposed to survive for eternity, for what the eye did not see was no longer important. For example, when the embalmers found that young Pedi Amun, who died at the age of seven and whose body is now kept in the Chicago Museum, was too big for his sarcophagus they simply removed his arms and broke his thighbone in the middle to make him shorter. Another body, which is now in the museum at Leiden, was too small for its container, so two tibias were borrowed from another corpse and wedged under its feet in order to fill up its coffin.

The embalmers were careless and often decomposition had set in before they completed their task, or else they missed out a stage and had to repair the damage as best they could afterwards: fragments of a decayed limb which had fallen off the body were used to stuff the stomach, while the missing limb was replaced with a makeshift one of cloth. A deceased person from this period presenting himself before the tribunal in the next world would have been lucky if he still had all his limbs and viscera with him, and certainly could not expect to have them in order. Of course accidents happened sometimes even during the best period of mummification, and the evidence of one embalmer's carelessness was found by Winlock in a mummy at Deir el-Bahri. It had no proper viscera so the embalmer had concocted false packets out of some string, a piece of leather and some rags, which he stuffed into the stomach together with the required statuettes of the four sons of Horus in order to observe the forms as far as possible. This however was an insignificant forgery compared to the stratagems resorted to in the declining period, when some unfortunate mummies consisted of nothing more than a skull and a few miserable rags mounted on a bundle of reeds.

This partly explains a funerary epigram written in Greek in the Late New Kingdom on a building in Tuna el-Gebel, which reads:

I am the son of Epimachus.
Do not pass by my tomb with indifference.
You will not be disturbed by the unpleasant odour of cedar oil.
Listen a while to the words of a dead man who smells good.
Death came to me through a cough, and I passed away as all men
    must.
So do not weep, my friend, I loathe tears.
It was for this reason that I asked my cousin, Philermes, to refrain
    from lamentation at my funeral.
Do not inter me in order to disinter me.
Bury me only once, without cedar oil.
The long funeral ceremonies, the women wailing, give me no
    pleasure.
For every man is destined to die.

Evidently this young boy, who died of tuberculosis at the age of twelve, refused to have an Egyptian funeral and was perhaps cremated as was beginning to happen in the Roman period. Embalming continued for a while longer, and was even practised by the Coptic Christians in spite of the fact that it was forbidden by their religion, but the techniques of embalming continued to decline. Soon the body was no longer cut open but was merely covered with a thick layer of natron or salt in order to dry it, and then dressed in its ordinary clothing and buried in the sand or beneath brick vaults. The end of mummification in Egypt was approaching.

WRAPPING THE BODY

To return to the mummy as we left it in the final stages of treatment, we can only conclude that it was allowed to remain exposed for a period before it was wrapped, for there is no other explanation for the quantities of eggs and pupae belonging to many varieties of flesh-eating insects, beetles and mosquitoes that infest the mummies.

When the embalmers embarked on the intricate and time-consuming task of wrapping the body, they were provided with three kinds of covering: shrouds or winding-sheets which enveloped the whole body, stuffing which filled the hollows and reduced the prominence of any projecting parts of the body, and bandages which held everything in place. Though there are often different qualities of material to be found on the same mummy, with the best invariably next to the skin, the material is always linen because wool was not allowed to be used in funerary ceremonies, or indeed ever by priests. A good many bandages bear inscriptions which have given valuable clues as to their origin and purpose, and some of these are pieces of clothing belonging to the deceased or his family, as is evident from the fringes which border them and the traces of mending and patching, or the owner's identifying marks which constant washing had faded.

The custom of using family clothing seems to go back to quite an early date, for Princess Aashayt, wife of Mentuhotep II of the Eleventh Dynasty, had two bandages bearing inscriptions, one "King Mentuhotep" and one "Fine Linen Shop." Extracts from the Book of the Dead were written on others, and these must have been specially manufactured for wrapping mummies and bought by the family for the occasion. We even have an account of funeral expenses in which one Thotataïs contracted to supply the embalmer with linen for the mummification of his son. Some of the materials used came from more unexpected sources such as a temple. Bandages bearing inscriptions such as "Holy linen from the temple of Amun" show that they must have been cut from the garments worn by the god's statue in the temple, which were customarily replaced with new ones whenever the king or a high priest led the ritual. The cloth belonged to the temple and bore marks indicating its origin. Once it had been worn by Amun it became sacred, and we can easily imagine that it was invested with various magic powers. Clearly it was a desirable accessory, for as we can read in Paheri's tomb at El Kab: "May you be wrapped in holy linen, fine material, and clothing taken from the bodies of the deities." Not only Amun, but other gods too imparted god-like qualities to their clothing, and there is a funerary papyrus in the Louvre which mentions bandaging belonging to Horus, the goddess Sekhmet, and the gods and goddesses of Karnak.

In Egypt magical powers were also supposed to belong to the number seven, so it is not surprising that the shrouds, bandages and amulets were often used in sevens. It was important too to have large numbers of pieces of cloth on the mummy, dozens if possible, like the mummy of Tausert, priestess of Amun, who had eighty-three.

Everything needful was prepared in the embalming chamber, and by the time the corpse was ready for bandaging there must have been hundreds of yards of bandaging and cloth carefully arranged in piles according to size and purpose by the scribe who was responsible for keeping the accounts. He wrote down what they were to be used for on the top of each pile. It seems that several bodies must have been wrapped at the same time, for one bandage which presumably came from the top of its pile bore the reminder "Bandages for three mummies." The shrouds measured on average five by nearly three and a half yards, longer than one would expect, to allow for them being knotted at the head and feet.

The first layer of wrapping was a large shroud of saffron yellow cloth which was held in place on the mummy by bandages. Then the embalmer would wind narrow linen bandages around each finger and toe separately. Next large numbers of tampons, each marked with the name of a god, had to be secured to the head by strips of cloth which were bound on crosswise, starting from the right shoulder. A special official entitled the Overseer of Mysteries chose the appropriate pieces of material from the piles to place on top of the skull and on the temples, ears, eyes and mouth. He made sure that they bore the right inscriptions, such as "the cloth from Sekhmet the Great, beloved of Ptah, to be rolled twice around the head . . ." The embalmer placed amulets between the layers of cloth.

The embalmer then returned to the hands, putting pieces of folded material into the palms, continued binding up the arms, and proceeded to wind material from the head crosswise round the thorax, down to the abdomen, and finished with the legs.

The operation of bandaging took around fifteen days to complete, as far as is known, and was extremely complex. On one occasion two little mice attracted by the smell of the ointments nibbled themselves a hole in the bandages of the mummy, but the embalmers never noticed, and it was only thirty centuries later that Winlock discovered the two skeletons between layers of wrapping when he was unwinding the mummy.

The gold finger-stalls which were placed over the bandages on some mummies were reserved for people of high rank. Tutankhamun had them on his last two finger joints; they were delicately engraved with the outline of a nail and the lines on the back of the fingers (Fig. 32).

While the wrapping was in progress, the bandages were im-

Fig. 32. Gold rings and finger-stalls on the hand of Tutankhamun's mummy.

pregnated with resin, as we see in four scenes depicted in Thui's tomb at Thebes, during the Nineteenth Dynasty. The door of the embalming workshop is on the left, and the mummy itself, stiff and already partly bandaged, is resting its neck and heels on two pedestals. Two embalmers stand at its head and feet, while a reader-priest is officiating between the door and the mummy. In the first scene, the bandages are being adjusted. The second scene is mutilated, but in the third we can see the embalmers holding a little bowl containing resin in one hand, and with the other applying liquid to the bandages with a brush. Under the mummy, there is a large vessel containing the rest of the resin, which they take as they need, while a similar pot is slowly warming on a small stove above the door (Fig. 33).

During the Greco-Roman period, the mummy's toilet was completed with the addition of a blood-red Osirian shroud, which was sewn up at the back. It was decorated with a web of long blue or green beads, and round white or yellow beads, though if the funeral was less costly the design was simply painted on. The material was only dyed when it was actually in place, with the result that the colour soaked through to the first layers of bandaging, though not to the fabric underneath. Sometimes one can still see the outline of the web drawn on the shroud in pencil after it had been put on the mummy. Sometimes too the name of the deceased was written on its forehead or stomach.

The final step in the whole operation was the fitting of the funerary mask. Of all the examples that have survived, indisputably the most beautiful belongs to Tutankhamun. Its splendour is without parallel in Egypt, or indeed in any civilisation elsewhere. It covers the head and shoulders of the mummy and is made of gold leaf, beaten, burnished and hammered into shape, and seems closely modelled on Tutankamun's actual features. On the forehead it bears the royal emblems of the vulture goddess Nekhbet, and the cobra. Its eyes are inlaid with semi-precious stones and the *nemes*, the funerary headdress of the pharaohs, is made of gold and blue glass in alternate stripes. The face is that of an adolescent, with a slightly upturned nose, fleshy lips, and a rather melancholy and touching look.

The other masks which we know from the Ptolemaic period seem very drab in comparison with Tutankhamun's royal adorn-

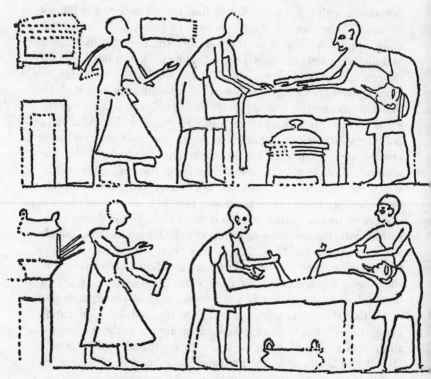

Fig. 33. Different stages of wrapping. Thui's tomb. Below, applying resin to the bandages.

ment. No doubt they were made in bulk in the workshops by placing several thicknesses of cloth plastered with stucco one over the other. This process was used in Upper Egypt where papyrus was not so common, whereas in Lower Egypt they used a kind of cardboard called cartonnage made from several layers of waste papyrus. Sometimes these layers came unstuck and in this way a number of texts have come to light which have provided interesting information.

During the Roman period the deceased's portrait was painted in encaustic on wooden boards which were inserted between the

bandages in front of the face. These are called Faiyum portraits
after the name of the region where they are found most abun-
dantly. They were not intended to resemble the deceased closely,
but rather to show his age, sex and marital status by various
symbolic details of the face, headdress and pectoral. The so-
called Antinoë Egypto-Roman masks looked more as if they had
been sculpted, and covered the head and chest of the female
mummies. The head was supported on a small cushion and leant
forward slightly, often crowned with roses, while a bunch of the
same flowers in stucco rested on the chest. These portraits replaced the upper portion of the lid of mummy-shaped sarcophaguses (Fig. 34).

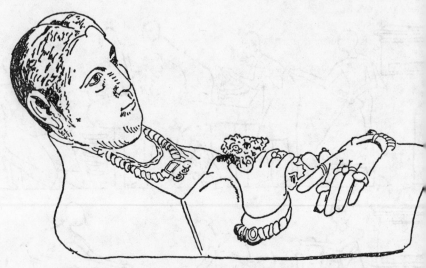

Fig. 34. Romano-Egyptian mask, known as Antinoë portrait, which in the Late New Kingdom replaced the upper part of the sarcophagus lid.

SEVENTY DAYS' WORK

Each stage of mummification took a great deal of time, so when we read in an inscription like the following from the Nineteenth or Twentieth Dynasty: "Year Six, the second month of summer, on the fifteenth day, Tahene died; she was buried on the seventeenth day," it is clear that none of the operations I have described can have been carried out. No doubt the woman was poor, and so was buried without any treatment. Mummification was a lengthy process which according to Herodotus required seventy days, which is corroborated in a phrase from the Eighteenth Dynasty: "When you have completed your seventy days in the embalming place, you shall have a good burial in peace." This period may also have had a symbolic value because it lasts for as long as the star Sothis, our Sirius, disappears when it is in conjunction with the sun, which is the same length that elapsed between the death of an individual and his resurrection. In fact this long period did not cover just the various physical stages of mummification, for as we can read in Genesis (50, 2–3): "And Joseph commanded his servants the physicians to embalm his father: and the physicains embalmed Israel. And forty days were fulfilled for him; for so are fulfilled the days of those which are embalmed: and the Egyptians mourned him for three score and ten days." It is probable that the time required for the actual embalming varied considerably, according to the grade chosen and the care taken.

The Fuad papyrus remarks that one woman was mummified and taken to another village in only nine days; this was in the year A.D. 64. We also have some very exact details about one Aan-em-her, whose embalming began four days after her death; when the embalmers had finished the evisceration, they left the body fifty-two days in natron, and then dried it; the next sixteen days were occupied with wrapping; and finally three days after the body was put in its coffin it was buried.

DISPOSING OF THE WASTE

Nothing which had been in contact with the deceased's flesh could be thrown away. Every piece of linen stained with blood or soiled with fluids, all the natron wadding which had absorbed the fats, each scrap of material which had been used to clean the body, even the natron in which the body had been buried and which was impregnated with the liquid exuded, all had to be preserved. There were vessels filled with used sawdust and pots of damp natron, jars of greasy stuffing material and vases of rags soaked in the discharges from the body. The embalming chamber was swept out and the rubbish put in sacks, so as not to lose even the tiniest particle of the dead person, in spite of the fact that the waste was all considered impure and had no connection with the ceremonies of osirification which were to make a god out of the dead man. It had to be kept separate from the mummy and was buried in a special small kind of sepulchre called an "embalming cache," at a little distance from the main tomb. Many of these caches have been discovered and some, such as one at Qurna, contain as many as a hundred sacks of natron which had been used to embalm a single person. The most famous cache of all was discovered in 1908 by Davis, a hundred or so yards away from the principal tomb: it contained the waste matter from Tutankhamun's mummification, put into twelve large earthware jars.

This completes the description of the technical processes involved in transforming the body from an ordinary corpse into a dehydrated and bandaged mummy. Now we must turn to the rites which accompanied each stage of mummification, and the ceremonies which preceded and followed it.

CHAPTER 7

THE RITES OF MUMMIFICATION

TWO MONTHS' MOURNING

When death struck in an Egyptian family, there was no need to send out any notification to friends because the widow's cries of anguish were immediately taken up by all the other women and servants in the household, who ran out into the little streets alerting the whole district with their lamentations. The news quickly spread from one person to another, and a long period of mourning then began (Fig. 35). Women rubbed handfuls of dust from the streets or mud from the Nile into their hair, which dripped down and stained the special tunics they wore as a sign of grief. The men stopped shaving, as we can see from a sketch found at El Amarna which shows King Akhenaten with his beard unkempt, in his sorrow (Fig. 36).

Right up to the moment of burial, food was kept to a strict minimum. There was nothing extravagant or abnormal about the terms of a letter written by a man to his dead wife, which is now kept in the museum at Leiden and which says: "And when you died, I neither ate nor drank for eight months, as was right and proper for a man."

Fig. 35. Mourning procession.

Diodorus confirms that when a king died the whole people were plunged into grief:

All the inhabitants were weeping and tearing their clothes; the temples were closed and the people abstained from making sacrifices and did not celebrate any feast-day for seventy-two days. Crowds of two or three hundred men and women wandered through the streets with their heads covered in mud and their clothes knotted like a belt beneath their breasts, singing funeral laments twice a day in praise of the dead man. They refused to eat wheat or meat, and abstained from all wine and good food. No-one took a bath,

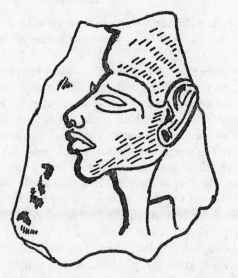

Fig. 36. Limestone tablet engraved with Akhenaten's profile; the small notches are drawn on it to show that his beard is being allowed to grow as a sign of mourning.

no-one applied any ointment, no-one took part in the pleasures of love. The seventy-two days passed in sorrow and lamentation, as if a beloved child had died.

CROSSING THE NILE

When someone died, the necropolis employees were at once informed and came to take the body over the river to the west bank. A large number of people were involved in reciting the innumerable rites and making the ceremonial gestures which accompanied them, as well as participating in the processions which took place between ceremonies. There are many texts which provide us with all the details, and in addition the ink sketches on the walls of the tomb of Pepi-Ankh the Vizir at Meir are a mine of information on the whole organisation of the processions. They are like strip cartoons, and even have the role of each person and the words they must pronounce explained in hieroglyphs.

When the porters came to the little room where the deceased had expired, they placed the body in a sarcophagus whose edges were decorated with moulding in the shape of palm leaves. This was not the proper coffin, which could not have been prepared in time, but was probably a sort of bier used to transport bodies over the river. The weeping family stayed at home while the porters carried the dead man to the quay where a group of boats were waiting. The corpse travelled in a boat made of large bundles of reeds bound together, where it was placed under a platform supported by four small thin columns. A master mariner stood on the poop, with a helmsman next to him who steered the boat with the aid of two long oars. Two mourners customarily crouched down next to the platform and began to wail. They were joined by an ordinary embalmer, and next to him sat the master embalmer who leaned proudly on the stick which was his badge of office. Another master mariner stood at the prow and manoeuvred the boat with a pole. Finally, a lector priest stood next to the sarcophagus, bringing to eight the number of people accompanying the corpse on the boat.

Two wooden boats towed the funeral craft, each with a crew of eight rowers, a helmsman and a sailor who guided their efforts, as well as a seated person whose function is not clear. Pictures show them calling to each other such remarks as "Hurry up with the towing," and, when they had completed the short journey and reached the far side, "All is well. The trip is over." At the landing-stage for the city of the dead the boats were pulled in and tied up, and a master mariner urged the crew to "hold tight to the rope."

Then three men placed the sarcophagus on a lion-shaped bier and carried it to the Purification Tent at the end of the quay. The lector priest marched at the head of the cortège holding his roll of papyrus, followed by the two embalmers and a woman mourner, two more embalmers, four priests who were to officiate at the funeral, and another lector priest.

FIRST CEREMONIAL PURIFICATION

In the Purification Tent, the corpse was first sprinkled with lustral water, which was probably a natron solution. According to early Heliopolis theology, this ceremony was intended to recall the birth of the Sun god who had emerged from a vast stretch of cold dark water called Nun. It obviously symbolised the rebirth of the dead man, and the ritual might have ended there if the Osirian creed had not added more elaborate observances later on.

There are very few pictures showing us this scene, for as we have already mentioned the Egyptians were reluctant to depict corpses. Those we have show us the dead man sitting on a large earthenware jar with his feet resting on two looped crosses which are the sign of life, or crouching at the edge of a rectangular basin. The most realistic portrait of the purification ceremony is to be found on one side of a sarcophagus belonging to a woman, Mutardis and shows a black corpse lying at the bottom of a kind of trough with a priest on each side throwing the contents of a vase over it (Fig. 37). The deceased was then anointed for the

Fig. 37. Sprinkling lustral water on the corpse. The deceased being purified is shown in black.

first time and dressed in clean clothes, and where appropriate ar-
rayed with the attributes and decorations of his station in life.
Sandals were placed on his feet, and he was lifted on to the lion-
shaped bier once more in readiness for a new funeral procession
from the Purification Tent to the embalming workshop, still accompanied by the same officials as before.

ENTER ANUBIS

By the time the procession arrived, the room was full of a plentiful supply of food and jars of wine. A lector priest recited from
his unrolled papyrus the words summoning the deceased to the
feast. Then the cortège dispersed and only those people essential
to mummification, the embalmers and the priests, remained.
Sometimes they were joined by two women who symbolised the
goddesses Isis and Nephthys, who as we know had participated
in the resurrection of Osiris. Each stage of the physical embalming process was accompanied and followed by the recitation of
ritual phrases wishing the deceased the recovery of his sight,
hearing, breathing, movement and other faculties he enjoyed on
earth and which mummification together with religious ceremony were intended to restore to him.

Wrapping was carried out under the direction of a master embalmer wearing a cartonnage mask in the shape of a jackal's
head, symbolising Anubis, the god who had put Osiris together
again (Fig. 38). It was not only the prayers, invocations and ad-
monitions which were necessary to the ritual, but also the gestures made by the participants, which were laid down in great
detail. We can take one example from chapter IX of the Ritual of
Embalming entitled "First wrapping of the hands."

Then, following this, continuing with the wrapping of the
god [the deceased], wrap his left hand whose closed fist will
already have been covered with the same oil as before. Add:
ankh-imy plant, one; Coptos bitumen, one; natron, one, inside. Next wrap his [?] with a bandage of royal linen and
then with a band of cloth. Put the gold seal-ring in place on

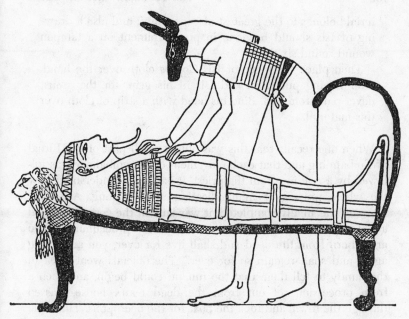

Fig. 38. Embalmer wearing an Anubis mask putting the final touches to the mummy.

his finger, and let his closed hand be gilded again after it has been given the right shape with a tampon of material. Cover the outside with oil up to the base of the fingers. Ankh-imy plants, natron, bitumen, seneb-netjery plant; make thirty-six packets, tie them up, and place them against his left hand. [This is a symbolic allusion to the thirty-six gods who accompany his ba and to the thirty-six *nomes* or districts of Egypt in which Osiris is honoured.]

Tie together a pod of the mensa plant and a branch of the aru-tree in his left hand, with the help of the seneb-netjery plant, remembering that the aru-tree is Osiris. At the same time make sure that all this stays firmly in his left hand with some aru-tree resin and a piece of cloth rolled round the outside of his left hand. An image of Hapi should be drawn on this material which enfolds the hands, for the ma-

terial belongs to the greatest of gods, Hapi; and also a drawing of Isis should be done in pure orpiment on a tampon
wound round six times.

Then place the piece of Isis Coptos cloth over the hand,
after having put Hapi and Isis in his grip, for they must
never part from him. Bind his hand with a strip of cloth over
this material.

When one recalls that this was only a small part of the Ritual
of Embalming and that each movement of the embalmer was followed by a reading from the priest, it is easy to understand how
the whole process of mummification took so long. After the
mummy was finally completed, it was laid on the ceremonial bed
and the priests showed their satisfaction by proclaiming: "You
are reborn from the dead and shall live for ever, you are young
again and shall remain so for ever." The officials went back to
the family to tell them that the funeral could begin, and then a
fresh procession set out from the dead man's house, passed
through the town, and took the boat for the necropolis. The same
people accompanied it as before, with the addition of the family
and friends. The picture we have of the scene shows a little
sailor clinging to a plank, who is telling the "Inspector of the embalmers" as he embarks: "I am holding the gangway safe." There
is a new sarcophagus on board to take the mummy.

Once at the necropolis, all these people moved in the direction
of the embalming workshop to fetch the body. In the picture,
three men carrying the empty coffin are saying to each other
"This procession shows he was a good man." Later, after they
have arrived in the embalming room, we see the piles of food
without which no funeral ceremony would be complete. The
mummy was then placed in its coffin, and the procession wound
its way towards the Purification Tent, joined by more people
who had missed the first part of the lengthy obsequies.

OPENING OF THE MOUTH

Here in the Purification Tent was where the essential rite of the
opening of the mouth took place, until the beginning of the New

Kingdom when it was transferred to the entrance to the tomb. A detailed study of how the practice developed has been made by Goyon, who found that initially it was only employed on royal or divine statues, who received the spirit magically through their mouths. Gradually the rite extended to other objects: the statues, so that they could join in tasting the food offerings; the figureheads on the sacred boats and the figures carved on the temple doors, so that they too could come to life; and even the amulets in the shape of "heart" scarabs. Very early on from the Thinite era corpses were reanimated in the same way. The ceremony was performed on the mummy itself, then on its coffin and then on the statues of its double. Its purpose was to restore the vital energy, the spark of life, which had escaped from the body, and to give the dead man back the use of his mouth so that he could again eat and drink, speak and breathe.

The phrase "opening of the mouth" is slightly misleading, because in fact the priest who was officiating touched all the orifices of the head. He used an object resembling an adze to do so, with which he imitated the gestures of carving a sculpture. Clearly this was intended to recreate the dead man. The principal part in the drama was played by the temple priest, who belonged to the temple of the god Ptah in Memphis and is recognisable by the panther skin which he wore on his breast. He was assisted by the lector priest and by an enlarged gathering of clergy for important ceremonies. Often the role of Horus, son of Osiris, was taken by the son of the deceased. Many implements were required such as ewers for pouring out libations to the gods and sprinkling holy water, different kinds of adzes, and a number of chisels resembling wood chisels, all of which give us a good indication of the priest's role. In addition there would be a gold finger, stone chisels, all kinds of scarves, and ointments.

Before the rites of reanimation started, incense was burned and there was more purification. An animal had to be sacrificed so that its heart and haunch could be used. When everything was ready the temple priest advanced towards the mummy and with the aid of the adze and chisel feigned several times to open the body's orifices (Fig. 39), and then brought the gold finger near the mummy's mouth. Afterwards the deceased was offered a bunch of grapes and a cup of wine, and was fanned with an ostrich feather until all his vital functions were deemed to be re-

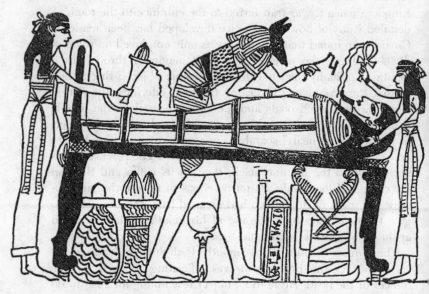

Fig. 39. The ritual of opening the mouth with the aid of an adze. Isis and Nephthys are sprinkling the mummy with lustral water. Under the bed, from left to right, are oils and perfumed ointments, chest of Ushabti figures and chest of canopic vases.

stored to him. The whole ceremony was performed twice with a few slight variations the second time, in tribute to the ancestral rites of the time when the country was still divided into Upper and Lower Egypt. Incense was again burnt, water was sprinkled on the mummy, and he was invited to partake of the feast with the living. When this was over and the temple priest had touched the corpse's mouth for the last time with his adze, the priests withdrew.

All through the ceremony special prayers were recited in order to produce the miracle of reanimation.

During the Old Kingdom period, religious texts were inscribed on the walls of the corridors and the rooms inside the pyramids in order to protect the king in the afterlife; these were called the "Book of the Pyramids." The texts we find painted inside the coffins of the Middle Kingdom are sacred or magical formulae of the same kind, while in the New Kingdom the custom developed of slipping a papyrus known as the "Book of the Dead" into the coffin beside the mummy, or later between its legs. This book was a collection of magic spells whose presence alone ensured the resurrection of the deceased, made his stay in the kingdom of Osiris a happy one, and enabled the little Ushabti figures to carry out the duties prescribed for a dead person.

Later, especially in the Theban region, it was the "Book of Breathing" which was placed near the mummy's head or under its feet. This contained all the necessary introductions to the supernatural beings the mummy would encounter, and instructions for avoiding the dangers he would meet along the way, as well as incantations to counteract the effects of the foul air and suffocating heat in the tombs, and prayers to render breathing easy.

LAST PROCESSION

The grandeur of the burial ceremonies varied greatly according to the status of the deceased. The poorest went to their last rest

Fig. 40. Carrying the mummy only (putting it into the grave).

Fig. 41. Transporting the sarcophagus, pulled by oxen. Women
        mourners accompany the cortège. On the right, the
        temple priests again carries out the ceremony of the
        opening of the mouth for the last time before the
        interment.

alone, just wrapped in matting, while the kings were borne in
state and accompanied by hundreds of porters (Fig. 40).

If we could follow one of these processions as it left the
Purification Tent, we would see that it was headed by a temple
priest who sprinkled water on the ground from an offering vase
while he intoned the ritual phrases. Next came men carrying
trays bearing jars of wine, beer and oil, bread and cakes of all
kinds, fruit, vegetables, and haunches of beef and antelope.
Others brought the funerary furniture which was to fill the
rooms in the tomb, while one man bore a box containing the
Ushabti figures.

The sarcophagus itself was placed in a heavy decorated cat-
afalque carried on a sledge drawn by four oxen (Fig. 41). A second sledge was laden with the canopic vases which contained
the entrails, and this was followed by priests dressed in white
linen, women mourners with their breasts bared, and then the
family and friends. The women wore long transparent veils, and
the widow covered her hair with a hair-net. Both men and
women had a white band tied round their foreheads and knotted

at the nape of their necks, while the sticks carried by the men were also decorated with a white bow.

If the dead man belonged to a guild, his colleagues were bound to attend the ceremony and contribute towards it. Indeed if they were absent without good cause they were liable to a fine.

On their side, the necropolis workers whose duty it was to transport the body were also well organised and certainly in the Late New Kingdom were capable of taking action to support their claims. We can still read in some papyri of the disputes which arose between six of them and the priests because they had not received all their wages, in spite of the fact that the money had been paid by the bereaved family. These men were in charge of lowering the heavy sarcophagus down the shaft by means of a complicated system of pulley-blocks and winches to where some of them were waiting to bring it into the tomb proper. They also had to bring down the funerary furniture and the offerings, all by the light of tiny oil lamps.

The offerings could be very extensive. Emery discovered at Saqqara an intact tomb belonging to a noble of the Second Dynasty which contained a veritable banquet cooked for the deceased, consisting of a triangular loaf, barley porridge, fish, pigeon stew, a quail, two kidneys, sides and legs of beef, fig stew, berries, little round honey cakes, cheese and wine. It was all displayed on dishes of unglazed pottery. Unfortunately this particular deceased woman may have been unable to appreciate the menu fully, because her jaw was so deformed that she would only have been able to chew on one side.

When everything was in place, a last prayer was uttered, and then the shaft was filled in and the mourners ceased their wailing. Silence reigned in the grave. At last the dead man could lie in peace.

The period of mourning for the deceased was now officially over. The provisions which had been transported from one procession to another, from the Purification Tent to the embalming workshop and finally to the tomb, had been apportioned between the gods, the priest and the deceased, and what remained at this stage could be consumed by the family and friends. There is plentiful evidence for these final meals taken near the sepulchre; the cachette near Tutankhamun's tomb, which as we have already seen contained the refuse from his embalming, also yielded big earthenware pots which held the remains of such a meal in the shape of dishes, bottles, and beef and poultry bones.

Wealthy people from the Egyptian upper class sometimes indulged in a highly expensive supplement to the funeral: a journey to Abydos, which was a holy city where it was thought that Osiris' head was buried and where the god supposedly had his tomb. To be buried here in the vicinity of the very deity who ruled over the kingdom of the dead, to participate in the ceremonies held in his honour and to share in the offerings, was naturally seen as highly desirable, but if for some reason it was not possible and the body had perforce to be buried elsewhere, then the family could make a pilgrimage to the sacred spot. The mummy was carried on to a boat and transported in it in state on the bridge, surrounded by priests and mourners (Fig. 42). If the family could not afford the journey, then it was possible to have a commemorative stela engraved and erected in Abydos instead.

KEEPING THE BODY AT HOME

In the Late New Kingdom it was not always the practice to bury the body after it had been mummified. Some families kept the

Fig. 42. Funerary barque transporting the deceased. Wooden
model coated with stucco and painted, from the
Middle Kingdom.

mummy at home with them in a special room fitted out for the
purpose, or even in one of the family rooms so that the dead person could be present at meals and symbolically take part. The
custom became quite widespread in the Roman period. Many
mummies found by Petrie bore signs of wear and tear as a result;
their portrait masks were damaged and the features sometimes
obliterated, the gilding worn away and the artificial eyes lost; the
cartonnage masks were torn or sometimes had obviously been
left out in the rain because all their colour was washed away, or
else they were stained with mud that had dripped from a damaged ceiling, while yet others were covered with bird droppings
or saturated with oil from an overturned jar. In some cases the
relatives had meticulously carried out repairs to a nose or panel,
in others the damage was left untouched. In any event the mummies must have had a fairly long stay above ground, possibly
lasting several years.

In the Greek era under the Ptolemies, funeral undertakers often had to keep mummies in temporary vaults because there was a shortage of space in the cemeteries. The competition for land and graves for the dead was so fierce that sometimes the temporary vaults were built on the right-hand side of the river, and contracts have been found which stipulate that the right to perform the burial ceremonies belonged to one undertaker before interment and another after. Obviously the macabre trade was a lucrative one.

Even more shocking to our modern sensibilities was the monetary value placed on mummies, which could serve to guarantee loans. You borrowed the money on the surety of the body of your father or mother or other ancestor, your brother or perhaps even your child. However, if you failed to discharge the debt disaster followed. You were regarded as completely dishonoured, and the disgrace was so great that when you died you were not allowed to be buried.

The only circumstances in which death imposed no financial burden were when the relative was drowned or devoured by a crocodile. The deceased then automatically became a god and only the Nile priests were permitted to touch the corpse, so the expense of the funeral ceremonies was borne by the civil authorities.

COFFINS AND TOMBS

As time passed, so the layers of material that protected the body increased in number. The plain piece of material thrown over the dead person in predynastic times gave way to a series of shrouds, and then to the complicated bandaging we have described. Coffins, which were used in Egypt from the dawn of history, also became more elaborate and multiplied in number.

During the Old Kingdom the sarcophagus was carved out of alabaster or granite and was rectangular in shape, with a lid that was either flat or slightly curved. Its sides were usually plain, but sometimes had the features of a palace façade outlined lightly on them, as for example on one Fifth Dynasty coffin discovered by

Bisson de la Roque at Abu-Roach, which is now in the Louvre. These sarcophaguses enclosed a wooden coffin which was sometimes covered with gold leaf, and contained the mummy.

During the first intermediate period and the Middle Kingdom, the outer case was also made of wood, and both the inner and outer coffins were decorated with inscriptions and lists of offerings which previously were to be found carved on the tomb walls. So that the double casing did not completely cut off the mummy's contact with the outside world, two symbolic eyes were painted on the outside on the left near the mummy's head to enable it to look out (Fig. 43). Similarly, the false door drawn under the eyes permitted the ba or spirit to leave the body when it so desired and either enter the funerary statue to animate it or take the form of a bird and fly up to the trees.

The decoration grew richer in the New Kingdom and for the first time the goddesses Isis and Nephthys made their appearance at the head and foot of the coffin, shielding the body with their wings. Now there were three coffins, which in this period were usually carved in human shape and closely fitted over the mummy. Some of these sheaths, like Tutankhamun's, were covered with gold, others were just varnished, and they were made either of wood, or of several thicknesses of papyrus glued together, or of material soaked in stucco. One unusual example was found at Deir el-Bahri belonging to Queen Nefertari: it had no cover and looked like an open box with the head and shoulders in the top half and the rest of the body in the bottom.

The mummy-shaped chests were usually large and enclosed in rectangular stone containers which were even bigger. From the Saite epoch onwards the latter were also carved in the shape of the mummy, and made from black granite or basalt which was beautifully polished and finely engraved. As a result the actual coffins became cruder and were only hastily decorated. The outer stone sarcophaguses continued to grow progressively larger until Greek and Roman times, when they gradually returned to more modest dimensions and again appeared with painted portraits and plaster masks.

For a long time it was the custom to place a board underneath the mummy and bind the two together with the last strips of bandaging so that the mummy did not slip. This must have been

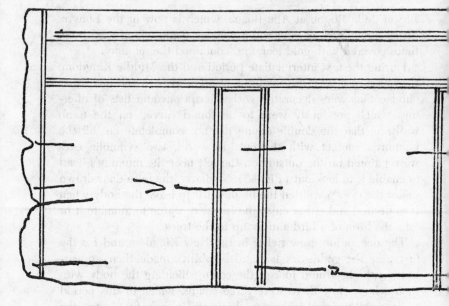

Fig. 43. Wooden sarcophagus, prior to the New Kingdom.
Near the head, symbolic eyes and the false door.

particularly necessary during the rite of the opening of the mouth, when to judge from the pictures we have the sarcophagus was raised to a standing position. Cairo Museum contains two such boards, roughly carved to fit the mummy and covered with inscriptions taken from the Book of the Dead. In other instances the wrapped body was glued to the bottom of the coffin with resin, which served too to seal the lid. Sometimes resin was poured all over the sarcophagus itself.

As fashions in coffins changed, so too did the graves, which as we have seen started just as pits dug in the sand and protected with wattle covering, and developed into magnificent tombs in the heart of the pyramids or hidden in the ground at the bottom of a deep shaft under a mastaba. From the beginning of the Eighteenth Dynasty these developments were influenced by a new problem which greatly preoccupied the pharaohs. Grave

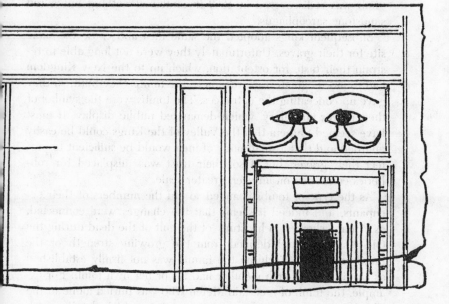

looting was on the increase, and they did not want their last rest-ing-places and least of all their mummified corpses violated by sacrilegious robbers.

It was Amenophis I who decided to break with tradition, and have his tomb hewn out of rock at the entrance to the Deir el-Bahri valley. The opening of the tomb was completely hidden from view so as to keep its existence secret, while the funerary temple was built on the other side of the hill. Ineni, the chief ar-chitect, had inscribed on the funerary chapel walls the phrase "I supervised the digging of His Majesty's tomb alone, without any-one seeing or hearing me," which shows how confidential the op-eration was, though it makes no mention of the difficulty posed by the workmen who had to carry out the building and decora-tion of the underground chamber, as well as the porters who transported the furniture and the sarcophagus. Howard Carter concluded that prisoners of war were employed who could be executed afterwards, but this seems to have no basis in fact. In any event the secret was not kept for very long, for when the tomb was rediscovered in 1889 it contained nothing but a red sandstone sarcophagus.

Subsequent kings adopted the same idea and chose the same site for their graves. Unfortunately they were not long able to restrain their taste for ostentation, which up to the New Kingdom had found its greatest expression in the tombs they built, so they gave up concealing the entrances. The tombs were the symbol of their power and glory, which demanded public display. It must have seemed to them that the Valley of the Kings could be easily guarded and that a small body of men would be sufficient to protect their graves, but if so, their trust was misplaced for robberies continued on an even greater scale.

As the type of tombs changed so did the numbers of their occupants, and indeed it seems that the changes were connected, as Pirenne showed in his study of the cult of the dead during the Old Kingdom, and derived from the growing strength of the family structure. Early on the family was not firmly established as a unit, and so each member had his or her own tomb. For example, the tomb of a certain Meten who was buried alone in the Third Dynasty was covered in inscriptions which details somewhat vaingloriously each brilliant stage of his career, but hardly mention his parents and children and completely ignore his wife. It seems that his last resting-place was maintained with money deducted from the income from his property and that it belonged solely to him and not to his children who would have had to construct their own tombs.

All this altered in the Fifth Dynasty when new customs grew up which became firmly established in the Sixth. They corresponded to new social and economic circumstances which reinforced family links, largely because the civil appointments made by the court now became hereditary. This meant that the benefits which accrued belonged to the whole family, so they could not be used to establish a cult of one member of the family alone, and in consequence the vault became a family vault and was to remain so for the whole of the rule of the pharaohs. Filial piety therefore became more important, both towards the father and the mother, and the eldest son became responsible for maintaining his father's memory. The wife was buried next to her husband, and later the children beside their parents, each with his or her own funerary stela and offerings table, and sometimes their own burial chamber.

In later periods there were considerable complications because every Egyptian family wanted its own tomb and the undertakers were swamped with business. We have already seen how they bought land and built temporary vaults to house the mummies, but even so there was not enough space in many necropolises, especially at Thebes. In addition it was extremely expensive to build a tomb, and some families who had already handed over their deceased relative to the embalmers could not then afford even a modest grave. In the Greco-Roman period therefore it became the custom to re-use old tombs from the times of the pharaohs. Deir el-Medina holds many examples, some of them found by Bataille when he investigated graves from the Middle and Late Kingdoms and discovered mummies wearing headbands inscribed in Greek, or lying in baked clay coffins decorated with vine leaves which are typical of the Roman period.

Sometimes extra rooms were added on to enlarge the sepulchre and to make room for new arrivals. Since the tombs were quite close to each other, they could be joined up by means of corridors which also provided more space. Elsewhere walls were hollowed out so that a tomb which had originally been constructed for one person or family became a veritable honeycomb of tombs containing hundreds of bodies.

The procedure was not altogether new, for when Queen Hatshepsut selected a site at Deir el-Bahri for her magnificent temple, her architect was forced to remove the occupants of tombs which had been there for centuries, and put them in a Middle Kingdom vault some distance away. By an appropriate twist of fate, the temple fell into ruins and itself became a cemetery in the Twenty-third Dynasty; but the dead who were buried there did not enjoy a lasting rest for they in turn had to make place in their sarcophaguses for Greek and Roman mummies.

Old mummies were not usually destroyed but were simply pushed to one side to make space for new ones. This explains how one can find, for example, in vault 1407 in Deir el-Medina a priest of Amun from the Late Kingdom, a mummy of an old man from the time of the pharaohs, and the embalmed bodies of a family from the second or third century of our own age. In any case it is most unlikely that the funeral undertakers or priests in charge of the worship of the dead would have suggested that one body which had already been promised immortality should be destroyed in order to make way for another one whom they intended to bestow the same promise. Who would have believed them? On the contrary, when ancient tombs were reopened some effort may even have been made to restore any mummies which had deteriorated.

Any site could be made to serve. North of the Theban necropolis at Dira Abu'n-Naga one group of vaults which had begun as private tombs in the Eighteenth Dynasty changed their use on several occasions. The private tombs made way for a vast catacomb of ibises and falcons, which were later removed during the Roman period and were replaced in their turn by a hundred or so human mummies. At Deir el-Medina, the great chamber in which the Saites preserved the sacred rams of Amun was transformed into a tomb for some twenty human bodies during the Ptolemaic period. Still the pressure for more space grew and burials became more costly, so hundreds of bodies were simply interred in the sand.

Within these communal tombs where funeral stelae were rare and coffins no longer inscribed with the deceased's name, some other means had to be found of identifying the body. During the Roman period a little wooden label was tied around the mummy's neck on which was marked the mummy's name and sometimes the dates of his birth and death and the name of the town from which he came. A few set formulae such as are found on funerary stelae would often complete this ultimate identity card, sometimes giving us a revealing picture of the times and beliefs of the dead. For instance, some Egyptian invocations in the demotic tongue read: "Your spirit lives," "May Hathor give you bread," "May Heset give you milk;" while some Greek phrases which were probably intended to be consoling in fact give a bleak impression of the afterlife: "Be not anxious," "No-one is immortal," and "In eternal memory." The first quiet intimations of the beginnings of the Christian religion appear in the words written next to a monogram of Christ, "He has gone to his rest" and "he has gone towards the light."

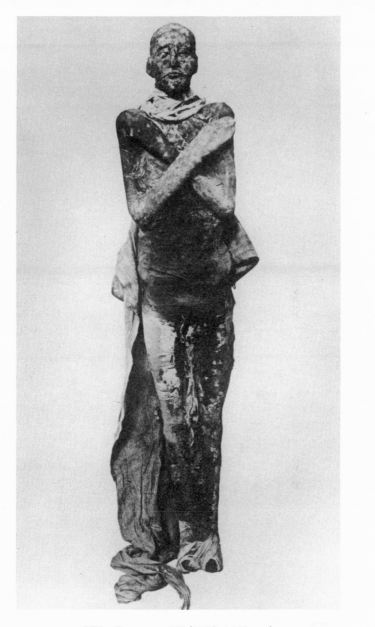

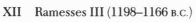

XII Ramesses III (1198–1166 B.C.)

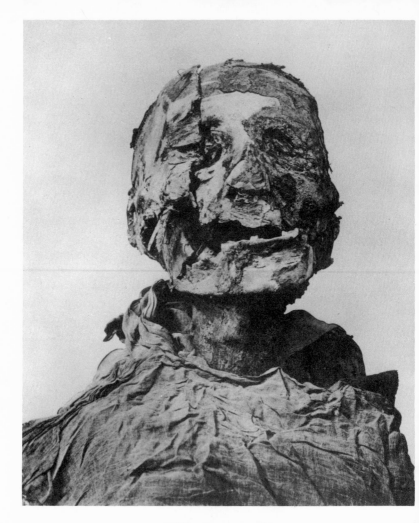

XIII   Ramesses VI

XIV   Wooden coffin containing a cat mummy, Late period, c 600 B.C.

XV   Gilded cartonnage headpiece of a mummy of a woman. Roman period

XVI   Mummy of a bearded man, with face covered with his portrait.
Roman period

XVII   Mummy of a youth, with portrait over face. Roman period

XVIII   Mummy of a baby in a reed coffin. From Gurob. c 1350 B.C.

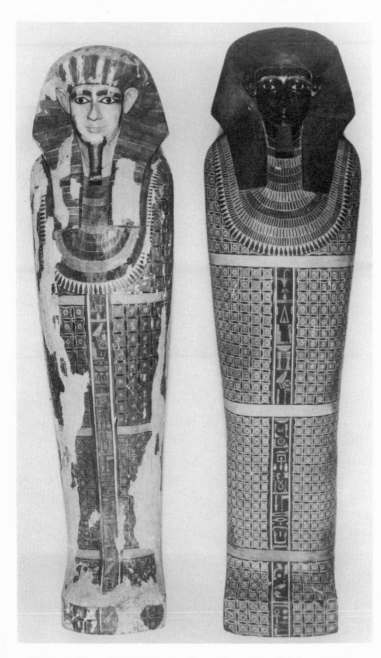

XIX   Coffins of The Two Brothers, from Der Rifeh. c 1900 B.C.

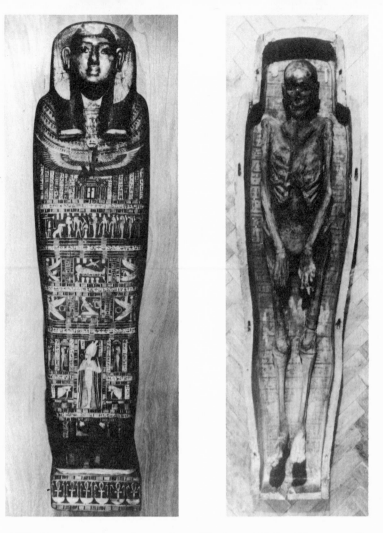

XX   Later and more decorative coffin Azru, Divine Chantress of Amun, c 750 B.C. (left).

XXI   Open coffin with unwrapped mummy of Azru (right).

OVERCROWDED CEMETERIES

Overcrowding in the cemeteries produced some very unpleasant results. Half-way between Thebes and Memphis there is a Greco-Egyptian town called Hermopolis which had its own necropolis on the left bank of the Nile at a place called Tuna el-Gebel. The necropolis was very popular because it contained the remains of Petosiris, a man revered as a saint, whom the inhabitants of the region were eager to have as their neighbour when they died. Numerous little white limestone chapels and more modest tombs sprang up near Petosiris' funerary temple which was built in the year 300 B.C., and was actually very elegant, though more in the Greek style than in the Egyptian. The area was excavated over a long period by Gabra, who was astonished one day to discover some half-mummified bodies which had been buried around the temple immediately next to the foundations. Evidently their families had not been able to afford a decent burial and so the unfortunate people had been laid to rest as near Petosiris as possible, so that they might at least derive some benefit from the religious observances carried on there. However, worse was to follow at the end of the Ptolemaic period when Tuna el-Gebel ceased to be a religious centre. During the subsequent Roman period bodies from Hermopolis were simply piled up in heaps with no respect for the dead and no regard for hygiene. G. Lefèvre was horrified by the sight that met his eyes when he cleared a way into Petosiris' chapel: it was filled with corpses to a height of over six feet, like a charnelhouse. All the other chapel-tombs turned out to be the same. As Gabra said, they were real jewels of architecture when seen from outside, but inside they were houses of decay, filled with ill-prepared mummies which lay in untidy heaps giving off a foul stench. Today the visitor who walks through the streets of this pleasant cemetery town and gazes at the chapels built to house the dead can hardly imagine the appalling task which faced the first archaeologists who had to clear the ground.

It was not an easy matter to keep the tombs in good repair, as Erman has shown, especially since it was not only a question of material upkeep but also of paying the priests in charge. The children could manage, and no doubt the grandchildren also, but with the passing of the centuries the number of ancestors in the family grew ever larger, and the expense involved in maintaining all those distant forbears and in paying for the worship of so many past generations became intolerable. And of course no priest who did not receive the offerings due to him could be expected to care for the abandoned tombs. Sometimes royal edicts were issued such as the one served on the provincial chiefs of Beni Hasan and el Bersha which compelled them to restore the tombs of seven generations of ancestors, from the Sixth to the Twelfth Dynasty, which must have cost them dear. Usually though the monuments were left to deteriorate and eventually no-one even remembered that a site had existed on the spot. For instance there is a group of Sixth Dynasty tombs at Saqqara which were built over the new tombs in the Late Kingdom; these in their turn disappeared and then the site was re-used for more graves in the Greek period.

All the same, there were some who kept up the practices of ancestor worship, and hoped thereby to win the favour of the gods. Among those who nobly took on the task of repairing ruined graves was Intef, Prince of Hermonthis during the Middle Kingdom, who wrote: "I found the chamber of offerings belonging to Prince Nekhti-Iker in a state of ruin; no-one any longer took care of it. I had it rebuilt and enlarged, its statues restored to their original state and its doors carved out of stone, so that his abode might surpass that of other princes."

CHAPTER 8

WHERE ARE THE MUMMIES NOW?

There must be few peoples who spent so much time and wealth in their lifetime in search of eternal rest, and yet who suffered so much disturbance after their death. It did not matter whether the dead were royal sovereigns or ordinary citizens, nobles or commoners, priests or laity, men or women, they all found that the very precautions that were taken to safeguard them defeated all their efforts by attracting attention to them. The wealthier the individual, the more his mummy suffered, and all the thousands of tons of stone used in the construction of the pyramids, the mastabas built up on top of the funerary shafts, and the secret labyrinths contrived inside the hypogeums that were dug out of the mountains, could not save him and his jewels and precious furniture from the depredations of thieves. There was no respite, from the time he was buried up to our own day. From the very beginning robbers pillaged the tombs in search of real or imaginary treasure, iconoclastic Christians then used the polytheism of the Egyptians as an excuse to disturb the mummies' slumbers, and the Arabs themselves rifled the tombs to extract whatever was left of value. During the Middle Ages and the Renaissance, doctors recommended the healing qualities of powder made from mummies, which led to a shameless trade in bodies by the Jews. Egyptomania took root, there was a vogue for collecting the odd and unusual, and so of course no collection of curiosities was complete without its mummy. Even today graves are still being secretly looted for profit in spite of all the archaeologists' care, and bodies are still being dispersed around the world with impious greed and stupidity.

SACRILEGIOUS DEEDS IN ANCIENT EGYPT

At the beginning of the Eighteenth Dynasty, there was not a single royal tomb which had not been pillaged. As we have seen, this was one of the reasons why the pharaohs decided to change their mode of burial and to dig hypogea in the Valley of the Kings, where they thought it would be easy to post guards to protect them from thieves. Unfortunately their efforts proved futile, and these tombs too were secretly excavated on more than one occasion. Thutmosis IV was buried for only a few years when his tomb was robbed, and King Horemheb had to restore it as we know from inscriptions he had carved on it in the eighth year of his reign which show that he commanded someone called Maya to "restore King Thutmosis IV's sepulchre in the Precious Habitation to the west of Thebes."

On the other hand Tutankhamun's tomb was spared, and the young king's mummy is perhaps the only one to have survived intact, in spite of the fact that robbers had twice managed to enter his tomb before Carter discovered all its riches. It was probably saved from worse depredations by the twenty-five foot long corridor which led from the outside to the antechamber, and which had been deliberately choked with rubble after the burial took place. When the robbers succeeded in hacking out a narrow passage through this, they still had to cut an opening in the heavy door which guarded the antechamber, before they could start hastily emptying the oils and precious ointments into the flasks they had brought for the purpose. In their rush they left behind fragments in the antechamber which show what happened. They must have been well informed as to the topography of the tomb, for they next proceeded to the northern chamber where they seized on the gold jewellery as quickly as possible, for very little air can have reached the interior through the narrow passage they had dug. Like the catburglars of today who scatter the contents of every drawer over the floor so as to seize on the valuables as quickly as possible, these ancient robbers tipped over the furniture in their frantic search, leaving the tomb in the chaos in which it was discovered by Carter. They may even have been disturbed at their work, and certainly they left the scene in a great hurry, to judge from the evidence of the little handkerchief containing a few rings which they dropped on the floor.

Every possible means, magical and material, was used to thwart the robbers and protect the dead. Threatening injunctions were carved on the walls, giving notice of the dire fate that would befall those who violated the tombs. "If anyone effaces my name in order to put his own in its place, God will repay him by obliterating his image on earth," warned one inscription, and "If he respects my name on this stela, God will treat him as he treated me" said another, appealing to the better side of man's nature. Curses were invoked against those who disturbed the mummy, and the robber was threatened with the prospect of paying the penalty before the tribunal of the "great god," or even with retribution by the deceased himself, who would fall on him and carry him off like a bird of prey. None of these precautions was of any avail, and indeed did not deter the pharaohs themselves from taking over the sarcophaguses of their predecessors and obliterating the original cartouches. Even the fact that Alexander was proclaimed son of Amun did not prevent Ptolemy XI from ravaging his tomb. Only in one instance do the threats seem to have been fulfilled, in a tomb at Meidum, where two bodies were found, one mummified and intact and one that of a thief who had been crushed by a heavy stone falling from the roof; an inscription reads, "The spirit of the dead will wring the robber's neck like a goose's."

Obviously the families who owned the tombs did not put great trust in the efficacity of magic formulae, for in addition they installed traps and blocks of stone like portcullises in the corridors, built false doors and tunnelled out numerous misleading passageways which turned out to be blind alleys. Their best efforts were all in vain. The robbers' determination overcame all obstacles, and succeeded even in finding the key to the great pyramid of Cheops, as Goyon has described. This pyramid was particularly well protected, as can be seen from the cross-section of the western side (Fig. 44). Once the pharaoh had been interred in the heart of the pyramid, the workmen blocked the entrance to the royal chamber with three heavy granite slabs which they lowered into position like portcullises by means of ropes passing over wooden rollers. They then blocked off the main gallery as they left by withdrawing wedges which held more granite blocks

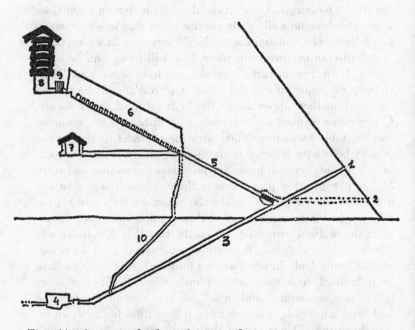

Fig. 44. Section of Cheops' pyramid. 1. Entrance. 2. Passage excavated by looters. 3. Downward-sloping corridor. 4. Underground chamber. 5. Upward-sloping corridor. 6. Grand gallery. 7. Queen's chamber. 8. King's chamber. 9. Portcullises. 10. Passage excavated by looters.

in place, and letting them slip slowly backwards down the upward-sloping passage, where they jammed themselves into the
narrow northern end. It was humanly quite impossible to penetrate this obstacle. Afterwards the workers only had to go back
along the downward-sloping passage in order to reach the entrance which opened to the north, at the level of the seventeenth
row of blocks. This was then finally sealed with a heavy stone,
and robbers would hardly dare to risk trying to break in at that
point because it was situated so high up on the façade that it
was clearly visible. Instead, what they did was to hack out their
own passage through the stone, starting at the fifth tier of blocks
and working at night only when they would not be seen. It must
have needed more than one night, and they would have had to
disguise the opening each time they left. However, once they
had tunnelled along for about twenty-two yards, they reached
the point where the downward and upward-sloping passages
met. They could not go up because the way was blocked, so they
went down to the underground chamber, which was empty, and
decided to dig another way up into the heart of the pyramid. As
they dug they removed the debris into the underground chamber, and when they reached the point where they had to start
going vertically upwards they were forced to construct little
landings where they could rest. Finally they succeeded in reaching the intersection of the upward-sloping passage with the
horizontal one which leads to the so-called Queen's chamber. The
fact that they emerged so accurately at the beginning of the
great gallery argues either that they themselves were familiar
with the lay-out of the pyramid, or that they had accomplices
who had worked on it. This was the work of a skilled team, not a
haphazard group of robbers.

Breaking in to the Step Pyramid of Zoser was also no easy
task. Here the funerary chambers were dug out underground,
and there are no rooms within the bulk of the pyramid itself.
The entrance was through a central shaft followed by a ramp
which penetrated laterally underground and led to a veritable
maze of corridors, ending in eleven funerary chambers. All access was blocked with stones which the robbers had to remove,
so they constructed an ingenious platform in the shaft on to
which they hauled the debris before transporting it outside.

When they reached their goal, they emptied the chambers of everything except a few stone vases which they did not consider valuable.

In other places such as the necropolis of Tuna el-Gebel where the ibises are entombed, robbers found a way into the galleries through a natural fault in the rock along which they could crawl, and indeed the first archaeologists who discovered the site entered the same way, before they found and cleared the great stairways which led inside.

Occasionally the robbers' efforts were discovered almost immediately, and measures were taken to foil further attempts. Maya, the "Superintendant of Building Works in the place of eternal rest," who had already restored Thutmosis IV, ordered an inspection of Tutankhamun's tomb which verified that the sarcophagus itself was untouched amid the chaos, which the inspectors vainly endeavoured to put right; then in order to prevent further depredations he had the stairway to the tomb filled in with rubble, which effectively hid the entrance. When workers' huts were put on the site, this successfully concealed the pharaoh's resting-place and allowed him to remain undisturbed until Carter arrived on the scene.

It did not help the pharaohs that the robbers were so afraid of discovery. On the contrary, in their haste to make off with their booty and their greed to plunder every jewel they would attack the mummies with axes in order to hack through the wrappings which were hard with resin, and use daggers to cut the shrouds, often cutting off limbs and heads in the process.

The most audacious theft was undoubtedly the one detected by Winlock in a tomb at Deir el-Bahri, where he found two mummies which at first sight seemed quite untouched. The shroud of Osiris was neatly sewn on to the bodies, and all the wrappings and bandages were carefully wound around the mummies, but when he began to unwrap them he found that all was not as it seemed; some linen was out of place, bandages had been torn, and then he came across the print of a falcon-shaped pectoral in the resin, and marks of dirty fingers on the cloth, which should have been clean. The piece of jewellery had been removed and replaced by a heart scarab which had no commercial value. There were no rings on the fingers either, and

Winlock came to the conclusion that the mummies had been despoiled even before the wrapping was finished.

In some cases the thieves were in a position to conduct their depredations without fear of being disturbed by the guards. For instance, the ones who raided Sekenenre's tomb had enough time carefully to scrape off all the gold from his coffin, and conceal the theft by repainting it yellow. Where precious stones were inlaid, they were removed and more paint was applied. Significantly, the gold on the religious or royal emblems was left untouched, and we can only conclude that this time the perpetrators of the theft were the priests themselves.

Usually, however, it was the necropolis workers who were to blame. They had the knowledge and the necessary skills in tunnelling, and when in addition they were forced to go on strike in order to obtain even their basic ration of food which was part of their due wages, it is hardly surprising that they succumbed to temptation. For them it was no problem to construct a tunnel from a new tomb they were building to the interior of an old tomb in the vicinity where they knew they would find treasures, and on occasion they even conspired together to make a secret way into a tomb which they could make use of later, or deliberately left a chink in the precautions which the architect had devised to make the place impregnable.

As time passed, the tombs suffered increasing violation. No less than sixteen papyri from the Nineteenth and Twentieth Dynasties have survived to tell us of these events, and out of these three, the Abbott, Leopold and Amherst Papyri, give us detailed information on the corruption and dereliction of duties connected with tomb robberies in those days. As we shall see from the account of a trial which took place at Thebes in the reign of Ramesses IX, around the year 115 B.C., the administration of the period was incapable of coping with crime on this scale, nor were the tribunals any more competent.

There were three principal characters involved: Pesiur, mayor of East Thebes, the city of the living, Pwero, mayor of West Thebes, the necropolis on the other side of the Nile, and the vizier Khamuese, representing the central administration. The two mayors heartily detested each other and each was only waiting for an opportunity to blacken the other's name in the sight of

the authorities. Finally the opportunity presented itself to Pesiur,
so he thought, in the shape of an unofficial report concerning
large-scale robberies in the city of the dead, of which his colleague was mayor. He conveniently forgot to notify Pwero, as
courtesy demanded, and went straight to their immediate superior, the vizier Khamuese, to inform him that he had got wind of
the violation of ten royal tombs, four tombs of priestesses, and
numerous private vaults, and to give him all the details. When
Pwero heard of the matter, he was unable to deal with it at such
short notice and was forced to refer to the vizier too, who set up a
commission to investigate the affair. This consisted of Pwero
himself at its head, who was thus well placed to cover up his
own responsibility in the matter, and two high officials, "Nesamon, carver to the king, scribe to the pharaoh and director of the
domains of the High Priestess of Amun, king of the gods, and
Neferkere-em-per-Amun, carver to the king and his adviser."
These three were assisted by two officers from Pwero's police, no
doubt personally committed to him, the vizier's scribe, and other
officials including some priests. They began their inspection in
the necropolis, paying particular attention to the tombs which
Pesiur claimed had been broken into, and when they produced
their detailed report this stated that out of the ten royal tombs
named by Pesiur only one had really been forcibly entered. The
report is a small masterpiece of administrative literature, and is
worth quoting for the sly attacks which Pwero makes on his
fellow-mayor, especially in the first paragraph:

1. The eternal horizon (the tomb) of King Amenophis
I, . . . about which the prince of the city, Pesiur, laid a
complaint to the vizier and governor of the city, Khamuese
. . . It was found intact by the inspectors.

2. The pyramid of the king, son of Re Intef the Elder
. . . it was found intact.

3. The pyramid of King Nubkheperre, son of Re Intef. It
was found that thieves had started to break in; they had dug
a hole of two cubits at the bottom, and another of one cubit
in the outer room of the ruined tomb of Yurai, director of
offerings in the temple of Amun; it was intact, the thieves
had not succeeded in entering.

4. The pyramid of King Sekhemre Upmaat, son of Re Intef the Elder; it was found that thieves had begun to make an opening at the spot where his stela was erected . . . it was found to be intact, the thieves had not succeeded in entering.

5. The pyramid of King Sekhemreseshedítaui, son of Re Sebekemsaf; it was found that thieves had opened it up and broken in with the aid of stone-cutters, at the base of the pyramid, starting at the entrance portico of the tomb of Nebamun, director of granaries under King Thutmosis II. It was found that the place of burial of his master the King had been pillaged, as had the place of burial of Queen Kasnub, his royal wife; the thieves had laid hands on them.

The vizier and the prince carvers to the king organised a detailed examination, which established the way in which the thieves had laid hands on the King and his royal wife. . . .

The conclusion of the enquiry led by Pwero into the royal tombs was eloquent in its baldness:

Pyramids of the ancestral tombs which were today examined by the inspectors:

Found intact: pyramids	9
Found open and broken into: pyramids	1
Total:	10

What a fuss about one pyramid, even if Pesiur had claimed that ten were involved! The vizier can hardly have been pleased at being put to so much trouble, even though two out of four tombs of the singers of the High Priestess of Amun had been entered, as well as the private tombs, of which "it was found that they had all been violated by thieves; the latter had pulled the corpses from their coffins and torn off their wrappings, thrown them on the ground and stolen the furniture and the articles of adornment which they found inside the bandages." This must have been such a common occurrence that it evoked no shock, the main point being that the majority of royal sepulchres remained intact.

For good measure, Pwero was also able to hand over the guilty parties at once. It looks as if he must have already known of their activities, or he would hardly have been able to arrest them so quickly, or else the group may have confessed to whatever was put to them in the course of "their interrogation after they had been given the bastinado and been caned on their hands and feet." There were eight of these well-organised brigands, of whom we know the names of five: Hapi, a stone-cutter, Iramen, an artisan, Amen-em-Heb, a peasant, Kemuese, a water-carrier, and Emnefer, a black slave. Their confession took up only a few lines: "Then we opened their coffins and the wrappings in which they were bandaged. We found the august mummy of the king. He had a large number of amulets and gold jewellery around his neck; his head was covered in a gold mask. The august mummy was completely covered with gold and the coffins were coated with gold and silver, outside and inside, and were inlaid with precious stones. We pulled off the gold we found on the august mummy of this god and the amulets which were around his neck and the bandages in which they were placed. We also found the king's wife and we pulled off everything we found on her in the same way. We took the objects which we found near them, that is to say the gold, silver and bronze vases. We shared everything among ourselves, and divided into eight portions the gold we had found on the two gods, on their mummies, and the amulets, jewellery and coverings." We know that the thieves were imprisoned, but we do not know the tribunal's verdict: it is probable that they were condemned to death unless there were extenuating circumstances which might have allowed them to escape with only amputation of the nose and ears.

Next day the vizier and Nesamon, carver to the king, went themselves to the same spot to enquire into another affair, this time involving a metal-worker known by the name of Pikhare. He was a serf from the temple of Ramesses III who had been condemned three years previously, after a hurried preliminary investigation, for having penetrated into the tomb of Isis, royal wife of Ramesses II. The vizier wanted to ascertain whether other sepulchres housing members of the royal family in that area, known as the "place of beauties," had been violated, and so he decided to set up a reconstruction of the crime, and brought

Pikhare blindfolded into the necropolis. The record states: "When the bandage was removed and he could see again, the princes told him: 'Walk in front of us to the tomb from which you stole something, according to your statement.' Doing as he was told, the metal-worker turned towards one of the tombs belonging to the children of King Ramesses II, in which no-one had ever been buried and which was open, and towards the dwelling of the necropolis worker Amenemone and said: 'See, these are the places where I went.'" This was not at all what the commission of enquiry expected, and immediately rods were brought out to lash the hands and feet of the unfortunate man, in the hope of extracting the truth from him. This time however he held out and did not renew the confessions which torture had forced from him the first time. "He swore, by the king, that they might cut off his nose and ears and impale him if he had any knowledge of any other place but the open tomb and the dwelling he had pointed out to them." His steadfastness was rewarded and the enquiry concluded that there were no grounds for prosecution. The princes finished their inspection of the "place of beauties" and declared themselves satisfied that the tombs were intact.

Pwero was exultant, and took full advantage of his triumph to dispatch to East Thebes an organised body of "inspectors, necropolis administrators, workers, police and all the labourers in the cemetery." He was determined that everyone should know that the honour of the necropolis was untarnished, in particular the inhabitants of the city of the living, where noisy demonstrations took place around the home of Pesiur, who had made the accusations originally. Pesiur himself was furious, for he suspected, not without reason, that there may have been some complicity between Pwero and the princes and he was certain that Pwero was profiting in some way from the pillage of the tombs. He therefore accused him of having falsified the results of the enquiry, and decided to bypass the vizier and go straight to the king with his complaint, claiming that he was in possession of new facts: "Hori-Shere, the scribe of the necropolis, came to my residence on the main side of the town and made three declarations to me about some very important matters. My scribe and the scribe of the two districts of the town kept a record of the proceedings. Then Pibes, the scribe of the necropolis, made two other declarations; thus, five in all. An official record was also kept of the two last. It is impossible to pass over them in silence. They involve crimes so grave that they merit the death penalty, impalement, and all kinds of punishment. I am now writing about them to the king, my master, so that he may send one of his men to arrest you." The vizier, who was doubtless Pwero's accomplice, was upset by this turn of events and worried too, but he could not stifle the whole affair so he decided to face up to Pesiur's threats by appointing another tribunal to investigate the three accused. This reported:

"Understand, the town governor and vizier Khamuese had brought before him the metal-worker Pikhare, the metal-worker Zaroy, and the metal-worker Pikamen, all three from the temple of Ramesses III. The vizier told the great princes of the city tribunal: 'this prince of the city made certain remarks to the inspectors and workers of the necropolis on 19th Hathor of the year 16, in the presence of the royal carver to the king, pharaoh's scribe Nesamon, and in the course of his remarks he spoke in a slanderous manner about the great places which are situated in the "place of beauties." But I, the vizier of this land, I went there together with the carver to the king, Nesamon, pharaoh's scribe. We examined the places where the prince of the city had said that the metal-workers from Ramesses III's temple in the dwelling of Amon had entered, and we found them intact. Thus everything that he had said was then seen to be inaccurate. See, the metal-workers now stand before you, let them recount everything which took place.' They were heard and it was ascertained that these people knew none of the parts of the necropolis about which this prince of the city had spoken. He was therefore found guilty on this point. The high priests spared the lives of the metal-workers of Ramesses III's temple . . ."

Pesiur found himself with his credibility seriously damaged by the vizier's evidence, and when he was accused of making false accusations he was forced to beat a retreat. If he had any further information, it was not sufficient to lay before the pharaoh, so the suspicion of public complicity in the embezzlement of treasures from the tombs remained unsubstantiated and Pesiur made a public apology. We shall probably never know the true details of this Egyptian scandal, which is not surprising since it involves the first trial in history of which the records have survived.

The outcome was not calculated to help put an end to the depredations, even though three years later some sixty robbers were brought to justice under Ramesses X, including a scribe of Amun's treasure and two priests. By that time tomb-robbing had become a virtual industry in its own right, and the government was so weak it seemed incapable of putting an end to it. True, guards were still posted around the private tombs, though they can hardly have been expected to keep watch effectively when it was known that the police were bribed to turn a blind eye to the goings-on, or even to lend a hand with the crime themselves. For this reason, from the Twenty-first Dynasty onwards efforts were concentrated on safe-guarding those royal mummies which had already suffered at the hands of looters. They were reduced to such a bad state that it was sometimes necessary to wrap them afresh, and to provide new coffins, which the inscriptions written in ink on the shrouds or traced directly onto the coffins refer to as "renewing the king's burial." Through the details they provide we can follow the unhappy journeyings forced on the mummies in the extraordinary game of hide and seek on which the priests embarked in the hope of foiling robbers. As soon as they thought a tomb was discovered, they would remove its occupant and place him in another pharaoh's hypogeum which was considered to be better protected.

During Pinedjem's term of office as high priest, he had to over-see the restoration of the mummies of Thutmosis I, Amenophis I, Seti I, Ramesses II and Ramesses III, but his efforts did not save the unfortunate Amenophis I from being attacked by thieves a second time, and this mummy was again rebandaged under the pontificate of Masaharte. Ahmosis, Queen Satkames and Prince Siamon all had to be reinterred. Under Menkheperre, Seti I was re-wrapped, and during the Twenty-first Dynasty Ramesses III was disturbed and reburied three times, while at the end of Pinedjem II's pontificate the mummies of Ramesses I, Ramesses II and Seti I were all removed from the latter's tomb where they had already been transferred once, and taken to the more modest resting-place of Queen Inhapi. Pinedjem II was himself soon to join them. Finally the High Priest Psusennes was inspired by a better idea than any of his predecessors, and took all those mentioned together with others to the famous cachette of Deir-el-Bahri, where they were at last allowed to rest in peace until they were rediscovered at the end of the last century.

By the Twenty-second Dynasty the pharaohs had established themselves in the Delta in the capital of Tanis, and though their mummies suffered considerably from the dampness of the region they and the nobles of their court did not all have to undergo the indignities endured by their predecessors. The mummies of Psusennes, his chief archer Unudjebaouendjebet, Amenemope and Sheshonq II completely escaped the unwelcome attentions of thieves, though on the other hand Osorkon II, Sheshonq III and Takelothis II all had violence inflicted on them. The north was no more free of greed than the south.

The situation continued to decline. Indeed, the looters could hardly have been expected to desist when so many coffins were sold on the open market with the name of their original owner obliterated that it looks as if the trade was, if not officially approved, at least condoned. There was a flourishing commerce in second-hand coffins of high quality from the best periods, the Eighteenth, Nineteenth and Twentieth Dynasties, and the supply was so well maintained by thieves that both rich and poor could aspire to one of their own. Indeed when in the 4th century B.C. the Persians and Macedonians ravaged the cemetery in Memphis the most magnificent sarcophaguses appeared on the market, with the names of their original owners obliterated, not only in Egypt but as far away as Phoenicia, Tyre and Sidon. What became of the mummies they had contained? Evidently neither the robbers nor the Persians suffered from any scruples in this regard.

MAGIC SPELLS

Towards the 2nd or 3rd century A.D., a new civilisation of Christian origin appeared in Egypt, the Coptic civilisation. Monasteries proliferated. The richest communities, evidently inspired by Roman models, broke with the pharaonic and hellenic traditions and created their own type of building, while the less well endowed established themselves in chapels and burial vaults alongside the mummies. It can hardly have been a happy arrangement, and no doubt many of the mummies were quietly removed to make way for the new inhabitants. Others would have been ejected by anchorites who took up their abode in their sepulchres and in tombs which were no longer regarded as sacred, in order to escape from the world. Some of them took a dislike to the mural paintings and one, a hermit in Thebes, effaced every picture of a woman from the walls in order to avoid the temptations of the flesh. On the whole, however, the Copts did very little damage and because they were not interested in acquiring wealth in this world they had no cause to exploit the cemeteries.

This did not apply to the Arabs, who seem to have become obsessed with the search for treasure, and were convinced that the Egyptian tombs were an inexhaustible source of fantastic fortunes buried by the ancient kings. Experts even compiled treatises on likely sites, and offered books of magic formulae to discover them as well as all kinds of spells to safeguard the seeker from the evil spirits who watched over all this fabulous wealth. So strong a hold did these ideas have on the popular imagination that when later it was decided to put a stop to ransacking tombs the first step that had to be taken was to deal with the books and ridiculous hopes they raised. The superstitions they had engendered did not prove easy to eradicate, especially when some writers maintained that the magic treatises had, as Mas'Oudi tells us, facilitated the discovery near the pyramids of statues whose eyes were "made out of all kinds of precious stones, such as rubies, emeralds, turquoises and some with a surface of gold and silver." Even though these reports were clearly exaggerated, the frantic search continued, and we are informed by Abd el-Latif that around 1200 a "crowd of people have no means of earning a living other than foraging through cemeteries and carrying off everything they find."

By this time looting was so common that it was no longer a crime, and indeed the authorities themselves, ever on the lookout for new sources of revenue, had no qualms over accepting the booty in payment of duties. As Ibn Khaldum points out, the moment "that taxes were imposed on various regions and different kinds of industry, they were also imposed on the people whose profession it is to seek for treasure." The old type of banditry was transformed into a respectable profession, and ravaging monuments was officially sanctioned by the state. Vansleb, a traveller who visited Alexandria in 1672, was astonished to find that Pompey's column which he had seen upright eight years previously was then leaning at an angle; the explanation was that in the meantime its pedestal had been excavated.

The princes themselves set the example. Caliph Al-Maamoun, son of the great Harun-al-Rashid, first removed the greater part of the exterior covering of the great pyramid of Cheops, in order to avoid going to the trouble of digging out stone slabs from a quarry, and then actually gave the order to seize Cheops' treasure. At first the searchers dug a tunnel into the pyramid, but it came out in the wrong place, so they then endeavoured to clear a way down through all the rubble. When they came to the section where the corridor was blocked with granite, they forced a way around and finally reached the great gallery, only to find that others had already passed the same way before them. Their disappointment must have been considerable but is hardly apparent from the hyperbole of the following poetic account: "When the workers reached the centre of the building, they made a wondrous discovery, a vessel full of dinars whose total exactly matched the sum that had been expended to reach the spot." It must have been an expensive expedition.

EATING MUMMY

In the Middle Ages and Renaissance in Europe, a great vogue grew up for mummy as a medicine, and Avicenna, one of the greatest doctors of antiquity, declared it to be a sovereign remedy against "abscesses and rashes, fractures, contusions, paralysis, migraine, epilepsy, hemoptysis, diseases of the throat, coughs, palpitations, weakness of the stomach, nausea, disorders of the liver and spleen, internal ulcers and also cases of poisoning." The list might have been shorter if he had told us when this panacea was not effective! The vogue was largely started by a Jewish doctor by the name of El-Magar who practised in Alexandria around 1300, and who began the custom of prescribing it for his patients.

The product was delivered to the apothecary's establishment either in the form of fragments of body or as a thick oily substance which was the residue from burning the mummies, or later as a blackish paste which in fact had nothing to do with embalmed bodies but was simply Judean bitumen or pissasphalt which was referred to as "funeral balm." Four kinds of mummy were distinguished by Schroder: "That of the Arabs, a sort of liquid composed of aloes, myrrh and balm extracted from the bodies which one finds in tombs; that of the Egyptians, a liquid which flows out of the bodies of the common people who have been embalmed with pissasphalt—one still finds these bodies whole; artificial pissasphalt, a mixture of pitch and bitumen which is sold as true mummy; and finally corpses buried in sand and dried in the heat of the sun." These last were much less prized because they were not impregnated with any of the resin or aromatic oils which rendered the properly embalmed mummy effective. At the beginning of the seventeenth century, Savary de Bruslon advised that the best mummy was one which was "the least shiny, really black, smelling pleasant, and which when burnt has no odour of pitch."

By the sixteenth century, only two out of the numerous afflictions for which Avicenna had indicated mummy as a remedy were still thought to respond to it: gastric pains, for which mummy was supposed to be taken internally, and ecchymoses and bruises to which mummy was applied externally. François I never moved without ensuring that his butlers carried an ample supply, and never left on a journey without first having hung a little leather bag containing a piece of mummy from his horse's saddle, in case of necessity. At the imperial court in Bohemia, there was even an entire mummy, "a whole fellow," as Christoph Harant tells us.

Only fifty years ago, Bruyère observed in the course of his excavations that the Arabs of Qurna still used mummy to stop haemorrhaging. In order to obtain a sufficient quantity of it, they broke the skulls so as to extract the resinous substance from it, burnt the limbs, and boiled up everything in vessels which were often the actual skulls of the corpses.

Fortunately, there were objections to the widespread use of mummy as far back as the Renaissance, when the great French surgeon Ambroise Paré made his distaste plain in a special chapter, "Discourse on mummy," which he devoted to the subject in his complete works. He was disgusted by the fact that people had so little respect for the religious customs of the ancient Egyptians, who had not embalmed bodies merely in order that they "might serve as food and drink for the living." According to Paré, "not only does this wretched drug do no good to the sick . . . but it causes them great pain in their stomachs, gives them evil-smelling breath, and brings on serious vomiting which is more likely to stir up the blood and worsen the haemorrhaging than to stop it." He considered that these "stinking lures" were good for nothing but fishing bait, and in his conclusion he stated forcefully that he would never prescribe mummy for anyone under any circumstances.

His pleas fell on deaf ears. There is no doubt that mummy continued to be widely used, not only because of a superstitious belief in its efficacy, but also because by this time powerful financial interests were involved and trafficking in the drug had become a highly organised business, starting in the Egyptian tombs and following a well-planned route to Europe.

The trade produced some puzzling effects for later archaeologists. Bruyère, for instance, when he was investigating the Theban necropolis at Deir el-Medina, remarked on the evidence of fires in nearly every vault. If they had only occurred in the occasional tomb, one might have concluded that the contents had been carelessly set alight by the torch of some clandestine graverobber, but their universal presence argued a more systematic purpose. Ancient looters would never have dared to risk discovery by lighting fires deliberately; a more feasible theory advanced was that the Coptic monks wanted to purify the place by destroying all evidence of any previous inhabitants, but this did not explain why rooms in some hypogea were left with all their pagan décor intact. In fact the only possible explanation lies in the preparation of mummy, which involved first of all bringing the corpses into rooms which served as storage chambers, and then sorting them out, breaking the skulls in order to extract the resin, and piling up the bandages and broken pieces of body in other rooms, either to be sent off as they were or in readiness for burning. Coffins were also brought to these dumping-rooms to break them up for fuel. Yet other rooms were used to incinerate the bodies and prepare the end product, and these rooms were black with smoke and still held ashes or half-carbonised bones on the floor.

This was the time when a Dutch traveller, Jan Sommer, gazed in amazement at the extraordinary spectacle provided by donkeys and camels transporting loads of mummies to the merchants of Cairo and Alexandria (either whole or treated and almost ready for consumption). The merchants then saw them on to the next stage of their illicit journey, on Portuguese or Venetian boats which seem to have specialised in this trade and which carried them on to France where the demand for mummy was much stronger than elsewhere. Here the centre of distribution seems to have been Lyons, which supplied apothecaries all over France with the last relics of the ancient Egyptians to retail at vastly inflated prices.

It was not always easy to obtain supplies, and as the penalties for trafficking in bodies grew harsher so the sources of genuine mummies dwindled, and some merchants took to fabricating their goods in order not to lose trade. They saw no harm in this, and indeed when in 1564 Guy de la Fontaine, doctor to the King of Navarre, asked to see the stock of the principal supplier in Alexandria the trader was only too happy to open up his doors and display the forty or so bodies inside. The doctor was surprised and enquired where the bodies came from and whether they originated from the ancient tombs, whereupon the trader began to laugh. None of the corpses, he affirmed, was more than four years old, and most of them had belonged to slaves. This worried Guy de la Fontaine, in case they had died of some infectious disease like leprosy, smallpox or the plague, so he asked for more information, and where the bodies originated. The reply was hardly reassuring, for he was told that the source of the bodies and whether they were young or old, male or female, was quite irrelevant; all that mattered was that they were available and not likely to be recognised or claimed once they were dead.

When the doctor asked how they were embalmed, he was told: "Quite simply, I just remove the brain and entrails and then I make long and deep incisions in the muscles and fill them with asphalt, then I take some old cloth which I soak in the same asphalt, put the cloth in the incisions and bandage up each part separately; then I wrap everything in a sheet. When they are ready, I let them pickle as they are for two or three months." What he did not explain, and which was perhaps the secret of his method, was how he dried the bodies out, whether in the heat of the sun or in an oven. Cynically, he derided the Christians who were "so fond of eating the bodies of the dead." Actually Christians were not above concocting mummies themselves and there were similar laboratories in France which obtained their supplies from the bodies of executed criminals or those who died in hospital and were not claimed by their families.

The bottom only finally fell out of the market in the seventeenth century, though the immediate cause of the collapse was neither medical nor moral. One of the suppliers of faked mummies, a Jewish trader from Daumiette, owned a Christian slave whom he was determined to make forswear his own religion and adopt the Jewish one. The slave was not anxious to offend his master, so he pretended to fall in with his wishes, and all went well until the trader insisted that his slave should be circumcised as proof of his change of heart. The slave could no longer maintain the pretence and refused point blank, with the result that he was subjected to all kinds of harassment and ill-treatment, to such a degree that he finally went to complain to the pasha. At the same time he denounced the illicit practices of his master, who was thrown into prison and condemned to pay three hundred gold sultans if he wished to regain his liberty. When the governors of other Egyptian towns like Alexandria and Rosetta heard of the incident they immediately realised that they had discovered a new source of revenue, and imposed a tax on all traders in mummies. This, combined with the fact that the demand for such goods was on the wane, proved too heavy a burden to sustain, and so the extraordinary traffic finally came to an end.

THE POET AND THE MUMMY

Western travellers in the sixteenth and seventeenth centuries were, as has already been mentioned, fascinated by mummies. At first they were interested in their pharmaceutical uses, but when these proved dubious they turned their attention to the mummies as objects of curiosity, much sought after to embellish their collections of exotica. Mummies were no longer exported in bulk, and only a few specimens continued to be transported clandestinely across the Mediterranean each year.

The tales brought back by travellers aroused great interest though, and particularly in the romantic period of literature each discovery stimulated fresh enthusiasm. Napoleon's expedition to Egypt and its finds made an impact on the imagination of many writers, including Flaubert and in particular Théophile Gautier, who was sufficiently impressed by one account to use it as the basis for one of his stories, which he called *Le pied de momie* (The mummy's foot). The account was written by a member of the expedition, Baron Vivant Denon, who in the depths of a tomb in the Valley of the Kings had come upon the tiny embalmed foot of a young woman which so intrigued him that he brought it home with him. His report was accompanied by a drawing, and the two together gave rise to the following description in Gautier's tale:

The toes were slender and delicate, ending in perfect nails which were as delicate and transparent as agates; the big toe was set slightly apart from the others and angled differently from them in the antique mode, which happily contrived to lend the foot an air of freedom, a bird-like suppleness; the sole of the foot, marked with the faintest of lines, showed that it had never touched the ground and had only come into contact with the finest Nile rush matting or the softest carpet of panther skins.

The tale was well received, and since Egypt was then very fashionable Gautier returned to the same theme in a much longer work, *Le roman de la momie*, published by Hachette in 1858. He was influenced in this by the conversations he held with Flaubert and Maxime du Camp, who had journeyed up the Nile, and also guided in his research by Ernest Feydeau on whose great work *Histoire des usages funèbres et des sèpultures des peuples anciens* he had published a report. Thus he came to read some of the best material produced by Egyptologists such as Champollion, Wilkinson, Rossellini and Lepsius, and his book is remarkable for the detailed knowledge it displays. If it does have any defects these are due to the gaps in information available at the time, not to any error on his own part, though he did tend to let his imagination run riot on occasion, especially when he was describing the discovery of the mummy of Tahoser by two experts, Rumphins and Everdale, in highly romantic and extravagant terms:

The last obstacle removed, the young woman appeared in all her chaste nudity and beauty, still, in spite of the lapse of so many centuries, displaying all the shapeliness of her figure and all the supple grace of her pure body. She lay in an attitude unusual for a mummy, like Venus de Milo, as if the embalmers wished to spare this sweet form the pain of a more death-like pose, and soften the rigid inflexibility of the corpse. One of her hands half concealed her virginal breast, while the other hid her mysterious beauties as if the dead girl's modesty was not sufficiently shielded by the protective shadows of the sepulchre . . . Never had Greek or Roman statue presented more elegant proportions; the particular features of the Egyptian ideal gave this beautiful body, so miraculously preserved, a lissomness and lightness that no antique marble possesses. The slenderness of her tapering hands, the distinction of her narrow feet ending in nails as brilliant as agates, the delicacy of her figure, the shape of her breast which is as small and upturned as the point of a tat-beb under its covering of gold leaf, the gently curved hip, the rounded thigh, her long, almost too long legs with their delicately moulded ankles, all recalled the slender grace of dancing-girls and musicians. . . .

Ten years after this effusion was penned, one of the Egyptian pavilions at the World Exhibition in Paris in 1867 received several cases of mummies, and Théophile Gautier was among the numerous doctors, scholars, artists and writers who were invited to watch one of the bodies being unwrapped. For the first time he set eyes on a genuine embalmed corpse, and the description it inspired was very different from the one in his novel, though it too was a woman called Nes-Khons. He wrote: "Her enamelled eyes gazed fixedly and terrifyingly ahead, her nose was pushed back at the tip in order to conceal the incision through which her brain had been extracted from her skull; gold leaf sealed her lips. Her trunk revealed reddish skin which developed a blue bloom when it came into contact with the air, like mould on pictures, and in her side could be seen the incision which served to allow the removal of her entrails and from which escaped a trail of aromatic sawdust mixed with resin in small grains resembling colophony, as if it were stuffing from a broken doll. Her thin arms were stretched out and her bony hands with their gilded nails copied the gesture of Venus de Milo with sepulchral modesty." This description is very far from the beautiful idealised mummy of Tahoser in his novel.

The famous French novelist Honoré de Balzac never succumbed to the romantic view of mummies. His references to the topic are obviously based on his actual experience of the bodies displayed at Passalacqua's exhibition, as for example in this comparison in *Le Père Goriot:* "Mademoiselle Michonneau, thin, dried up and cold as a mummy." There are no slender figures or rounded thighs here, no poetic fancies to persuade us of the mummy's attractions, just the cold eye of the realist who in another book, *Les Illusions Perdues,* writes: "Monsieur de Rastignac, who was very well versed in the affairs of Angoulême, had already made two theatre boxes laugh at the expense of that silly mummy whom the Marchionness called 'her cousin.'" Only a poet could be fanciful enough to persuade us that mummies are beautiful.

MUMMIES STILL NOT AT REST

In the nineteenth and twentieth centuries, the mummies still knew no rest. Early archaeological excavations aroused less of a thirst for knowledge than an acquisitive desire to collect objects, an Egyptomania which led in turn to a great expansion in the tomb-robbing industry. Jomard recounts a spine-chilling tale about one of these encounters when he was investigating a hypogeum. It happened when he had already been inside it for some hours, making his way through rooms and galleries heaped with mummies. All of a sudden he heard a noise at the end of a tunnel which he could not explain; as it continued he grew more anxious, and then as he perceived in the darkness a white figure waving a lamp among the corpses his heart nearly failed him. It was a little while before he could gather his senses together and come to the conclusion that the apparition was in fact an Arab clothed in his burnous, who had come to collect his daily supply of goods to sell on the black market. It would have been comic if it were not such a tragic waste of material. At this time too mummies provided fuel for the local people, who would make huge bonfires, visible for quite some distance, at the entrance to the monuments in order to keep themselves warm at night, while in Europe people like Piccini, an Italian merchant, vandalised ancient coffins to provide themselves with panelling for making doors, windows, staircases and floors. Baron Minutoli was not ashamed to admit that all his food was cooked on fires of sarcophagus wood, which was apparently the only wood that his servants could obtain; it was supplied to him by the camel-load, as many as six at a time.

The practice of making fires in tombs continued until quite recent times, with the result that what was recorded by the early archaeologists has in some instances completely vanished. For example, there were some very interesting texts and scenes in the sepulchre of Anher-Khaui at Thebes, which were copied by the German Egyptologist Lepsius, but when Bruyère visited the same spot a few dozen years later he found only blackened ruins destroyed by fire.

The same Bruyère had an unexpected stroke of good fortune when he visited a group of workmen's huts in 1930, and found a whole collection of ancient objects and splendid ornaments from the dim past. The dwellings had in fact been constructed on the site of a cemetery in Deir el-Medina which dated from the Ramessean period, and they were built on top of the tombs because the vaults sheltered people from the heat of the day and provided some protection against cold at night. Families passed on their homes and their precious contents from generation to generation down to the present day.

The final resting-place of the mummies transported away from their native land was often very strange, and none can have been stranger than the one allotted to a group of bodies which were donated to the Louvre by Napoleon's expedition. During the reign of Charles X they began to deteriorate in their coffins, to such an extent that they had to be removed from the reserve collections because they were causing an unbearable smell. They were taken to the nearest burial ground, the gardens of the Louvre beside Perrault's colonnade, and interred for a second time, but were soon disturbed again when those revolutionaries who fell at the barricades nearby during the "three glorious days" of the revolution in 1830 were buried in exactly the same spot. In due course a pillar was erected in the Place de la Bastille to commemorate the three days, and after it was finished in 1840 five hundred and four of those who had died were buried with great ceremony at the foot of the pillar. Not every one of them though was a victim of the revolution, for when the gravediggers came to dig up the bodies they found themselves quite unable to distinguish the French bodies from the Egyptian ones. A few years under the earth had reduced them all to the same condition, so they were all perforce reburied together, which is why some Egyptian mummies came to lie beneath the Bastille column.*

Other mummies suffered the indignity of public unwrapping,

* J. Hillairet: *Dictionnaire historique des rues de Paris*

which was popularised in England around 1830 by a surgeon
and professor of anatomy, T. J. Pettigrew. W. R. Dawson has
recounted how Pettigrew made his first attempt privately at
home in Spring Gardens, with a mummy he had bought at a
public sale. Unfortunately it had been badly embalmed in the
Ptolemaic period and was not in good condition, so there was
very little information he could glean from it. Eventually he obtained two more, one which he bought himself for £23 at an
auction at Sothebys, and one which his friend Saunders had bid
£36 for at the same event. Since his own residence was not really suitable for the task he envisaged, he decided to transfer the
scene of operations to the lecture-hall of Charing Cross Hospital,
where he taught anatomy, and invited a large audience of lords
and other nobility, doctors, archaeologists and travellers to view
the spectacle. From this beginning he went on to examine the
remains of a priestess of the Twenty-first Dynasty which another
of his friends had acquired during the same auction, until finally
after a succession of public unveilings he reached his greatest triumph at a theatre in the Royal College of Surgeons where the
demand for seats was so great that entry had to be restricted to
ticket-holders, and even then such important personalities as the
Archbishop of Canterbury and the Bishop of London failed to
obtain places. In spite of the crowded auditorium there was ab-
solute silence when at one o'clock precisely on Thursday 6 January 1834 Pettigrew and his assistants entered the hall, preceded
by the president and members of the council of the College. The
operation was received with acclaim, and so much enthusiasm
was aroused that Pettigrew decided to present a series of public
lectures on embalming, each one of which would culminate in
the unwrapping of a mummy.

In spite of the publicity which accompanied these events, Pettigrew did in fact contribute a great deal to our knowledge of
the technical process of mummification. There was only one occasion on which he really let his integrity as a scientist suffer,
when he accepted an invitation from a speculator called Athanasi who offered to let him perform an autopsy on a mummy he
owned. Perhaps it was simply an error of judgment on Pettigrew's part. In any event, let us hope that he was not a party to
drawing up the prospectus for the event, which announced:

"Giovanni d'Athanasi respectfully informs the public that on the evening of Monday 10 April next at five o'clock, the most interesting mummy which has ever been discovered in Egypt will be unwrapped in the large room at Exeter Hall." Right at the end, in small letters, was written: "Tickets, with a description of the mummy, are now on sale from Giovanni d'Athanasi, at No. 3, Wellington Street, Strand. A limited number of seats will be reserved immediately around the tables on which the mummy will be placed, at a price of six shillings. Places on the balcony and on the platform, four shillings. All other places, in the middle of the hall and in the gallery: two shillings and six pence." On the appointed day five or six hundred people crowded into the hall to watch Pettigrew at grips with the mummy, which proved to be the hardest he had dealt with in his career. All his efforts with hammer, chisel and knife failed to crack the hard shell of resin which encased the mummy, and after three hours of struggling it had to be announced that the operation would be continued elsewhere and the results announced later. Nonetheless Pettigrew's reputation was unscathed, and he was even obliged on one occasion to conduct the operation in reverse, as it were, and himself make a mummy. This was at the request of Alexander, tenth Duke of Hamilton, who before his death on 18 August 1852 in London had had himself built an enormous mausoleum in the gardens of his residence, and specified in his will that he should be embalmed by Pettigrew and placed in an Egyptian sarcophagus. This strange request was duly fulfilled.

The United States also had an interest in mummies, though in one particular case it was more financial than scientific, and led to some unfortunate consequences. Pulp for making paper could be produced from the shrouds and bandages of mummies, and towards the end of the nineteenth century an astute American dealer, Augustus Stanwood, who owned some paper mills in Maine, started producing paper from rags, which is very profitable. All went well until he had the idea of using linen and material from mummies, which he procured from Bedouins who were accustomed to trading in mummies. Unfortunately the resin in the cloth caused the paper to come out brown, and Stanwood could devise no method of whitening it. He was determined not to discard it, so he turned it into brown wrapping-paper and sold it to food retailers. Again the enterprise was successful, American housewives bought their meat or their groceries oblivious of the fact that they were wrapped in paper made from Egyptian funerary linen, and all might have continued happily if an epidemic of cholera had not broken out, which was soon traced by the authorities back to Stanwood's mill. No more paper was made from mummies, and nothing is known of the fate of the actual bodies.‡

Even mummies whose final destination was to be a museum abroad often did not arrive there without undergoing further trials and tribulations. The great royal mummies from the cachette at Deir el-Bahri, whom we last left neatly lined up in rows at the entrance to their sepulchre as Brugsch and Ahmed Effendi Kamal were organising the workers bringing them out and taking stock of the objects with them, were next taken from the Valley of the Kings to Luxor, which meant that they had to traverse the dusty plains of Thebes in the paralysing July heat. It took more than a dozen men to lift each coffin, and the journey from the mountain to the riverside took an exhausting seven or eight hours. Even under these circumstances, a few small objects were stolen from the mummies and disappeared during the journey, but the police were watching and soon recovered them, all except a basket containing some fifty figurines in blue enamel which now probably grace the private collections of a privileged few. By the evening of 11 July 1881, the entire caravan of mummies, coffins and tomb-equipment had reached Luxor. The mummies were carefully wrapped in matting, ready to leave again by boat, but it was three days before the steamer Menshieh which belonged to Cairo Museum arrived. Everything was quickly transported aboard and the boat set out again along the Nile, passing for the first twenty miles of its journey from Luxor to Qift between lines of wild-haired women uttering piercing wails and men firing off guns. Thus the fellahin saluted the final passing of their ancient kings.

When they arrived in Cairo at the Boulaq Museum, the former Museum of Egyptian Antiquities, the rooms were so crowded that it was difficult to find place for them and so the bodies were

‡ M. M. Pace, *Wrapped for Eternity*, MacGraw Hill, 1974

put temporarily in a central hall and the objects with them into store. It took four years to make a detailed inventory of everything from the hypogeum, during which time the museum was enlarged, extra rooms were added, and twelve glass cases were installed to take the most interesting mummies, while the best of the other items were put in cabinets.

Soon after the mummies arrived Brugsch, without telling Maspéro, took it upon himself to unwrap the mummy of Thutmosis III, an offence which he repeated in September 1873 when he did the same for Queen Nefertari, though with more excuse because decomposition had set in and the mummy was beginning to smell badly. This decided Maspéro to examine all the mummies, which he did, beginning with Ramesses II and leaving out only Amenophis I whose bandaging was exceptionally fine. Even then in 1914, just thirty-three years after the mummies had been brought out of their tombs, they were in poor condition, and Maspéro wrote: "They have suffered a great deal since they were discovered, and however much care was taken to protect them with preservatives, most of them have been subject to attack by insects; the day is not far off when they may be totally destroyed." However, today's visitors can still view them in the new Egyptian Museum in Room 52, where they were transferred from the Boulaq Museum.

One of the few mummies to remain in his tomb is Tutankhamun, although most of his funerary equipment and adornments were taken away. Amenophis II had an equally troubled though different fate after he had been discovered by Loret in 1898 among the find of Eighteenth Dynasty pharaohs who had been missing from the Deir el-Bahri cachette. Loret was ordered by the Minister to leave the mummies as they were and to wall up the hypogeum. Even in 1900 when permission was eventually given to reopen the tomb and bring the royal mummies to the museum, Amenophis was excepted and remained entombed in his sarcophagus along with four other anonymous mummies, of which three were put back in the recess where they had been found originally and one which was a black corpse with a contorted face and a split skull, possibly a robber, was laid in a funerary barque. A footbridge was erected to allow tourists to cross the dangerous shafts on the way to the royal mummy, and solid wrought iron gates were placed in position to safeguard the treasures outside visiting hours. Whoever devised the precautions, however, did not take into account the rumours which were spreading locally, to the effect that the mummies were laden with jewellery. The temptation was strong, and soon the inevitable occurred.

It was on 24 November 1901 that three night watchmen who were eating their dinner peacefully in tomb no. 10 were surprised by thirteen armed and masked men. They were forced to stay where they were, guarded at gun-point by six of the men while the other seven departed for Amenophis II's tomb, and soon returned with their booty. All the bandits then fled along a path across the hills in the direction of Medinet Habu, courageously chased by the watchmen until the latter were deterred by gun-shots and wisely decided to turn back and finish their dinner. One of them then went off to tell the whole story to an inspector, who immediately rushed to the scene and established that the black mummy on the boat had been broken into pieces, the boat stolen, and the king's mummy itself torn open.

The next day under a stream of questions the watchmen admitted that they had recognised three men among the thirteen, the same Mohamed Abd el-Rassul whom we have already encountered stealing in the first chapter of this book and two others, Abdrachman Ahmed Abd el-Rassul and Mohamed Abdrachman, all three from Qurna. They were immediately arrested, but the police decided to keep an eye on the three watchmen as they suspected that some of the details of their story were not accurate. Indeed, when Carter examined Amenophis II he realised that the bandages had been cut in the exact places where jewellery would be found, and that the damage must therefore have been carried out by people with expert knowledge. He at once resolved to carry out a full investigation to establish precisely what had happened, and soon discovered that the padlock on the entrance gate had been closed by the robbers with such care that they had even disguised the marks of their break-in with little strips of lead and resin, in exactly the same way they had done a few days earlier in a private tomb. It was clear that this did not tally with the watchmen's story of a hasty flight after the robbery. Further examination of the scene provided confirmation of Mohamed Abd el-Rassul's presence in the tomb, for he had left behind perfect prints of his bare feet, but it did not help to clarify the watchmen's role. It was possible that they had been asleep, or had left their posts for a short while. Other watchmen posted at a distance away confirmed that shots had been fired on the night of the robbery but were unable to say by whom, and so it was only when the tomb watchmen's guns were examined that it was proved that they had been recently fired, and consequently that the watchmen must have been accomplices in the crime.

Only a few minor obstacles now stood in Amenophis II's way before he could reach his last home in the Museum where he was to be placed in 1931 in a glass case well protected from thieves and amidst his peers. He was brought by boat to the gates of Cairo, only to be faced with a demand for payment of the city dues which were exacted on all goods entering the city. The official had some difficulty in deciding on the amount as mummies, royal or otherwise, did not figure under any heading in his register, but he insisted that a charge must be paid and finally assessed the sum by reference to the nearest commodity he could find—dried fish.

Not all voyages made by mummies had such a happy ending, and certainly not the one made by a mummy belonging to an English lord which crossed the Atlantic in April 1912. This mummy had a particularly magnificent wooden sarcophagus, and as a special concession in view of its value it had been stowed behind the captain's bridge rather than in an ordinary baggage room.† Unfortunately this precaution proved worthless when the ship entered an icefield near Newfoundland and on the night of the 14 April came into collision with a gigantic iceberg which ripped it open for a hundred yards down its side. Less than three hours later the ship's stern rose up into the air while the vessel gradually sank, bow first, into the water, taking with her four thousand one hundred and ninety passengers and one mummy. That vessel was the famous Titanic, and so it was that an ancient Egyptian came to his last resting-place three miles under the Atlantic.

† P. Vandenberg: *La Malédiction des momies*, 1975, Belfond

Even if a mummy survived for thousands of years and escaped damage from looters looking for treasure, avoided incineration, was sufficiently well embalmed not to fall to dust when taken out of its tomb, and did not succumb to the hazards of a long journey to some museum, it was not immune to other accidents. One very ancient mummy which Egyptologists were particularly anxious to preserve was literally blasted out of its glass case in the Royal College of Surgeons in London when a bomb fell on it in 1941 and pulverised everything.

Even today, the authorities have not succeeded in their efforts to stamp out theft from archaeological sites which are being excavated. No regulations can prevent the occasional workman from pilfering objects, not even if they were to revert to the methods of the nineteenth century when one English explorer compelled his workers to swallow a purgative because he suspected them of stealing some scarab-amulets. During the Second World War the authorities relaxed their vigilance, which led to the loss of some valuable items especially from the site at Tanis which Montet had been investigating up to 1939. Much of his valuable find from the Twenty-first Dynasty tombs had already been transported by lorry to Cairo Museum, but after he left the remainder was guarded only by a few soldiers who later slackened their surveillance when it was thought that the French mission was never going to return. Soon burglars forced an entry into Montet's home near the site, rifled the store-rooms and made a clean sweep of all the valuable objects which had not been removed. Thieves also broke into Psusenne's tomb, but fortunately they did not discover its treasures which were only brought to light when the French Egyptologists resumed their exploration in 1946.

Theft was not always a profitable occupation. The bare skeleton of a man found by Egyptologists excavating at Giza in 1969 was obviously that of a robber who had either died of natural causes while he was on the point of leaving with the booty or was killed by watchmen who surprised him in the act. He was lying inside the sarcophagus in a curious position, with one arm raised towards the lid which had been partially pushed back, and his hand hanging down inside. At first he was presumed to be a tomb robber from ancient times, but when archaeologists looked more closely at the rotted scraps of clothing which still clung to his body they found to their astonishment fragments of a diary whose date was still decipherable: 1944. Clearly he was a contemporary thief who, if he had not been overtaken by the vengeance of the Egyptian gods, had certainly met with a brutally sudden end.‡

In modern times the most extraordinary robbery must be the one revealed in February 1973 by a German press agency which announced that five thousand tombs of the pharaonic period had been rifled. The number was undoubtedly exaggerated but the report itself was not without foundation. As Vandenberg recounts the story†, the police first became suspicious when they were told that shots had been heard at Beni Suef, seventy-five miles to the south of Cairo. When they went to investigate at dusk the same day their searchlight revealed extensive diggings in the middle of the desert. They were lucky enough to catch three men as they were coming back up a ladder which led down into a grave, and these quickly confessed all. Apparently they had found a tomb a few months previously which was richly equipped and had never been touched. One discovery led to another, and soon they all gave up their jobs at the cotton factory where they were employed in order to concentrate on extracting the utmost from their unexpected find. It proved to be so rich that they had to take on additional labour which was employed in shifts working day and night. In the space of a short time their lives changed completely, and instead of being miserably poor they found themselves wealthier than they had ever dreamed. Unfortunately for them, they fell out among themselves, as so often happens. The occasion of their downfall was actually the discovery of another tomb more splendid than any of the others, containing treasure which the newly-employed labourers thought they had a right to share. The original finders selfishly decided to appropriate most of the contents themselves by excavating the tomb secretly without informing their companions who, however, were suspicious and decided to keep a look-out. When the deception was discovered, there was a flurry

‡ M. M. Pace: *op. cit.*
† P. Vandenberg: *op. cit.*

of gun-shots which finally gave the game away and led to the apprehension of the thieves.

On this occasion the crime was discovered, but for every clandestine excavation which comes to light there must be many others which are never exposed. Such huge profits can be made from the ancient Egyptian tombs that there is no hope of suppressing the frantic search for treasure. It is frightening to think how many vital documents may have been lost or destroyed by thieves who know that they have little monetary value when offered for sale illicitly.

CHAPTER 9

END OF THE LEGENDS

People who are attracted to the occult have always found something peculiarly fascinating in Egyptian civilisation and its religion. They want to believe in the existence of a supernatural force whose workings are beyond their comprehension so they fasten eagerly on to the mysteries of Egypt and fail to notice that there is often a perfectly simple explanation for the strange phenomena they encounter. In their enthusiasm they ignore the laws of nature and forget their knowledge of history and religion. Such people fall an easy prey to the mystique which maintains that Egyptian priests somehow held the key to all the secrets of the universe, which needless to say they guarded jealously for themselves, and that they were the privileged recipients of lore which would make our own scientific progress look insignificant by comparison. It is not difficult to produce correlations between objects, beings and the cosmos which lend verisimilitude to these theories.

One particular branch of the resulting pseudo-science, pyramidology, has given rise to the most extraordinary hotchpotch of esoteric hypotheses based on a calculation of the relationship between figures derived from the Bible and the dimensions of the pyramids, the angle of their walls, the arrangement of their inner chambers, and the direction of the corridors inside. These are ingeniously manipulated to arrive at various geodesic and astronomic conclusions which were no doubt very far from the minds of the original builders. It is highly probable that one could produce similar interesting results by juggling with the measurements of any well-known building such as the Tower of London or the Empire State Building.

It is worth noting that the alleged science of symbolist Egyptology, like all other branches of the occult, has never brought to light any fresh information or opened up any avenues of enquiry that did not already exist. On the contrary, it has merely battened on to new discoveries after the event and made use of them to demonstrate what has been proved already. For instance when Hertzian waves were discovered, immediately mysterious waves were found to be emanating from objects uncovered in the course of excavation; and when X-rays were invented, the same objects started giving off rays; while the advance of atomic science has produced claims that the ancient Egyptians had prior knowledge of atoms too.

The layman is easily deceived by a concoction of magic and mystery, overlaid with a few apparently scientific facts slanted to lend authenticity to the brew, and flavoured with a soupçon of some real knowledge to give it a genuine tang. Even if he is incredulous to start with, he can eventually be convinced without a shadow of definite proof if he is bombarded with constant reiteration of so-called facts. It is hard in this troubled day and age to resist the consolations offered by the pseudo-sciences, and no-one can be blamed for succumbing. Nevertheless, it is preferable to take a stand on the side of objective reality, however thankless such a stand may be.

MIRACULOUSLY PRESERVED CORN

The myth that the Egyptians had discovered some miraculous method of preserving corn derives from the fact that the little figurines of Osiris found in tombs were sometimes covered with dried-up vegetation (Fig. 45). These figurines were either statuettes modelled from clay in the shape of the god and lying on a little bed, or they were Osiris-shaped moulds filled with sand or earth, in which a few seeds were sown and watered. Inside the tomb the grain germinated, transforming the god into a small field of greenery in the shape of his silhouette, and clearly illustrating that Osiris was not only the god of death but also, through his resurrection, a powerful instrument of earth's destiny. At the time of the floods, he was the water which made the fields green again, he died at the end of the harvest and he was reborn with the following year's growth. The functions of the god of death were inextricably linked with the rebirth of nature, so clearly the Osiris figurines had a very important significance for mummies.

Some enthusiasts proceeded from these facts to claim that the grains of corn or barley found in tombs are cable of germination. Count Sternberg, for example, announced that he had succeeded in germinating two grains from pharaonic times. It is quite true that these grains, which were purposely placed in sachets or vases in the tombs to nourish the dead, often looked in good condition even if they had gone a little brown, and several botanists thought that they had successfully grown plants from them. From this it was but a short step to the theory that the Egyptians had invented a method of preserving seeds indefinitely, though the fact of the matter was that none of the seeds was older than a few months and the experimenters had been deceived. It took the persistent efforts of scientists such as Brocq-Rousseu and

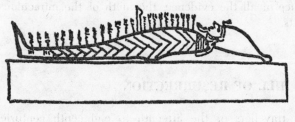

Fig. 45. Osiris sprouting vegetation.

Gain to show that the theories were absurd, by taking seeds from various sources and trying to grow them under the best of conditions. No matter whether the seeds they planted came from the Boulaq Museum and were from two to five thousand years old, or from the Pachacamac cemetery in Peru, around five hundred years old, or from an eighteenth century herbarium of our own civilisation, not one of them sprouted. Even with grains only fifteen years old, the proportion that could be made to germinate was minute; Alphonse de Candolle was successful with only seventeen out of three hundred and sxity-eight different kinds. The most ancient seed to have survived was one from the Tournefort herbarium, which sprouted after a hundred years.

It is common knowledge that a seed is basically made up of two parts, the embryo which will develop into the future plant, and the albumen which is a store of food to nourish the embryo when it starts to grow. During the early stages the little plant manufactures enzymes to break down the albumen for itself, and no matter how old the seed is its food stores remain intact and useable, the starch retains its properties and could still be used in bread-making. On the other hand the enzymes are much more fragile and though they have been found in nineteenth century seeds they are completely absent from seeds dating from further back. This means that the embryo could no longer make use of its food stores and so could never develop. In addition, though the network of plant cells may survive, the actual cells deteriorate with age and no longer show signs of life.

A great deal of research has been carried out since the beginning of the century in this area. The most recent experiment was carried out by an Englishman, Parker, whose seeds simply shrivelled up and went mouldy after fifteen days. Nonetheless, in the face of all the evidence, the myth of the miraculous grain persists.

THE HILL OF RESURRECTION

Many travellers of the fifteenth to eighteenth centuries who visited Egypt recounted the tale of a "miracle" which took place every year on Good Friday or a few days before or after, on a little sandy hill not far to the south of Cairo. The details of the happening recalled the resurrection of Christ, and it was said that on this spot near the Nile one could see the dead rising from their tombs. Crowds of Christians gathered in the cemetery there every year to see the spectacle, joined by some Jews and even Turks, of whom Thévenot wrote in 1727: "They came in procession with all their banners, because there was a Sheik buried there whose bones, so they said, rose up every year. Like the others, they go to say their prayers devoutly."

Not all the travellers who described these events had actually seen them with their own eyes, and indeed some of them introduced a distinctly sceptical note into their accounts. Finally one of them succeeded in exposing the swindle. He, like the rest, had made the journey to the spot and was walking along the sand when suddenly a local man pointed behind him. He turned round, and there in the sand was an arm, a leg, sometimes a head and sometimes a whole trunk protruding from the ground. It was an amazing sight, though curiously no-one had ever succeeded in catching sight of a mummy actually emerging from the sand, either because the mummies were there beforehand or because the traveller was looking in another direction at the crucial moment. This particular traveller, a Frenchman, was determined to unveil the fraud if there was one, so he cunningly turned round suddenly before any signal was made to him, and saw an Egyptian holding a mummy's limb under his jacket. It turned out that the local people used to steal mummies from the cemetery, and then plant bits of them here and there to deceive the gullible visitors. The whole show was put on by boatmen who used to prepare the ground the night before and then make their profits the following day from those who wished to cross the Nile to view the apparitions.

THE MUMMY THAT MOVED

Another curious incident concerned one of the bodies of the pharaohs which Maspéro had removed from the cachette at Deir el-Bahri in 1881. When the mummies were first brought out into the open they were left under strict surveillance at the entrance to the tombs, and then had to be moved along as more bodies were recovered. One of the biggest was Ramesses I, a tall mummy in a very good state of preservation, who was carefully placed in a shady spot to await transfer on to the boat. He lay there so peacefully, with his arms stretched out down his sides, that he almost looked as if he was asleep like the labourers who had stopped working at mid-day to take a siesta while the sun was at its height. When they woke up and returned to collect the pharaoh, they were terrified to see that one of his arms was raised and pointing at them as if he was threatening them. All their old superstitions flooded back into their minds, panic set in, and it took the directors of the excavations to exert sufficient authority to calm them. When they set about investigating what had really happened, they perceived that the mummy, which started off in the shade, had later received the full rays of the sun and its tissues had retracted in the heat so much that its arm rose up. The unnerving phenomenon was soon explained to everyone's satisfaction, though it proved very difficult to bring the arm back down to its original position.

THE PENALTY FOR SACRILEGE

We have seen that native Egyptians often used to build their dwellings on top of a tomb, and the necropolis at Dira Abu 'n-Naga provided a convenient site for various families to take up residence. One man, Ahmed ibn Soliman, built his little house on the slope of the hill in such a way that the room at the back of it was in fact part of an ancient tomb dug out of the rock and served both as a stable and a storeroom, which was convenient because it was cool.

The family had a relative called Ali Yunis who one day early in November 1905 came to clear out the cave. While he was working, he stumbled across a long-forgotten hidden entrance to a corridor which led down under the earth and conceivably to buried treasure. Immediately he started on the task of clearing away the earth and stone slabs, without telling his relatives what he was doing, and one day when no-one was at home he finally succeeded in clearing a narrow passage into the secret room. He never emerged again. Naturally his wife was alarmed when he did not return home, but it was the following day before she went to the cave to see if she could find out what had happened to him. Of course she soon saw the tunnel leading down into the earth, and decided to see where it led. She too was never seen alive again. By this time tongues were beginning to wag, and the next person to investigate was Ali Yunis' mother-in-law who took two of Ali's cousins with her. They also disappeared and did not return, to the general alarm of the neighbourhood. Two courageous men volunteered to try and see what could have occurred, and set off sensibly carrying candles. After they had gone three yards the tunnel turned sharply to the left and then almost immediately left again. By this time the candles were beginning to quiver, but by their dim light the two men could just make out one of the cousins, barely alive and gasping for breath. They pulled him out into the fresh air but he died a few seconds later.

The authorities were alerted to the mysterious disappearances and sent the police together with Mursi Effendi Halim, district inspector of antiquities, to investigate the affair. The latter took four policemen with him and started down the corridor, past the spot where the dying cousin had been discovered, around a few more corners, and into a room whose ceiling was supported by crudely carved pillars. The air was thick with fumes and the light from their oil-lamps was fading, but they managed to catch a glimpse of the bodies of the other unfortunate people who had ventured in before them. They made a superhuman effort to reach them, but the air was so poisonous that they were overcome with nausea and had to drag themselves out. When they staggered from the cave they were in such a dreadful state that no-one else dared venture inside, and the rumour quickly spread that an evil genie who guarded the riches in the cave had strangled the unwelcome visitors.

In fact of course the deaths were due to inhaling the poisonous gases which had accumulated in the tomb, a fact which was soon discovered by the health department. Weigall, the archaeologist, suggested bringing in a machine to pump out the air but in the end the Minister of the Interior decided to leave the bodies where they lay and to wall up the passage. Now the bodies of four present-day Egyptians lie inside a pharaoh's tomb, providing fuel for more myths about the unhappy fate which awaits those who venture to disturb the ancient mummies' rest.

A similar accident nearly befell Gabra, the Egyptologist, and his assistants when they were investigating the great gallery of the ibis cemetery at Tuna el-Gebel. After they had succeeded in clearing the seventy-five steps of the monumental stairway, they eagerly entered the tunnel to explore, but as soon as they reached the antechamber they found themselves stricken by terrible headaches and had to make their way outside as quickly as possible. It took three days before they felt well enough to venture inside again, and by this time the air had cleared and they could carry on their excavations without any ill effects. However, the workers were convinced that there was a magic spell inscribed on the gallery wall which condemned to death all those who committed the sacrilege of entering the sanctuary, which was reserved for the priests of the god Thoth.

These strange incidents and others like them have given rise to a plethora of superstitious myths and pseudo-scientific theories, the former due to man's fascination with the supernatural and the latter to the belief that Egyptian priests were the possessors of a secret store of knowledge. It has been seriously suggested that the priests knew how to produce prussic acid—the same as used in capital punishment in the United States—which was brushed onto the mummies and gave off poisonous fumes which would have killed anyone daring to profane the tombs. As proof, the ancient tomb-robbers were supposed to have pierced a fist-sized opening into the walls of a tomb to allow the gases to escape from the airtight chamber before they entered it. Of course it is possible that the Egyptians knew about this acid, and possible to cite as additional evidence a sentence found in an old papyrus in the Louvre which says: "Do not pronounce the name of Iao on pain of death from the peach-tree." This phrase has been interpreted as meaning that to pronounce the god's name, or to reveal his holy secrets, is to incur death by poisoning, and it is true that prussic acid can be extracted from the leaf and kernel of the peach. However, if the embalmers had really brushed the mummy bandaging with oil from bitter almonds, which gives off prussic acid when it comes into contact with the air, then they themselves would have died in the process. In any case, no other papyrus has yielded a similar clue, and no trace of oil of bitter almonds has been found on mummies.

It is much more likely that in tombs which had been sealed for thousands of years the combination of lack of oxygen, shown by the candles going out, and an accumulation of gases from decomposed bodies proved lethal. There is no basis for supposing that the secret wisdom of the priests had anything to do with the matter.

THE CURSE OF TUTANKHAMUN

Perhaps the most famous legend of all concerns Tutankhamun, and began with the death of one of those most intimately connected with his discovery, Lord Carnarvon. Lord Carnarvon was a wealthy Englishman who, in spite of his poor physical health, had a passion for motor sports and owned several fast cars which he used to race. Then unfortunately one day he skidded and crashed in Germany. He was dangerously burned and in a coma for some time after he was rescued, and indeed only recovered after he had undergone several operations. After a lengthy convalescence it was clear he would never be fit enough to race his cars again, yet he was still avid for new experiences. Unfortunately respiratory troubles continued to plague him, so in the end on the advice of his doctor he decided to visit Egypt, where it was hoped that the warm dry climate would improve his health.

He arrived there in 1902 and was immediately attracted to Egyptology. Not only was his curiosity aroused, but he also thought that funding excavations might prove a convenient way of increasing his wealth. Consequently he soon persuaded Maspéro, who was then Director of the Antiquities Service, to give a concession to himself and Howard Carter, a well-known Egyptologist. The partnership between the latter and his wealthy patron was destined to become famous throughout the world.

At first, Lord Carnarvon visited the site infrequently, and he was not present when Carter finally discovered the entrance to Tutankhamun's tomb on 4 November 1922. A message was hastily dispatched to Highclere, his residence in England to which he had returned for the hunting season. Immediately Carnarvon set out for Luxor, where he arrived on 23 November, and two days later he reached the tomb and participated in the opening. He was so impressed by what he saw that he returned to England only for the Christmas festivities, and then travelled straight back to Egypt to assist in disinterring the funerary equipment from the tomb in the Valley of the Kings.

Towards mid-March he was bitten by a mosquito. At first he thought nothing of it, but then the infection began to spread and he had to be taken to Cairo. For a while his health showed an improvement, until pneumonia set in, when it began to look as if his weak constitution could not withstand the illness. His son, the young Lord Porchester, was summoned from India where he was an officer in the army, and such was Lord Carnarvon's prestige that a boat was specially diverted to bring him as quickly as possible to Egypt. During the whole journey Moslem pilgrims prayed on the bridge of the boat for the noble lord's recovery, but their prayers were in vain for he had already lost consciousness by the time his son arrived in Cairo. His wife, Lady Almina, and Howard Carter had both collapsed at his bedside. At five to two in the early hours of the morning of 5 April 1922 he died, and so he never saw the mummy of the young king himself or his dazzling sarcophaguses.

An exact diagnosis of the disease which killed him is not possible at such a distance in time, though the evidence we possess suggests that the infection which started from a bite on his face could easily have spread to the veins in his brain, as was quite common at that time, or else it might have given to rise to septicaemia which in those days before the advent of antibiotics was usually fatal.

After his death his son, the sixth Earl of Carnarvon, related two very strange tales, based on the kind of coincidences which persuade the credulous that supernatural forces must be involved. In the first, he said that just as Lord Carnarvon was breathing his last all the lights of Cairo suddenly went out, and though the break-down lasted for three minutes no-one in the electricity service was able to provide any explanation. At the same time, the deceased man's faithful dog far away in Highclere uttered a long drawn out howl, without any apparent reason, and then sat up on its hind legs and died. There were very few witnesses to the dog's death, but even if we admit that it took place there can be no possible connection with the curse of the pharaohs. As for the other coincidence, one can only say that in any large city there will be one or more deaths which take place at the same time as any electricity break-down, in Lord Carnarvon's case or any other. The facts as they stand are simply not sufficient to justify any conjectures about the evil influence of some power beyond the grave.

Nevertheless the conjectures spread, and were given added fuel when six months later Lord Carnarvon's half-brother, Colonel Aubrey, and the nurse who kept watch over Carnarvon while he was dying both expired. The deaths were given sensational treatment in the press. Soon they were able to add another fatality to their list, when Dr. Archibald Douglas Reed died in 1924 after he had returned to England from a trip to Egypt to x-ray Tutankhamun's mummy. He was followed by Jay-Gould, an American millionaire and friend of Lord Carnarvon, who was afflicted with a terrible fever the day after he had persuaded Carter to show him the tomb, and died twenty-four hours later. Doctors declared that he had died of the plague, but this perfectly natural explanation did not satisfy people who were persuaded that some supernatural power was at work. No doubt they thought their views were vindicated when Joel Woolf, an English businessman, died in identical circumstances, though on this occasion the victim did not succumb immediately but died on the boat on his way home. The next on the list was a Canadian tourist. Professor La Fleur, who was a professor of English literature and had no connection with Egyptology. He simply paid a visit to the tomb as a result of the world-wide publicity it had received, and died twenty-four hours later. Then in 1926 Georges Bénédite, head Keeper of the Department of Antiquities of the Louvre, perished of pneumonia that he had contracted in the Valley of the Kings, followed quite shortly by Arthur C. Mace, assistant keeper in the Metropolitan Museum of Art in New York, who had helped Carter to break through the wall of the funerary chamber. This of course was said to have signed his death warrant!

For three years the pharaoh's anger seemed to have abated, until in 1929 it erupted again. First to die was Lady Almina, Lord Carnarvon's wife, and then came Richard Bethell, Carter's secretary, who was discovered dead in bed one morning from a heart attack. According to Vandenberg, Bethell's father was so grieved that he threw himself out of a seventh floor window. Unfortunately the trail of death did not end with him, for the hearse carrying Bethell senior's coffin ran over an innocent little boy.

In all, between seventeen and twenty-five victims are alleged to have paid the penalty for profaning Tutankhamun's grave. Some of them like Bethell and Mace were comparatively young when they died—Bethell was only forty-five and Mace was fifty-two. As against that, others had reached a good age. Lord Carnarvon and Bénédite, for instance, were aged respectively fifty-seven and sixty-nine years. Also, it is very odd that the man who first violated the tomb and who was the author of the whole enterprise, Carter himself, entirely escaped Tutankhamun's wrath and lived on for sixteen years until he died in 1939 at the age of sixty-five. Dr. Evelyn White, one of the first to have entered the grave, survived for another twenty years after that, though it is true that the way in which she died provided further nourishment for the myth of the curse. She hanged herself tragically after writing to her family: "I have succumbed to a curse which has forced me to depart from this life." Her fate may have been unusual but it is not inexplicable. After all, even Egyptologists may be driven to commit suicide by a serious bout of depression, and it is not surprising in these circumstances that the preoccupations Dr. White displayed in her last letter were closely connected with her work.

Others who died include Hall, an artist, and Callender, Carter's assistant, who perished in 1930 and 1931 respectively, though there was another artist called Hauser who survived until

1960. P. Lacau, who had been present at the opening of the tomb and who had deciphered many of the inscriptions was still working at the age of eighty-four. He died in 1963. Sir Alan Gardner, the English author of a famous Egyptian grammar, who had also attended the opening, remained active up to the age of seventy-four, when he died in the same year as Lacau. Dr. Douglas Derry, who had committed the sacrilege of unwrapping the pharaoh, also lived for many years pursuing his career until he died peacefully aged eighty. Others may not have lived for so long, but it would be stretching coincidence to claim that it was the effect of a curse which brought Lucas to his death twenty-two years after the tomb was opened. Lucas was the chemist attached to the Cairo Antiquities Service through whose hands passed most of the valuable items from the tomb. Engelbach, Chief Inspector of Antiquities in Upper Egypt, died twenty-three years after the event while the expedition's photographer, Burton, only died after the second world war. Gustave Lefèvre, who as Head Keeper of Cairo Museum had organised the display of all treasures, enjoyed a full life and died in 1957 at the age of sixty-eight.

For someone whose wrath was reputed to be so fearful, Tutankhamun seems to have displayed a remarkable indulgence towards many of those who violated his last rest. Whether it was he or a god watching over him who was responsibile for putting the curse into effect, the results were very erratic. Of course all the stories are pure moonshine, though if you believe in them it ought to seem odd to you that it was only Tutankhamun who displayed these extraordinary powers, while none of the other great royal mummies from Deir el-Bahri and Tanis exacted any retribution for the damage they suffered.

Some people have sought a more rational explanation for the unusual circumstances surrounding several of the deaths, and have put forward the theory that the cause lay in an unknown virus which could have been harboured by the mummy. At first the theory looked attractive, especially when it was proved that a Coptic mummy was the source of a virus which started a small epidemic in the Antiquities Service in 1962. However, it transpired in the end that the virus had been passed on by a man who was already afflicted with the disease when he handled the mummy in question. It is not easy to cultivate a virus, even on living tissue, and it would be impossible to do so on dead tissue, so in the absence of any evidence that Tutankhamum was handled by someone who was already infected this theory must be dismissed.

Another suggestion blames the deaths on something like the histoplasmosis which attacks speleologists. This is a disease of the lungs which produces symptoms similar to pneumonia and is caused by a microscopic fungus with an affinity for the intestine of the bat. It is found in bats' droppings in caves, and infects man when he breathes in the particles floating in the air. This is an ingenious idea, and explains why the disease does not attack everyone by virtue of the fact that people like Lord Carnarvon and Bénédite who are known to have suffered previously from lung infections would naturally be more vulnerable. Unfortunately it is not the answer to the mystery because as we know Tutankhamum's tomb had been hermetically sealed for nearly three thousand years and could not possibly have harboured either bats or living fungi for that length of time.

So far therefore neither medical science nor supernatural agencies have been able to furnish a common cause for all the deaths connected with the discovery of Tutankhamun's tomb, and really there is no reason to suppose that they should.

In the last analysis all these mysterious phenomena turn out to have quite a rational explanation. Nonetheless a substantial body of esoteric literature has grown up around the subject of mummies, and mummification continues to exert a compelling attraction. Even without the trappings of magic and the occult sciences, the unvarnished truth is sufficiently fascinating to satisfy the dreams of all who aspire to uncover the secrets of Ancient Egypt.

CHAPTER 10

SOURCES OF OUR KNOWLEDGE

The sources of our information about mummification range from the earliest written Egyptian documents that have survived, through the accounts that have come down to us from Greek and Roman times, the adventures of early European explorers in Egypt, down to the more sober expeditions which were the forerunners of today's teams of researchers. The fascination of the subject has never dwindled, and where in 1929 Dawson called attention to no less than one hundred and sixty references in a bibliography of publications about mummification (which was not an exhaustive list), the total now would certainly exceed a thousand.

THE EARLIEST GUIDE TO EMBALMING

One would expect most details of the method of embalming corpses to come from the Egyptians themselves, but unfortunately they seem to have written very little on the subject. There is the well-known "Ritual of opening the mouth," which is depicted in Theban tombs in the form of murals with written commentaries: this is a funeral rite concerned not with actual mummification but with the gestures to perform just before the burial so as to give life to the mouth. In the same way the "Books of Breathing" from a later period are intended to show how to restore the mummy's respiratory functions. Then there are a few inscriptions on stelae or on the inside walls of Old Kingdom tombs, which call on the living, the funeral priests and especially the "people of the embalming chamber" to prepare the corpse and watch over it, but the set formulae they use are concerned to intimidate or encourage the living to carry out their duties and do not detail the actual techniques of mummification.

There are only two manuscripts extant which, if they had been complete, might have spelled out for us the ways of preserving bodies in use in ancient Egypt. Unfortunately the beginning of both of them is missing, so we shall never know what significant information they might have contained. The first one is preserved in Cairo Museum under the name Third Boulaq Papyrus, and came from a collective tomb from the later Theban period. Unrolled, it measures more than two yards long and eleven inches wide, while the second, of unknown origin and preserved in the Louvre Museum as exhibit No. 5 158 is barely nineteen inches long; it is even less complete and consists of only the last pages of the Third Boulaq Papyrus. The Louvre papyrus certainly seems to have been used by an embalmer, perhaps as a manual, for it is covered with manuscript notes in demotic writing summing up each paragraph.

The two documents, which deal with the same topic, are together referred to as the "Rites of Embalming." Paleographic studies have shown them to date only from the first century of our era, but the particular phraseology which they both use leaves no doubt that they are copies of an older document from the New Kingdom (1580–1085 B.C.). Both are divided into paragraphs marked by headings in red ink, and each paragraph is itself subdivided into two parts: the first is a technical statement of the different stages of embalming and wrapping, introduced by the phrase "Following that . . ."; the second lists the corresponding ritual formulae to be pronounced, beginning "Words to say after that . . ." the sections laying down the various liturgies are of unequal length, since for example the text to be recited during a simple anointing of the head is a great deal shorter than that for the long operation of wrapping the legs. One is tempted to imagine that the missing part of the text described the different stages of evisceration, removal of the brain and dehydration, but it would be a dangerous assumption for the Egyptians virtually never showed the first steps of embalming in their reliefs or their paintings. Perhaps there were religious or magical prohibitions which would account for the absence of illustrations of the early stages of mummification.

The Rites of Embalming deals with its subject under the ten following headings:

—First anointing of the head.
—Perfuming the body (except for the head).
—Depositing the viscera in a vase.
—Preparing the back by rubbing in oil, and beginning the wrapping.
—Technical instructions as to how to avoid spilling the liquids used into the visceral cavities.
—Placing gold finger-stalls on the hands and feet.
—Final anointing and wrapping of the head.
—First wrapping of the hands.
—Anointing and wrapping of the legs.

GREEKS, ROMANS AND CHURCH FATHERS

The Egyptian texts may be sparing in their information on mummification, but happily some Greek ones are more forthcoming. The most famous author of these, Herodotus, received his information at first hand from the priests of Memphis, Heliopolis and Thebes, and no doubt also had contacts with the suppliers of embalming materials. However, his writings are really only valid for the later age in which he himself lived, and the greatest care must be taken in extrapolating from them to previous ages. It is rather as if we were to draw conclusions about the burial practices of our own forbears of long ago from a modern funeral in a big city today, though of course it would be true to say that Egyptian civilisation developed at a much slower pace than our own. As described earlier Herodotus said that families could choose from three methods of preserving the body of the deceased: in the first and most costly, the brain and viscera were extracted, the abdominal cavity filled with aromatic substances, and then the body treated with natron, rubbed with oil, and lastly bandaged; in the second, the viscera were not removed but were merely dissolved by injecting cedar oil through the anus; and in the case of the least wealthy families, cedar oil was replaced by a cheaper product.

Four hundred years later, in the year 56 B.C., Diodorus of Sicily paid a visit to Egypt, and wrote a highly coloured account of the customs he observed there. On several points his version confirms that of Herodotus, who may indeed have given him his inspiration, but he is the first to mention the use of bitumen: "The barbarians who trade in this asphalt (bitumen from the Dead Sea) transport it to Egypt where it is purchased for use in embalming the dead; for if they do not mix it with the other aromatic spices they use, the corpses cannot long be preserved from decay." This assertion must be treated with caution, for chemical analysis has only very rarely revealed traces of bitumen on mummies. It is possible that Diodorus was deceived by the blackish colouring of the bodies.

Another debatable point was made by Plutarch and Porphyry, who claimed that the entrails were thrown into the river, whereas as we shall see the Egyptians took very great care of them and buried them with the body. It may be that this was the practice in the Greek period but it was certainly not so earlier.

Those same Greeks who seem so amazed at Egyptian customs had in fact themselves made some attempts to save a few of their own dead from decay. One account states that Alexander the Great was preserved in honey while Plutarch recounts that the mortal remains of Agesilas, King of Sparta, were covered not in honey but in melted wax. Later, in Roman times, Tacitus wrote of the beautiful Poppaea, Nero's favourite, that "her body was not destroyed by fire according to Roman custom but was embalmed following the fashion of foreign kings, and impregnated with aromatic oils." Indeed every age of mankind has tried to find some way of preserving its illustrious dead, though not always meeting with universal approval.

The Greeks and Romans never found Egyptian burial customs reprehensible, though they may have been astonished by them, whereas the early Church fathers were furiously opposed to the preservation of bodies and waxed highly indignant in their writings. When Christianity reached Egypt from Rome, it wanted to impose its own rites and beliefs, and St. Anthony inveighed against mummification: "Never allow my body to be taken to the Egyptians. I do not wish them to have it in their houses . . . You know how often I have berated those who carry on these practices and how often I have urged them to do away with these customs . . ." The great St. Augustine also took part in the controversy and in one of his sermons thundered against mummification, forcefully affirming that the survival of the soul was not the prerogative of embalmed Egyptians and that immortality had nothing to do with preservation of the body. Nevertheless, in spite of all these authoritative voices, the Copts, who were Egyptian Christians, continued for several centuries to have themselves embalmed.

THE FIRST EUROPEAN TOURISTS

From an early date the exotic attractions of Egypt aroused Western curiosity, to such an extent that in the centuries between 1400 and 1700 more than two hundred and fifty travellers from every social class and every European country took the trouble to record the tale of their journeys, which to the modern tourist sound more like fictional adventure stories than accounts of real life. Pierre Belon, for example, was a doctor from Le Mans who accompanied a diplomatic mission in 1547; he visited the tombs which he found full of flies and referred to the bodies as "corps confits" (a rather charming expression in French but which comes out quaintly in English as pickled or candied corpses). Another visitor was the poet Jean Palerne from the Forèze region who braved the worst of the heat from July to September 1581, and also saw mummies being brought out from "small box-

rooms." Soon afterwards Germans and Austrians began to visit
Egypt too.

In those days travellers had to be prepared to face unknown
difficulties and dangers in the course of their journeys. Even to
let oneself be lowered into a funerary shaft by a rope was no
trivial matter, as Kiechel made clear when he described the risks
taken by his compatriot Lichtenstein who was so eager to see the
ancient Egyptians face to face that he ignored the danger of the
poorly shored-up walls crumbling. Hans Christoph Teufel had
even greater reason to be terrified, when he found himself
crawling with his candle in his hand through a long gallery
heaped with mummies whose bandages had been rendered
highly inflammable by the embalming fluids.

Some visitors were not content just to view the mummies, but
came with pre-arranged plans to bring back one or more of these
extraordinary objects as souvenirs of their journey. This was certainly the aim of Reinhold-Lubenau, a native of Könisberg, when
he arrived in Alexandria and went to visit the Venetian consul.
However, he was given to understand that it would be extremely
difficult to bring his purchase home because the sailors were so
superstitious that they would not accept embalmed corpses on
board ship, and if perchance a captain were to authorise the
transport of one he would not hesitate to throw it overboard into
the sea if a storm arose, blaming it for attracting the fury of the
elements. Thus many of the mummies transported overseas during this period had to be smuggled on their way.

Towards the end of the sixteenth century, it became almost a
tradition for those returning from a pilgrimage to the Holy Land
to travel via Egypt and to go and have one or two tombs in the
Saqqara region opened for their inspection. Lord Villamont, who
did this in 1591, noted the presence of two kinds of mummies:
one looked black and was embalmed with salt and pitch, while
the other was more elaborate and was preserved in myrrh and
aloes, and had its nails gilded or hennaed. Jean Sommer, another
traveller from Holland, almost failed to reach his destination
when he was captured by Turks during a stop in Cyprus, but in
the end he succeeded in escaping and reached Egypt in 1592.
There he learnt that the market rate for a well-prepared corpse

in good condition was from four to five hundred crowns, though the dessicated bodies of the unfortunate Arabs who had got lost in the desert and had been overtaken by sandstorms fetched a great deal less.

In 1598 three Czechs, Christophe Harant, Polzic and Bezdruzic also reached Saqqara. They had the good fortune to be taken on a specially organised tourist trip by the local people, who brought them to a shaft whose walls had been repaired and shored up with planks, and which led through underground corridors cut out of the rock to rooms containing thousands of mummified corpses.

By this time the trade in mummies and treasure was developing to an extent which shocked an English visitor who stayed in Memphis in 1611. George Sandys, son of the Archbishop of York, was horrified at the widespread practice of despoiling tombs, though he retained his equanimity sufficiently to record his astonishment at the skill with which the mummies were wrapped. The presence of hieroglyphs on the bandages aroused his intense curiosity. A year later a compatriot of his, William Lithgrow, followed him to Egypt.

Odd motives impelled some of these early travellers. Pietro della Valle, a wealthy Roman aristocrat, decided to embark on a visit to Egypt because of an unhappy love affair which threatened to drive him to suicide if he did not remove himself from the scene. He was away from Italy for twelve years between 1614 and 1626, and seems to have been successful in curing his broken heart since he was married in Baghdad. When he reached Egypt he stayed in Cairo, from where he went on a trip to the little village of Saqqara whose inhabitants made their living from the tombs. There he announced that he was ready to pay money to anyone who could direct him to an interesting find, and after he had eliminated the claims of some fifty fellahin who brought him idols or tempted him with promises of attractive sites, he agreed to follow one of them who offered him the prospect of obtaining a very beautiful mummy. When he arrived at the site of the discovery he was shown a corpse dating from the Ptolemaic period and adorned with a mask, necklace, gold medallion and many other ornaments. So modest was the purchase price of three piastres that he suggested he might buy a second mummy, and immediately another body was brought out, perfectly preserved, as well as one of a young girl. However he did not think the latter was in sufficiently good condition to be included in a collection, so he broke it into tiny pieces in order, he said, "to see how the bitumen was mixed with the bones" and to look for amulets, of which there were none.

The cupidity of the collectors was soon matched by the jealous determination of the local inhabitants to guard the treasures for their own profit.

When Pietro della Valle made his journey, he had had to so-licit the Turks for a military escort, and when Jean Coppin went to Egypt, which he did twice between 1638 and 1646, he es-tablished himself near Saqqara in military style on a little hill. As befitted a lieutenant-captain of the cavalry, he had the French flag hoisted, and organised his companions to take turns standing guard. In spite of the dangers, mummies continued to be acquired, and in 1646 Balthazar de Montconys wrote to one of his friends that he was about to bring home one of "the most beautiful mummies to be seen in France, all painted and gilded." The rate of despoliation accelerated in this period in response to the demand, not only from collectors of curiosities, but also from people believing in the curative properties of mummies.

Meanwhile the collectors of curiosities predominated. One of these who had a genuine scholarly interest in the field was Nicolas Claude Fabri Peiresc, a councillor who sat in the assem-bly at Aixen-Provence around the 1600s, a strange character who was obsessed with a desire to accumulate knowledge on every possible subject. The breadth of his curiosity, his erudition and his wide research made him almost a Renaissance personality. He never actually left Aix, but kept himself informed of foreign events and maintained a correspondence with scholars from all over Europe and from the countries bordering on the Mediter-ranean sea. He ordered books which he often recopied (his li-brary contained no less than five thousand volumes), and at great expense built up a collection of curiosities. The prize ex-hibits in this collection, which outshone all the other extraor-dinary items he had acquired, were sent to him from Egypt by one of his correspondents around 1630. They were two mummies, one of which was later used by Rubens as a model for a drawing.

For all his enthusiasm, such an amateur could never compete with the great men of the times such as Cardnial Richelieu. Mazarin, Chancellor Séguier and Colbert, who all encouraged archaeological expeditions with the help of their diplomatic representatives in Egypt. They were not as well organised, scrupulous and disinterested as they would be today, but nevertheless the orders governing the excavations stipulated even then that all discoveries should be carefully described. The quest for treasure was not overlooked either. Lucas, who was sent on an expedition by Louis XIV in 1714, was given instructions which read: "It is required that you should open a small (pyramid) . . . Something valuable may be found for even in ordinary tombs there are sometimes idols and other curiosities worthy to be included in the collections of our kings."

Among the Government ministers, Secretary Fouquet already possessed two magnificent sarcophaguses which were eventually acquired by the Louvre Museum after having passed through the hands of various owners. They were housed near the Minister's office, where they often diverted waiting callers for a while, including the poet La Fontaine who was inspired to describe them in one of his poems. Mistakenly, he attributed them to Chephren and Cheops, the builders of the great pyramids themselves:

> And if I see you are engaged,
> I'll wait here peacefully, content
> In this superb establishment,
> Where someone brought from lands afar
> From resting-places strange, bizarre,
> (At great expense, and with much toil)
> The coffin, tomb or bier of pharaohs royal,
> The kings of Egypt, Cheops and Chephren,
> Whose bodies now to dust have fallen;
> And that the point I wished to make.

Towards the end of the seventeenth century Benoît de Maillet, the French consul in Cairo, arranged to have a mummy unwrapped. He was not motivated by any desire for gain but by genuine interest. While he was examining the bandages he very astutely observed that underneath the hieroglyphic characters which he expected to find there was a second line written in different characters; perhaps it was a Coptic or demotic inscription. De Maillet informed the Minister himself, Ponchartrain, who assured him of the great importance he attached to this discovery in a letter of 16th September 1698. Nevertheless, nearly one hundred and twenty-five years were to elapse before Champollion was able to reveal the principles of Egyptian writing to the Académie Française.

Individual travellers continued to visit Egypt in spite of the dangers which awaited them. Apart from Saqqara, one of the most fascinating areas was the famous Valley of the Kings, Biban el-Moluk, where the pharaohs of the New Kingdom dug their underground vaults in the heart of the mountainous country which dominates Thebes from the west. These tombs are called hypogea, and fourteen of them were listed by Richard Pocoke, an English traveller who visited the area in 1743. He also drew up plans of the ones which were not obstructed by masses of fallen earth. However, even such a hasty exploration required a certain amount of courage, so he did not stay long in the impoverished countryside. This may account for the fact that he found so few tombs compared to the forty seen by Strabo when he journeyed up the Nile in the year 25 B.C. In 1737 one of Pocoke's compatriots, Norden, had stopped at the Ramesseum rather than going on to brave the hordes of bandits who were safely ensconced in grottoes hollowed out in the surrounding hills, from which they could control the region. Another traveller, Bruce, came into contact with these outlaws in 1769. The Governor had tried hard to get rid of them by filling their caves with dry brushwood and setting light to it, but it was to no avail; for the few who died were replaced by others even bolder than the first. On his way back from the tomb of Ramesses III in the dusk, Bruce was abandoned by his terrified guides and then attacked with stones. He had to flee to safety, swearing never to return to such an inhospitable region.

NAPOLEON IN EGYPT

When Napoleon undertook his great expedition to Egypt, as the first stage in his dream of an eastern empire, he achieved no military triumphs: his naval fleet was sunk by Nelson at Abuquir, his commanding general had to return home prematurely, Kléber was assassinated, and the French were finally expelled. Nonetheless it was in this disastrous campaign that the seeds of Egyptology were sown, for Napoleon had the great wisdom to take numerous scientists with him. The Commission of Arts and Sciences selected a hundred and sixty-seven experts to take part, among them geographers, historians, naturalists and archaeologists. They had very strained relations with the army representatives who had no conception of the significance of their work and resented the salaries they were paid and the funds they were allotted. The soldiers used to take malicious delight at the command issued at the critical point of battle: "On guard against the Mameluks, form squares! Donkeys and scholars in the middle!" The same scholars however knew how to use arms if they had to, and during the four years of campaigning from June 1798 to September 1802 they left thirty-four of their number on Egyptian soil.

Preceded by Vivant Denon, there were two Commissions which were directed by Costaz and Fourier and which surveyed Egypt from south to north, from Aswan to Cairo, during a whole summer. They gathered a mass of notes, an enormous quantity of sketches, plans and drawings, and considerably added to their archaeological and scientific collections. The final fruit of their labours, the monumental *Description de l'Égypte,* comprised no less than nine volumes of text and fourteen huge volumes of folio plates.

By this time, there were only eleven tomb entrances to be seen in the Valley of the Kings, together with the tomb of Amenophis III more to the west. The account of one member of the expedition, Jomard, who explored these Theban hypogeums, makes terrifying reading. Inside all the burial vaults there was chaos;

mummies lay in heaps on the ground and you could feel them
crack under your weight as you walked; sometimes your feet
were caught in the remains or in the bandages. At times you had
to crawl on your belly clutching your candle in your hand and
hoping that the bodies would not catch fire. The whole macabre
expedition was punctuated by the hiss of bats flying and swoop-
ing over the visitors; the beating of their wings disturbed the
warm damp atmosphere which was thick with the fetid smell of
their excrement which had accumulated over the centuries; the
candles threatened to go out; and the heat was suffocating, from
22° to 25° C. in the underground tunnels. Jomard's accuracy can
be checked on this point at least, for though the contemporary
tourist can now walk peacefully through the royal tombs along
corridors which have been swept clean and emptied of bats, the
temperature remains as hot as ever. Lucas confirmed Jomard's
observations when he measured the heat and the amount of
water vapour in the air in 1924: the highest temperature, 29° C.,
was found at the far end of Amenophis II's tomb; the highest humidity in Thutmosis IV's tomb. Suffocation was not the only danger in these tunnels, and Jomard had a number of other narrow
escapes. Once he was nearly killed when part of a pillar
collapsed just as he was drawing it, and grazed his head as it
fell, and in another tomb his torch caused a fire and he had to
leave hastily.

However, it was two of his companions who ran the greatest
risk in the hypogeum of Amenophis III. They were proceeding
down a gallery, each carrying a candle, when some distance from
the entrance they came to a hole about ten yards deep, which extended almost the entire width of the corridor; they were only
able to cross it by sitting on the edge and progressing on their
hands. This was just a foretaste of the perils to come, and several
more holes had to be traversed in the same manner. As they
were wending their dangerous way, a bat flew past and unfortunately the beating of its wings extinguished the candles. Now the
two, in total darkness, and with only the vaguest recollection of
the path they had come, had to retrace their steps and endeavour to avoid the mortal danger of the holes. Holding each
other by the hand, feeling the walls, testing the ground in front
of them with a foot at each step and taking every precaution,

they were making slow progress when after some hundred paces they suddenly lost contact with the walls. They had arrived at a cross-roads, and had to decide which way to go. Fortunately for them they took the right-hand turn which avoided the holes and led them safely to a point from which they could see the faint glow of light from the hypogeum's main entrance.

Some of the treasures which were brought back to France from these expeditions found their way into the royal collections, so it is not surprising that the inventory taken at Malmaison after the death of the Empress Josephine included some Egyptian souvenirs; but after they had been distributed in accordance with her will all trace of them was lost. Nine objects were mentioned, among them "two Egyptian mummies each enclosed in a walnut chest five and a half feet long; the head of a female mummy; three mummified ibises inside earthen vessels."

EXCAVATIONS AND PILLAGING

The French discoveries and the publication of Vivant Denon's *Voyage* and his *Description de l'Égypte* inspired many people to take up archaeology, and aroused the commercial appetites of others. When Mehemet Ali seized power in Egypt he began to open up the country and establish commercial relations with the West, to which he exported huge quantities of cereal and used the considerable profits he gained to build up his army. Next the ports were opened to Europeans, and soon anyone who requested it was granted an unconditional firman, or permit, to carry out excavations. This led of course to an influx of adventurers, with consequent widespread abuse of the system and pillaging of Egyptian treasures. It will never be known how many works of art were sacrificed, how many painted walls smashed in order to extract the desired piece, and how many landmarks in Egyptian history irrevocably destroyed.

The most picturesque adventurer of the beginning of the nineteenth century was undoubtedly Jean-Baptiste Belzoni. He was born in Padua in 1778 of a respectable Roman family and had been intended for the priesthood, but from the very first he refused to conform to his family's wishes and at one stage in his career even landed up in England in a circus where his gigantic stature and unusual strength led him to perform as the circus strong man. He was also an engineer, or so he claimed, and he did in fact build a hydraulic wheel which could do the work of four men. It was when he tried to interest the Egyptians in his invention, to no avail, that in 1815 he met Salt, the British consul, for whom he carried out several excavations. France should be duly grateful to Belzoni, for the magnificent Salt collection of four thousand items was eventually left to the Louvre Museum. Belzoni himself continued digging on his own account, and made his most exciting discovery in 1817. This was the tomb of Seti I, from which the mummy of the king himself was missing but which still contained the magnificent sarcophagus of transparent alabaster. In 1821 Belzoni took it to London and showed it in an exhibition which was so successful that he decided to mount it in Paris as well.

Meanwhile Champollion, who was then quite unknown, was working at deciphering Egyptian inscriptions, and it was on 27th September 1822 that he quietly presented his short treatise, *Lettre à Monsieur Dacier relative à l'alphabet des hiéroglyphes phonétiques,* to the Académie des Inscriptions et Belles Lettres. This was followed a year later by his *Précis du système hiéroglyphique.* It was a tremendous achievement which caused a sensation in well-informed circles, but publicly it was overshadowed by Belzoni's collection which on the very same day passed beneath the Academy's windows in a barge. The Italian adventurer was about to amaze the whole of Paris. He set up his material in the Boulevard des Italiens, where with the help of two Italian artists who worked on the project for twenty-seven months he reconstructed the main chambers of Seti I's tomb. The marvellous setting, the weird and wonderful objects, the mummies themselves and the sarcophagus could not fail to arouse general curiosity, and when they were finally revealed to the public they made a tremendous impact which was not even surpassed by the excitement of the discovery of Tutankhamun's tomb a hundred years later.

Others soon saw in Belzoni's success a way to make their own fortune. One of these was a dealer from Trieste called Passalac-

SOURCES OF OUR KNOWLEDGE

qua whose business had collapsed, and who immediately set out
on the antiquities trail. After scouring the Theban region for
mummies and other items he obtained a sufficiently large haul to
bring them to Paris and exhibit them at 52 Passage Vivienne in
1826. All went well and the event must have made a considerable impact for there is even a mention of it in a book of the
time, Balzac's *La Maison Nucingen* which describes one character in the following terms: "Malvina has nothing . . . Tall, dark,
thin and dried-up, she resembles a mummy which has escaped
from Passalacqua's collection to walk the streets of Paris." In
spite of the collection's high quality, the French government refused to pay the price of four hundred thousand francs to
acquire it, and it was Frederick William IV, King of Prussia, who
succeeded in obtaining it at a quarter of its value by the simple
means of promising Passalacqua the post of Keeper of Egyptian
Antiquities in Berlin.

Meanwhile Champollion returned to Egypt from 1828 to 1829,
and stayed in the Valley of the Kings, where he boldly set
up his camp in the tomb of Ramesses IV. He was not looking
for mummies, but was there to decipher texts, copy inscriptions,
and see how they compared from one tomb to another. Thanks
to his efforts the hypogeums, which up to then had been given
names such as tomb of the harpists or tomb of the transmigration
of souls, which alluded to some distinguishing feature of their
décor, now recovered their true ascriptions. However as his investigations continued and the extent of the damage caused by
both traders and collectors became clear, Champollion became
increasingly horrified. He appealed for the creation of an administrative authority to protect antiquities, but in vain.

The Egyptian collections of Paris, London and Turin were
now rivalled by Prussia, who sent a mission from 1842 to 1845
directed by Richard Lepsius. Today's standards of meticulous archaeological research were still far from being met, and many
more monuments were despoiled.

It was only in 1858 when Mariette was accorded the title of
"mamour" of antiquities by Said Pasha that an Antiquities Service was set up in Egypt to exercise control over all excavations.
The crowning event in Mariette's own life was his discovery of
the Serapeum of Memphis, the burial ground of the sacred bulls.

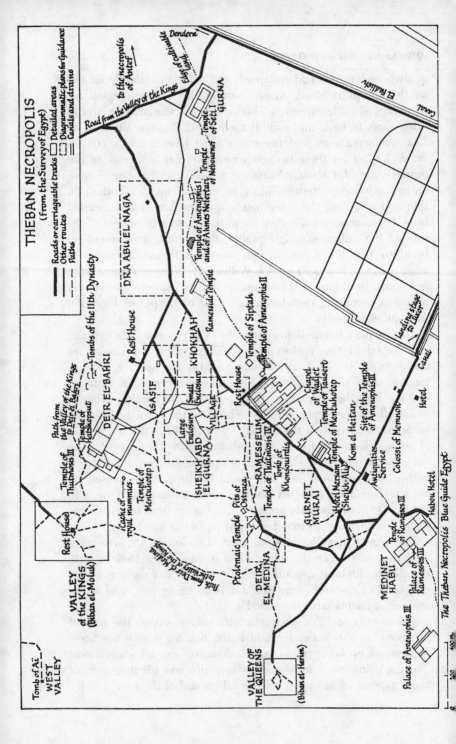

THEBAN NECROPOLIS
(from the Survey of Egypt)

☐ Detailed areas
┌┄┐ Diagrammatic plans for guidance
└┄┘
═══ Canals and drains

━━━ Roads or carriageable tracks
┄┄┄ Other routes
---- Paths

Dendera
El Fadliya
to the necropolis of Antef
Edge of cultivable lands
Canal
GURNA
Temple of Seti I
Road from the Valley of the Kings
Temple of Nebouenef
Temple of Amenophis I and of Ahmes Nefertari
DRA ABU EL NAGA
Ramessid Temple
Temple of Siptah
Temple of Amenophis II
landing-stage to Luxor
Canal
Rest House
Path from the Valley of the Kings to Deir el Bahri
DEIR EL-BAHRI
Temple of Thuthmosis III
Temple of Hatshepsut
Tombs of the 11th Dynasty
ASASIF
KHOKHAH
Small Enclosure
Large Enclosure
VILLAGE
Rest House
Chapel of Wadiet
Temple of Tausert
Temple of Montuhotep
Temple of Menuhotep I
SHEIKH ABD EL GURNA
Cache of royal mummies
VALLEY of the Kings (Biban el-Moluk)
Rest House
Temple of Thuthmosis IV
RAMESSEUM
Tomb of Khonsouirdis
Tomb of Khaemhet(?)
Ptolemaic Temple
Pits of Ostraca
DEIR EL MEDINA
Path from Deir el Medina to the Valley of the Kings
Kom el Heitan
Hotel Marsam Temple of Amenophis III
GURNET MURAI
Hotel Victoria (Sheikh-Ali)
Site of the Temple of Amenophis III
Antiquities Service
Colossi of Memnon
Hotel
Hotel
Canal
Tomb of Aï WEST VALLEY
Rest House
VALLEY OF THE QUEENS (Biban el-Harim)
Palace of Amenophis III
MEDINET HABU
Palace of Ramesses III
Temple of Ramesses III
Habou Hotel
Temple of Amenophis III

0   200   400 m.

The Theban Necropolis Blue Guide Egypt

Mariette was succeeded as head of the Antiquities Service by Maspéro, one of the great names of Egyptology. His discovery of the royal mummies of the Eighteenth Dynasty, referred to as the "first Deir el-Bahri find" is worth recounting in detail, for historically it is even more important than Tutankhamun's tomb.

Maspéro knew that the tombs in the Valley of the Kings had been pillaged and no longer contained the mummies of the pharaohs, but it was not certain whether their bodies had been systematically destroyed, so he was very excited when in 1875 there appeared on the market a few statuettes of blue enamel, bearing the name of Kheperkare on the seal. He knew that this name could only have belonged to two kings, Sesostris II of the Twelfth Dynasty and Pinedjem of the Twenty-first Dynasty, and decided that all the indications pointed to the latter. A year later, he was shown the hieratic ritual of the High Priest of Amun and King Pinedjem which the English General Campbell had bought at Thebes for four hundred pounds, and then de Saulcy lent him the photograph of a long papyrus which has since been divided among France, England and Bavaria, and which had belonged to Queen Not-Mit, mother of Herihor, who was the second sovereign to rule in the Twenty-first Dynasty. Around the same period, funerary statuettes inscribed with Pinedjem's name were being offered to collectors of antiquities. It was clear that all these objects must have come from a secret hoard, probably in one or more of the royal hypogeams of the Twenty-first Dynasty, which were being systematically looted.

With great patience and regardless of the time involved Maspéro set about questioning the purchasers, and tourists who had been covertly offered the treasures. His enquiries took him to two Egyptian brothers, Ahmed and Mohamed Abd el-Rassul, who lived in the little village of el-Qurna situated half way between the Ramesseum and the Temple of Hatshepsut, and to a third person, Moustapha Agha Ayat, vice-consul of England, Belgium and Russia at Luxor. The latter could not be brought to trial because he possessed diplomatic immunity, so pressure was brought to bear on the two Arabs. On the orders of the Luxor police Ahmed was taken in by two policemen and his interrogation began on 6 April 1881; however, he would admit nothing and indeed many people from his village testified in his favor, including the mayor and notables. There was so much evidence to say that he was innocent and so little proof of his guilt (for not one compromising object was found in his home), that after one and a half months he had to be released.

However, the Abd el-Rassul family had begun to have doubts. The vice-consul was still insisting on gathering in antiquities from the Theban region as the price of his protection, but it had become clear that he could not extend his own immunity to his associates. After all, Ahmed had been incarcerated for over a month, and Maspéro had threatened to start investigations again with the onset of winter. Mohamed was in favour of confessing everything to the museum administration, though Ahmed still believed there was no risk in continuing their gainful operations. The discord between the two brothers grew sharper when they came to divide up their latest haul, for Ahmed laid claim to a larger share as a recompense for the six weeks he had spent in prison. Finally the elder brother, Mohamed, growing weary of the quarrels and feeling that the net was closing in on him, decided to disclose the family secret. His revelations made such an impact that the affair was taken up at ever higher levels until it reached the Khedive Caliph. Since Maspéro was held up in Europe just then it was Émile Brugsch, the assistant keeper, who was dispatched to the spot which he reached on 6 July. There, in a hollow of the hill facing the village of el-Qurna, less than a mile from the home of the two plunderers, he found what he was looking for. A hole had been dug on a ledge in the rockface, very near the Deir el-Bahri temple and only some sixty-six yards from cultivated land. This hole was about twelve yards deep and two across, and led to a narrow corridor through which one had to crawl for a few yards until it widened, turned abruptly towards the north, and then continued for a bit until it reached an irregularly shaped room a little longer than eight yards.

By the wavering light of the candles Émile Brugsch and the members of the Antiquities Service who accompanied him first discovered a white and yellow coffin bearing the name of Nibsni, near the entrance. Venturing into the narrow corridor, they were then able to read the names of Sekenenre, a king of the Seventeenth Dynasty, Queen Tiuhator Honttui, and Seti I. Their sacrophaguses were surrounded with numerous objects scattered all over the ground, which made it difficult to proceed. The chaos in the large corridor and in the room was indescribable, and the investigators had to crawl along round canopic jars, chests and statuettes in order to examine the coffins and mummies, which belonged to some of the most famous kings known to Egypt: Sekenenre, from the Seventeenth Dynasty; Ahmosis, Amenophis I, Thutmosis I and Thutmosis III, from the Eighteenth; Ramesses I, Seti I and Ramesses II from the Nineteenth; Ramesses III and Ramesses X from the Twentieth; and from the Twenty-first, the well-known Pinedjem himself whose belongings had originally put Maspéro on the track of the robbers. They were accompanied by members of their families: Queen Ahhotep, wife of Sekenenre, Siamon, son of Ahmosis, and his mother Ahmosis-Nefertari, sister and wife of Ahmosis, who occupied a huge coffin, and many others.

It seems extraordinary that the great raves of the Valley of Biban-el-Moluk should lie empty, while this narrow passage contained so many royal personages. The answer lies in the organised bands of plunderers who flourished at the end of the New Kingdom and made their living by robbing the tombs of their treasures. No religious respect or fear restrained them, and they violated large and small tombs alike. We have already referred to the tribulations of these pharaohs who were moved from grave to grave until they reached their ultimate abode in such a lowly hiding-place. It really was a hiding-place too, for the site was so well chosen and the secret so well kept that after it had been sealed at the end of the Twenty-first Dynasty it escaped the greed of the ancient Egyptians, and the Arab robbers, and even the archaeologists, until the Abd el-Rassul depredations in 1875. The pharaohs had enjoyed an eternal rest lasting barely more than two thousand eight hundred years, though this was long in comparison with the forty-eight hours it took to remove them from the grave before they were transported to Cairo Museum. However, that is another story.

Ten years later the same Mohamed Abd el-Rassul, who seems to have been gifted with a most unusual flair, discovered a second cachette at a little distance from Queen Hatshepsut's temple which became known as the "second Deir el-Bahri find." He showed it to Grebaut, Maspéro's successor as head of the

Antiquities Service. The entrance was through a wide shaft which had been blocked up with stone, brick, clay and sand, and completely concealed beneath the paving. Thirteen yards down, at the bottom, a long gallery in which a man could stand upright extended for over a hundred yards and was joined by another shorter corridor. A strange collection of coffins, chests, vases, dried fruit and flowers were scattered over the floor, and amid them lay a hundred and fifty-three mummies, some piled in heaps on top of each other and others arranged in two rows along the walls. They included the bodies of the servants of the Amun cult from the beginning of the Twenty-second Dynasty, priests and priestesses, female singers, and members of their families. It took several months to clear the place completely, and such was the profusion of mummies that the Egyptian government sent a hundred of them to museums all over the world.

After several other directors of the Antiquities Service had come and gone, the last to be appointed in 1898 was Victor Loret. He decided to start a fresh search in the Valley of the Kings, so he followed clues left by clandestine diggers which led him to a site that had previously been neglected. There he discovered the entrance to a hypogeum, and after having gone down and then up several flights of stairs and having traversed various corridors and rooms he reached a large room where he saw a sumptuous sarcophagus of red quartzite rising from a pile of broken objects. Inside it was a wooden coffin. When he lifted the lid, he was amazed to discover a complete mummy, that of Amenophis II, garlanded with foilage and flowers, and with a little bunch of mimosa placed on his chest. The room with the sarcophagus was flanked by four narrower chambers, two on the left and two on the right, and in the first one on the right lay a woman, a man and a child (no doubt a prince, to judge from his hair-style), unwrapped on the ground. However, Loret had not yet come to the greatest marvel; he still had to explore the last room on the right, whose walled-up door had been partly smashed by blows from the robbers' picks. There he found nine wooden coffins, of which four had lost their lids. Two contained nameless mummies, but the remaining seven belonged to the pharaohs who were missing from the first hiding-place in Deir el-Bahri. They were Thutmosis IV and Amenophis III from the

Eighteenth Dynasty; Merneptah and Siptah from the Nineteenth; and Setnakht, Ramesses IV and Ramesses V from the
Twentieth. The list was not complete but the collection of kings
was nonetheless growing.

Five years after this discovery, T. A. Davis started systematic
excavations in the Valley of the Kings. He made many discoveries, but the most controversial came from tomb No. 55
which housed a mummy whose origins were much disputed. The
mummy rested in a sarcophagus in the name of Meryet-Amon,
daughter of Akhenaten, but this was clearly incorrect and for a
little while the body was thought to belong to Queen Tiyi, royal
wife of Amenophis III and mother of Akhenaten. However it
soon became apparent that the mummy was in fact a man, who
on the strength of some badly interpreted inscriptions was first
believed to be the heretical Pharaoh Akhenaten himself, and
then finally with the aid of proper medical analysis proved to be
in reality Smenkhkare, Akhenaten's nephew and son-in-law.

The most touching scene that Davis came across was in a little
room with bare walls, hollowed out in the rock, where he discovered Yuia and Tjuia, the father and mother of Tiyi. Their coffins
had simply been placed on a layer of fine sand, but the room was
embellished with some of the most beautiful pieces of furniture
yet discovered. The tomb had in fact been robbed and the jewels
removed from the mummies, but the plunderers had been extremely careful not to disturb anything, down to the gilding on
the furniture, so that the archaeologist at first thought that he
was entering an untouched chamber.

Theodore Davis decided to abandon the search in the Valley
of the Kings in 1912. Some mummies were still missing, but it was
thought that they must have been destroyed, and every royal
tomb had been found, explored and described. Davis was even
convinced that in 1907 he had discovered Tutankhamun's tomb,
for he had found a chamber near Horemheb's grave which contained a wooden coffin decorated with a picture of the king and
his wife Ankhesenamun. No trace of any body remained so
Davis simply concluded that the tomb had been robbed. A hundred yards away, ignored by Davis, a trench no more than two
yards long held a dozen large pots full of embalming materials
and closed with stoppers bearing the royal seal.

This was one of the finds that convinced Howard Carter that Davis could have come to the wrong conclusion. His enthusiasm led him to undertake the task of starting a new area of operations in the Valley of the Kings, near the tomb of Ramesses VI, and he was backed in his endeavours by a wealthy patron of Egyptology, Lord Carnarvon. For many years he had scarcely any success. Lord Carnarvon's concession, which he had obtained in 1917, was coming to an end, and there seemed little hope of finding Tutankhamun's tomb, when one morning after the workmen had removed the remains of a private dwelling from the Twentieth Dynasty they uncovered a step, the beginning of a stairway which led to a rough wall marked with the young king's seal, still intact. Once the wall had been knocked down Carter found himself in a short passage which sloped gently down to another wall bearing the same seals. On 26 November 1922, Carter removed a stone from the wall and shone his electric torch through the hole. "Can you see anything?" asked Lord Carnarvon. It took Carter a few moments to recover from his stupefaction sufficiently to utter a single, very ordinary phrase: "Yes, marvellous things." Indeed there were so many wonderful things that it took a dozen years for the teams of researchers to catalogue all the two thousand or so objects which were brought out from the grave. They are among the most beautiful items of Egyptian art that have survived to the present day. The furniture, jars, jewellery, cloth and statues filled four rooms, while in the funerary chamber itself four shrines of gilded wood, one inside another, protected the coffins. The first coffin lay inside a chest of yellow quartzite, with a second inside it shaped like a mummy and carved in the likeness of the king, covered with gold leaf and encrusted with semi-precious stones and glass paste. Yet more marvellous was the third coffin, which was of solid gold weighing well over a ton; it too reproduced Tutankhamun's features, his arms folded on his chest, and his hands holding the two sceptres which were the symbols of his authority. Inside this lay the blackened mummy, laden with jewels and gold amulets. Once it was unwrapped it appeared in a fairly good state of preservation, and the age at death could be established at about twenty.

Far from the Valley of the Kings, in the Delta, lay another

burial ground where one more exciting discovery was to be made. Here the kings of the Twenty-first Dynasty had decided to build the city of Tanis on the ruins of Avaris, the ancient Hyksos capital. They were so attached to the town that they also had their tombs built there, though later generations pulled down the structures above the ground and constructed private buildings on the site. Fortunately the galleries remained, and were redis-covered by Montet in 1939 as a result of a lucky blow from a pick. The first tomb he found proved to belong to Osorkon II, of the Twenty-second Dynasty; its enormous sarcophagus was carved in the likeness of a colossal statue of Ramesses II, and still contained the mummy. In the three adjoining chambers hewn out from the limestone Montet found prince Hornekht, son of Osorkon II, who had died very young, Takelothis II son and successor of Osorkon, and an unknown mummy which is thought to be that of Sheshonq III. The state of preservation of these bodies was not very good, and Takelothis and Sheshonq were both reduced to skeletons. In addition, all the sarcophaguses had suffered from the depredations of robbers.

Montet carried on his search until May 1940, when he discov-ered two blocked-up doors in a wall of Sheshonq III's chamber. They were completely hidden from view by a layer of plaster covered with paintings. These doors led to two vaults, of which the first contained a large granite sarcophagus with the name of Psusennes I, of the Twenty-first Dynasty, written all over its sides. In fact the Pharaoh had appropriated a monument which did not belong to him by destroying the name of its true owner wherever it was carved and having his own title inscribed in its place; but the workman who was given the task had omitted to efface one cartouche, from which we know that the huge chest had in fact been hewn out for Merneptah, Ramesses II's succes-sor. This kind of theft was not unusual and is explained by the comparative poverty of the kings in this troubled period. The second vault also held a sarcophagus of silver which contained the mummy of Amenemope, Psusennes' successor, who was liter-ally covered with jewels. Here again the sarcophagus had been re-used, for the name of Mutnejem, Psusennes' mother had been overlooked at the small end of the coffin; she had been buried next to her son, and then dislodged in favour of Amenemope.

The accumulation of royal personages in the Tanis cachette shows that the mummies of pharaohs buried in the Delta were no less likely than the ones buried in the Valley of the Kings to suffer from looting, and they had clearly been moved from grave to grave before finishing in a common tomb.

CHAPTER NOTES

CHAPTER I: WHY MUMMIES?

Explanations of the practice of dismembering bodies are to be found in "Numen," 3, 1956, by A. Hermann, in the *Guide to Cairo Museum*, 1915 edition by G. Maspéro, and in *Préhistoire et histoire de l'Égypte* by R. Massoulard, Institut d'ethnologie, Paris, 1949. The latter also gives the facts about the development of predynastic tombs. *Ame et vie d'outre-tombe chez lesÉgyptiens de l'Ancien Empire* by J. Pirenne, CdE, 34, 1959, explains clearly the idea of the Ka and the Ba.

CHAPTER 2: MUMMIES AND SCIENCE

The latest scientific techniques form the basis of *Death and disease in ancient Egypt,* by A. Cockburn, "Science," 181, 1973, pp. 470–471 and *Autopsy of an Egyptian mummy* by A. Cockburn, R. A. Barraco, T. A. Reyman and W. H. Peck, "Science," 187, 1975, pp. 1,155–1,160. Details of the x-ray process are given by P. H. K. Gray in *Radiological aspects of the mummies of ancient Egyptians in the Rijksmuseum Van Oudheden, Leiden,* O.M.R.O., 47, 1966, pp. 1–29. The story of histology, paying particular tribute to Sandison's work, is to be found in *La conservazione dei tessuti nelle mummie egiziane* by B. Chiarelli and E. Rabino-Massa, "Rivista Antropologica," 54, 1967, pp. 167–170. Chemical developments are discussed in Lucas, *op. cit.,* and in *Temporary stuffing materials used in the process of mummification in ancient Egypt,* by Z. Iskander and Abdel Moeiz Shaheen, A.S.A.E., 58, 1964, pp. 197–208. For mummies' blood groups, see *Kinship of Semenkhkare and Tut-Ankh-Amen demonstrated serologically,* by R. C. Connoly, "Nature," 224, 1969, pp. 325–326.

CHAPTER 3:   MUMMIES, THEIR LIVES AND TIMES
Part I: Civilisation and pathology

For amulets, read *Life and Death of a Pharaoh* by C. Desroches-Noblecourt, Penguin, London, 1965. Most of the references to sickness and injury can be followed up in *La méde-cine égyptienne au temps des Pharaons* by A. P. Leca, Dacosta, Paris, 1971. For dental disease and diet, consult *L'odonto-stomatologie dans l'ancienne Égypte* by Gisèle Brunschweig, Paris 1973, and *Bread of the Pharaoh's baker* by F. F. Leek, Newsletter of the American Research Center in Egypt, April 1971, p. 2. The basic study on tattooing is L. Kheimer's *Remarques sur le tatouage dans l'Égypte ancienne*, in "Mémoires présentés à l'Institut d'Égypte," vol. 53. Cairo 1948.

Part II: Historical connections

Descriptions and illustrations of the royal mummies will be found in *The royal mummies* by G. E. Smith, in the "General Catalogue of Egyptian Antiquities in Cairo Museum," 1912. See too *X Raying the Pharaohs*, by J. E. Harris and K. R. Weeks, C. Scribner, New York, 1973 and, for their history, Drioton and Vandier, *op. cit.* For the sixty unknown soldiers, read *The slain soldiers of Neb-hepet-Rê Mentu-Hotep*, by H. E. Winlock, M.M.A. Egyptian Expeditions Publications, New York, 1945. Details of the executed men in trenches will be found in *The archaeological survey of Nubia*, by G. E. Smith, F. Wood-Jones and G. Reisner, Bulletins 1–4, National Printing Department, Cairo, 1908. The essential article to consult on the virgin and child is J. Yoyotte's *Les adoratrices de la troisième période intermédiaire*, Bull. Soc. Fran, d'Égyptologie, 64, June 1972, pp. 31–52.

CHAPTER 4:   ANIMAL MUMMIES

An essential work on this subject is *La faune momifiée*, by G. Daressy and G. Gaillard, "General Catalogue of Egyptian Antiquities in Cairo Museum," 1905. On the sacred bulls, see *Théodule Deveria (1831–1871). Notice biographique*, by G. Deveria, Bibliothèque égyptologique IV, Deveria, I; *Mariette à Saqqarah. Du Sérapeum à la direction des Antiquités*, by J.-P.

Lauer, B.I.F.A.O., 32, 1961, pp. 3–56; *Le Sérapeum de Memphis,* by A. Mariette, Paris, 1882; and in particular *The Bucheum* by Sir Robert Mond and Oliver H. Myers, Egypt Exploration Society, London, 1934. On other ruminants, see *La Nécropole prédynastique d'Héliopolis,* (1950 excavations), by F. Debono, A.S.A.E., 52, 1954, pp. 625–652. On the Mendes ram, see *Memphis et le taureau Apis dans le papyrus Jumilhac* by J. Vandier. I.F.A.O., 32 (Mélanges Mariette), 1961, pp. 105–123. For the cats and dogs, see *Chats sacrés,* by J. Capart, CdE, 18, 1943, pp. 36–37; Debono, *op. cit.: Bubastis,* by E. Naville, 8th Memoir of the Egypt Exploration Fund, London, 1891, and *The cemeteries of Abydos II,* by T. E. Peet, 34th Memoir of the Egypt Exploration Fund, London, 1914. For the ibises and baboons, see *Chez les derniers adorateurs du Trismegiste. La Nécropole d'Hermopolis. Tounah el Gebel,* by S. Gabra, Société égyptienne, Cairo, 1971; *The ibis cemetery at Abydos,* by T. Whittemore, J.E.A., I, 1914, pp. 248–249; *Sur les oiseaux momifiés,* by Lortet and Gaillard, A.S.A.E., 3, 1902, pp. 18–21. For other animals, see *The great Egyptian crocodile mystery,* by G. Bagnani, "Archaeology," 5, 1952, pp. 75–78; *Lettre sur deux tombeaux de crocodiles découverts au Fayoum,* by M. X. de Gorostarzu, A.S.A.E., 2, 1901, pp. 182–184; *Sur les poissons momifiés,* by Lortet and Hugounenq, A.S.A.E., 3, 1902, pp. 18–21.

CHAPTER 5: MUMMIES AND THEIR MAKERS

Two essential works of reference are *Les Memnonia. Recherches de papyrologie et d'épigraphie grecques sur la Nécropole de la Thèbes d'Égypte aux époques hellénistique et romaine* by André Bataille, R.A.P.H., 1952, and the account of B. Bruyère's excavations at Deir el-Medina in F.I.F.A.O., especially in vol. II, pp. 24–29, 1925; vol. X, p. 84, 1934–35; and vol. XVI, p. 14 1939. For the purification tent, see the analysis of B. Groseloff's work in A.S.A.E. 40, pp. 1,007–1,014, 1940, by E. Drioton, and the *Manuel d'archéologie égyptienne* by J. Vandier, vol. II 1 pp. 54 and 141 and vol. II 2, p. 568. H. Meulénaère explains how mummies are made in an article on the excavations in the Assassif hills published in the Newsletter of the American Research Center in Egypt, No. 82, July 1972, p. 8. On embalming beds, most of the information is to be found in *An embalming bed of Amenhotep, Steward of Memphis under Amenophis III* by L. Habachi, M.D.I.A.K., 22, 1967, pp. 42–47. For the organisation of the Theban necropolis, see *Une enquête judiciaire à Thèbes au temps de la XX⁰ Dynastie. Étude sur le papyrus Abbott,* by G. Maspéro, Imprimerie Nationale, Paris, 1871; *Taxes funéraires égyptiennes à l'époque gréco-romaine* by M. Malinine, Mélanges Mariette, pp. 137–168; and *"Paiements" du Président de la Nécropole* by E. Jelinkova-Reymond, B.I.F.A.O., 55, 1956, pp. 33–55.

CHAPTER 6: PREPARING THE MUMMY

Among numerous works on this subject, two essential ones are *Making a mummy* by W. R. Dawson, J.E.A., 13, 1927, pp. 40–49, and *Ancient Egyptian materials and industries* by A. Lucas, W. J. Mackay & Co., London, 1972, pp. 270–326. For the bandaging, see especially Bataille, *op. cit.,* as well as *Une tombe gréco-romaine de Deir el-Medineh* by G. Bruyère and A. Bataille, B.I.F.A.O., 38, 1939, pp. 73–107. The latter also contains details on cartonnage masks. On the waste from mummification, consult *Données nouvelles sur la momification de l'Égypte ancienne,* by J. P. Lauer and Z. Iskander, A.S.A.E., 53, 1955, pp. 167–194, as well as *Materials used at the embalming of King Tut-Ankh-Amen* by H. E. Winlock, New York, 1941, reprinted by Arno Press, 1973.

CHAPTER 7: THE RITES OF MUMMIFICATION

The two essential works are *Rituels funéraires* by J.-C. Goyon and *Les Memnonia* by A. Bataille, already cited. On mourning, see also *Une coutume égyptienne méconnue* by C. Desroches-Noblecourt, B.I.F.A.O., 45, 1946, pp. 185–232. For the funeral procession, see *The Rock Tombs of Meir,* by M. Blackward and R. Apted, R. O. Faulkner, London, 1953, Part V. For death at home, see *Hawara, Biahmu and Arsinoë,* by W. F. Flinders Petrie, Fields and Teuer, 1889. For changes in tombs, see *Les recherches archéologiques en Égypte* by G. Daressy, La Science Moderne, 3, 1926, no. 3, pp. 141–149. For changes in coffins, see *Les Pharaons à la conquête de l'art* by Etienne Drioton and Pierre du Bourguet, Desclée de Brouwer, Paris, 1965.

CHAPTER 8: WHERE ARE THE MUMMIES NOW?

For accounts of sacrileges committed in ancient Egypt, read *Une enquête judiciaire à Thèbes au temps de la XXᵉ Dynastie. Étude sur le papyrus Abbott,* by G. Maspéro, Imprimerie Nationale, Paris, 1871: *Le mécanisme de fermeture à la pyramide de Chéops,* by G. Goyon, "Revue Archéologique," 2, 1963, pp. 1–24; *Excavations at Deir el Bahari,* by H. E. Winlock, Macmillan, New York, 1942; *The Royal Necropolis at Thebes,* by Elisabeth Thomas, Princeton, 1966. For Arab looting, consult Khater, *op. cit.* for the use of mummy in medicine, see *The Works of Ambrose Parey. Treatise on mummy,* London, 1634, which can be supplemented by *A History of Egyptian mummies and an account of the worship and embalming of the sacred animals by the Egyptians,* by Thomas Joseph Pettigrew, Longman, London, 1834. Further information on references to mummies in poetry can be found in *L'Égypte et le vocabulaire de Balzac et de Théophile Gautier,* a lecture given on Friday 16th November 1945 to the Institut de France and in *Voyageurs et écrivains franqis en Égypte,* by J.-M. Carré, R.A.P.H., 4, 1932. For contemporary accounts of excavations and pillaging, see *Les momies royales de Deir el-Bahari,* by G. Maspéro, M.M.A.F., I, part 4, 1889, pp. 511–787; Montet, *op. cit.;* and *Report on the suffocation of five persons in a tomb of Egyptology,* by A. E. P. Weigall, J.E.A., 20, 1934, pp. 170–182.

CHAPTER 9: END OF THE LEGENDS

On the corn found in tombs, see *Sur la durée des peroxydiastases des graines,* by Brocq-Rousseu and E. Gain, A.S.A.E. II, 1911, pp. 40–43, and *Blé de momie,* by H. de Varigny, CdE, 3, 1927–1928, pp. 100–101. On the hill of resurrection, see *Villes et légendes d'Égypte,* by S. Sauneron, B.I.F.A.O., 69, 1971, pp. 43–51 and 200–205, which brings together all the travellers' tales. The mummy that moved is described in G. Maspéro's *Les Momies royales.* Essential references to the penalties imposed for sacrilege and to the pharaohs' curse will be found in notes at the bottom of the page in the text of this book, and in *La malédiction de Toutankhamon,* by F. Destaing, "Panorama médical," no. 37, pp. 1–5.

CHAPTER 10:   SOURCES OF OUR KNOWLEDGE

A good study of the Egyptian texts is to be found in *Rituels funéraires de l'ancienne Égypte*, by Jean-Claude Goyon, Editions de Cerf, Paris, 1972. *Le Rituel de l'Embaumement* by Serge Sauneron, Imprimerie Nationale, Cairo, 1952 is a specialist analysis of the embalming rites. For the Greek and Latin authors, one can consult translations of Herodotus, Diodorus of Sicily and Strabo, and also read *Textes latins et grecs relatifs à l'embaumement* by M. Mercier and A. Seguin, Thalès, 4, 1937–1939. For the Renaissance explorers, besides *Le régime juridique des fouilles et des antiquités en Égypte* by A. Khater, R.A.P.H., 1962, vol. xii, see the series of travel accounts, *Voyages en Égypte*, published in Cairo between 1970 and 1973 by the F.I.F.A.O., of which nine volumes have appeared to date. For Napoleon's expedition, see *Isis ou à la recherche de l'Égypte ensevelie* by Pierre Montet, Hachette, Paris, 1956, and above all *Description de l'Égypte; description générale de Thèbes*, vol. III, by E. Jomard, Paris, 1821. For contemporary accounts of discoveries see Montet, *op. cit.*; *La trouvaille de Deir el-Bahari* by Gustave Maspéro, Imprimerie Nationale, Cairo, 1881; *The tomb of Tut-Ankh-Amen* by Howard Carter and A. Mace, Cassel, London, 1923.

BRIEF BIBLIOGRAPHY

There is no space in a work of this nature to refer to every source which was used in its compilation.

Much of the material derives from journals of Egyptology such as: A.S.A.E., Annales du Service des Antiquités de l'Égypte, Cairo; B.I.F.A.O., Bulletin de l'Institut Franąis d'Archéologie Orientale, Cairo; CdE, Chronique d'Égypte; F.I.F.A.O., Fouilles de l'Institut Franąis d'Archéologie Orientale du Caire; J.E.A., Journal of Egyptian Archaeology; M.D.I.A.K., Mitteilungen des deutschen Instituts für ägyptische Altertumskunde in Kairo; M.M.A.F., Mémoires publiés par les membres de la mission archéologique franąise du Caire; O.M.R.O., Oudheidkundige Mededelingen uit het Rijksmuseum van Oudheden te Leiden; RdE, Revue d'égyptologie; R.A.P.H., Recherches d'Archéologie, de Philologie et d'Histoire; Rec. Trav., Recueil de travaux relatifs à la Philologie et à l'Archéologie égyptiennes et assyriennes, Paris; Z.A.S., Zeitschrift für ägyptische Sprache und Alertumskunde.

Some of it comes from specialist medical journals.

The reader who has no prior knowledge of Egyptology should consult the following: for a general history of Egypt, *L'Égypte*, by Etienne Drioton and Jacques Vandier, P.U.F., Paris, 1962; for a view of Egyptian civilisation presented in easy reference form, *Dictionary of Egyptian Civilisation*, by Georges Posener, Serge Sauneron and Jean Yoyotte, Methuen, London, 1962, and also *La civilisation égyptienne*, by A. Erman and H. Ranke, Payot, Paris, 1963; and for details of the archaeological sites, *Guide Blue de l'Égypte*, Hachette, Paris 1967. These four basic works are easy

to consult and will provide the reader with a framework in time
and space for each chapter in this book. They can be supplemented by *The mummy; chapters on Egyptian funeral archaeology* by E. A. W. Budge, Biblo and Tannen, New York, 1964.

INDEX